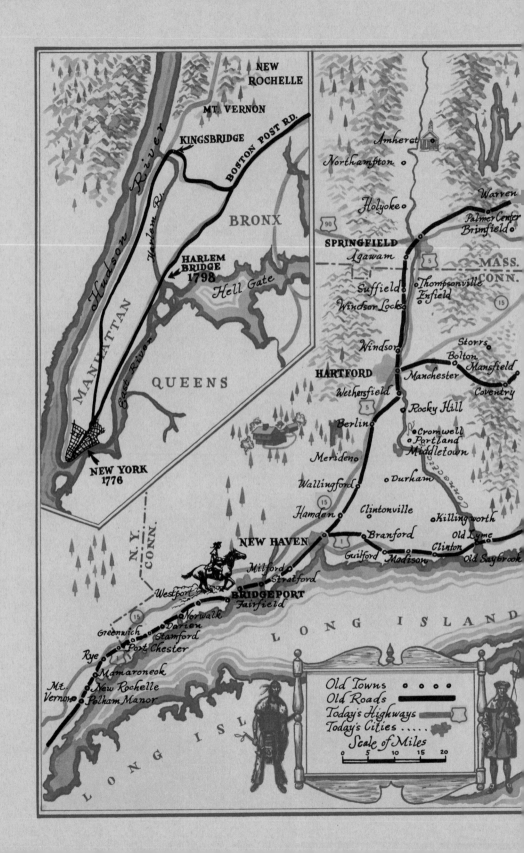

NEW ROCHELLE

MT. VERNON

KINGSBRIDGE

BOSTON POST RD.

BRONX

Hudson River

Harlem R.

HARLEM BRIDGE 1798

Hell Gate

East River

MANHATTAN

QUEENS

NEW YORK 1776

N.Y. CONN.

Amherst

Northampton

Holyoke

Warren

90

Palmer Center
Brimfield

SPRINGFIELD

Agawam

5

MASS.
CONN.

Thompsonville
Enfield

Suffield

Windsor Locks

15

Windsor

Storrs

Bolton

Mansfield

HARTFORD

Manchester

Coventry

Wethersfield

5

Rocky Hill

Berlin

Cromwell
Portland
Middletown

Meriden

Durham

Wallingford

15

Connecticut

Clintonville

Hamden

Killingworth

1

Branford

Old Lyme

NEW HAVEN

Guilford

Clinton

Milford

Madison

Old Saybrook

Stratford

Westport

BRIDGEPORT

Fairfield

15

Norwalk

Darien

Greenwich

Stamford

Port Chester

Rye

Mamaroneck

Mt.
Vernon

New Rochelle

Pelham Manor

LONG ISLAND

LONG ISL

Old Towns ● ● ● ●
Old Roads ▬▬▬▬
Today's Highways 🛣
Today's Cities .....
Scale of Miles

0   5   10   15   20

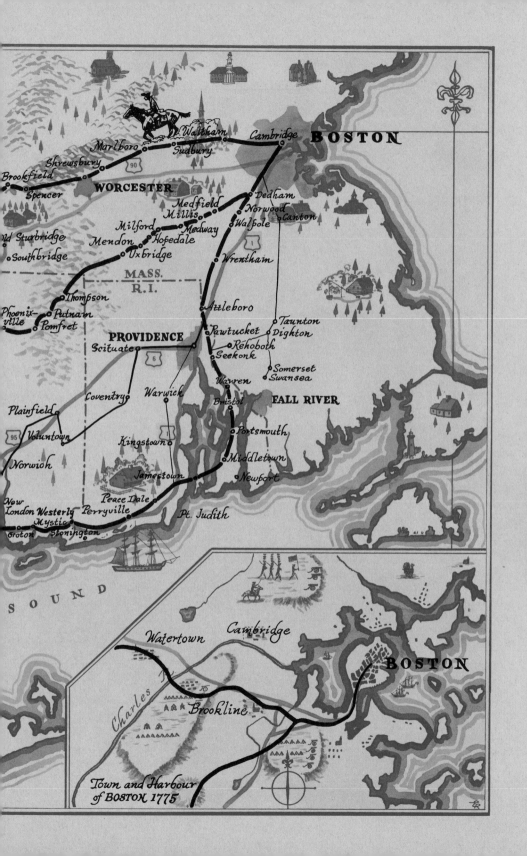

Town and Harbour of BOSTON 1775

*Books in the
American Trails Series*

━━━━━━━━━━

Subjects in Preparation

━━━━━━━━━━

The Story of the Boston Post Road
by STEWART H. HOLBROOK

The Old Post Road

McGRAW-HILL BOOK COMPANY, INC.
New York   Toronto   London

For Sibyl

THE OLD POST ROAD
The Story of the Boston Post Road

Copyright © 1962 by Stewart H. Holbrook.
Printed in the United States of America.
All rights reserved. This book or parts
thereof may not be reproduced in any form
without written permission of the publishers.

Library of Congress Catalog Card Number: 62-9989

Chapter headpieces by LARRY LURIN

First Edition

29535

Eighth Printing

Contents

Chapter 1

How It Began

THE FIRST MAIL in North America was dispatched from New York City on January 22, 1673, and arrived in Boston on or about February 5. The name of this first postrider on the continent is unfortunately not now known, but the path he took is of record. He rode by way of New Haven, Hartford, Springfield, Brookfield, Worcester, and Cambridge. His route has since been known, in both terminal cities, as the Old Boston Post Road.

I should like readers to know that this book is in no manner to be considered a guidebook. It is rather an account of selected places, people, things, and events which seem to have been of some special significance in the life of the first post road in the present United States. One might think of it as the first link in a 3,000-mile chain of trails and roads that were at last to reach the shore of the Pacific, the Great South Sea itself, where the waves were coming in from China.

The Old Post Road

This pioneer mail carrier rode at the command of Charles II, king of England, transmitted through his royal governors, Francis Lovelace of New York and John Winthrop of neighboring Connecticut. In an official communication to Lovelace late in 1672, "His Sacred Majestie" had "injoined his American subjects to enter into a close correspondency with each other." Governor Lovelace thereupon passed the word along to Governor Winthrop, adding that he himself looked upon the idea "as the most compendious means to beget a mutual understanding."

How right he was! Mutual understanding achieved its ultimate purpose, in colonial eyes, when somewhat later, Horseman Paul Revere came tearing down the Boston Post Road in '74, carrying to the Continental Congress the notorious Suffolk Resolves, the most inflammatory document before the Declaration of Independence; and only a little later came another horseman, Ebenezer Hurd, bringing the news of Lexington and Concord.

By the time the Revolution had turned into a fighting war, the Old Boston Post Road had been used for a century, though it had passed through difficult periods lasting for weeks, even months, when few if any postriders were seen over much of its 250 miles. These bad times were due to circumstances wholly beyond the control of what for the sake of brevity may be called the Post-office Department. Governors Lovelace and Winthrop happened to be among the most energetic officials of all the colonies. They had planned wisely and well for the first mail service in the new world.

Almost as soon as he received the King's wishes about a "close correspondency" among his American provinces, Lovelace set out on horseback to discuss the matter with Winthrop in Hartford. The New York Governor proposed that the postrider should be "a stout fellow, active and indefatigable, and sworne as to his fidelity." He should be paid an annual salary which, together with stated charges for letters and "other small portable packes, should afford him a handsome livelyhood." He mentioned Hartford as "the first stage I have designed him to change his horse, where I expect he should have a fresh one lye."

Each first Monday of the month, the rider was to set out from

2

How It Began

New York "and return within the month from Boston to us againe." The mail was to be in "divers baggs, according to the townes the letters are designed to . . . all sealed up till their arrivement, with the seal of the Secretairie's Office, whose care it is on Saturday night to seal them up." Letters from intermediate points were to be in an open bag, and dispensed by the way.

Lovelace hoped that Governor Winthrop would advise the carrier to whom he should report in Boston, and likewise aid him in getting letters and packages for the return trip. It would also be advantageous "to our design if in the interval you discoursed with some of the most able woodmen, to make the most facile way for a post, which in the process of tyme would be the King's best highway; as likewise passages and acomodations [sic] at Rivers, fords, or other necessary places."

The two governors agreed that the postrider be required to direct travelers, who might choose to accompany him, to the best roads and the most commodious stopping places. He was to select the most convenient places for leaving letters and packets for gathering.

It was planned that the first mail should leave New York on the first day of January, 1673. Yet, even so soon, there came a delay, owing to the failure of some Albany dispatches to reach New York in time. The postrider did not get away till the twenty-second day of the month. It is known that he arrived in Boston on or about February 5, where he delivered his mail and also "received congratulations on the success of his journey."

Has no American artist been inspired to paint this man, this first postrider? We've had the Pilgrims landing on the Rock. We've had the Wilderness Road, with Daniel Boone leading some emigrants west through Cumberland Gap. Surely, that lonely first postrider, the first on the continent, is a figure worth attention. When he reached Boston, then only forty years founded, he had come alone more than 200 miles through a trackless wilderness as dangerous (because of the Pequots) as anything in North America.

Paint this stout fellow, active, indefatigable, sworn as to his fi-

3

delity, perhaps standing on the east bank of a great river, the Connecticut, contemplating the surging wild rapids near present Windsor (or Enfield), wondering where and how he should find a fordable stretch. Or, paint him lost and all but immobile, amid the chaos of tangled, wind-felled timber near present Brookfield, Massachusetts. Or, place him triumphant at last on top of Beacon Hill, debating how best to lead his mount down this mountain to the cluster of huts near the shore of Massachusetts Bay.

I have seen fine post-office murals of rolling, rocking mail coaches, of lightning express trains, of RFD buggies, even of deliveries by air. Is it merely by chance that I have never seen "The First Postrider"?

That Governor Lovelace's heroic fellow got to Boston in two weeks with the first mail must have been counted as something of a marvel, even by the officials responsible. Mark the three physical qualifications he must possess. Note, too, that Governor Lovelace asked Governor Winthrop to discover the most able woodmen in New England to help to make a "facile way" for the Post, in other words to provide something nearer to a road than a blaze here and there along a dim moccasin path used by the few settlers who had already been striking out for the Connecticut River Valley from Plymouth, Boston, and Salem.

It seems probable that Winthrop knew where to find "the most able woodmen." He himself was a notable pioneer. He had walked through the forest into New Hampshire and Maine. He had been one of the founders of Ipswich, Massachusetts, and had walked from there to found an ironworks in New Haven Colony; then he had moved to Hartford, where he was to be elected governor of Connecticut Colony no less than seventeen times. One can believe that in the two years of life left to him, Winthrop managed to do something to improve the wilderness path from Hartford to Boston. It would have mattered little just then, anyway: the Dutch had returned to Manhattan Island, which became New Amsterdam all over again.

4

How It Began

Governor Lovelace, the second English governor of New York, had taken office in 1668, only four years after it had been surrendered to England by the Dutch, and its name changed. In 1673, while Lovelace was away in Hartford on a second visit to Governor Winthrop to promote the laudable project of a continuous post road, a Dutch naval squadron suddenly appeared in New York harbor. The city surrendered. A historian wrote that even if Lovelace had been at his fort "and used all the meager resources he had," the capitulation could not have been prevented. Yet, because the unlucky official was not at his post, Lovelace suffered disgrace with the King, and "was impoverished and degraded."

It was natural that the Dutch "did not desire communication" with their eastern neighbors in New England, hence the postrider ceased his trips to Boston. And although the Dutch gave up New York again in little more than a year, the mail carrier did not resume his rounds at once. He was prevented by another king, Philip, one of the ablest and most remarkable Indian chiefs in America, who attacked Swansea, near Plymouth, and massacred all the settlers there, men, women, and children.

That was in June, 1675. By August, Philip's band had destroyed Brookfield, later an important station on the Boston Post Road. By September, Deerfield had been burned by the savages, and sporadic attacks continued during the winter. In February, Philip killed every man in Lancaster, Massachusetts, took the women and children prisoners, and fired the town. He himself was killed in August. The war was declared ended by the settlers, yet the raids dragged on for another two years.

The widespread devastation of more than four years had confined public interest pretty much to military matters. Nothing was done in New England to resume activity on the Boston Post Road, and nothing in New York, until a new royal governor, Thomas Dongan, revived it. He also set up a sort of post office in what was called the Fort—later called the Battery—at the southern tip of Manhattan Island, and fixed the charge of three pence for distances not exceeding one hundred miles.

Meanwhile, by an act of the Massachusetts General Court, the legislature sought to prevent the miscarriage of letters, and named Richard Fairbanks, "his House in Boston, as the place appointed to receive all letters from beyond seas or to be sent thither."

Nothing was said about domestic mail, but later a Boston post office was established at the head of King (now State) Street, and the legislature took notice of the too free and easy manner in which letters were handled; they were often "thrown upon the exchange and whoever will may take them up." So, John Hayward, called "the scrivener," was appointed to take in and convey letters according to their directions.

Interest in the "correspondency" of the King's subjects in America and in the King's highways, continued. In 1691 the post became a sort of business monopoly when a royal patent was granted to Thomas Neale, who never came to America, to "control the post offices for twenty-one years." Andrew Hamilton of Philadelphia was appointed Neale's deputy in the colonies. Described as a typical Scot—canny, moderate, diplomatic, and courageous—Hamilton induced several of the colonies to pass laws to encourage the post.

There is no need here to trace the many steps by which the post office in America gradually took form, save to remark that Hamilton promoted the monopoly of the mails by stipulating rates of carriage and by providing that only his several postmasters could hire post-riders and horses. All other persons were subject to a penalty for violation of "one hundred pounds current money for every offense."

The colonial mails were still slow, expensive, and undependable when, in 1751, the Crown appointed William Hunter and Benjamin Franklin to be "Joint Deputy Postmasters and Managers of his Majesty's Provinces and Dominions on the Continent of North America." The general post office had been in Virginia since 1730. Now, under the new arrangement, Hunter was to act for the Southern colonies at Williamsburg, and Franklin at Philadelphia for the Northern. They were to split a salary of £600 between them, to be paid out of the monies arising from the postage of letters. That is, if there should be any left over from paying operating expenses.

The two men worked in harmony, and to some purpose. In 1761 they were able to pay back to themselves what they had advanced and could remit to the post office in London the first money the American department had ever earned. To accomplish as much, Franklin had completely reorganized the colonial post office. He systematized accounts, selected roads, fords, and ferries. Though he had continued the practice of using postriders to distribute newspapers free of charge, he thought this unfair and abolished it. Henceforth, all newspapers, including his own, might be mailed; all must pay postage.

Franklin also began to display his great ingenuity in post-office affairs. In the summer of 1753, he spent ten weeks in New England and, possibly because of constant wrangling between post-office clerks and patrons about estimated distances, (letters were charged by the mile) and between postriders and the post office itself, he either invented or adapted an odometer, an instrument for measuring distances. "Then, in a chaise of his own design," and followed by men with carts loaded with stones, he drove over the Boston Post Road, where the stones were marked and placed at intervals of one mile.

The milestones were of infinite aid in regulating postal rates. They were a fine advertisement, too, not only because the public found them useful in matters having nothing to do with postage, but also because they added tone to official post roads, giving them a new dignity. They also played a part in helping to report movements of the enemy. Colonel Stephen Moylan wrote General Washington, in 1777, to say that he had seen Hessians "collecting grain from every farm as far as the 8th Milestone"; and Thomas Paine reported the exact location of a marker "near which the American Army began its all-night march on Germantown."

Franklin had long since printed in his *Gazette* newspaper the names of persons who had letters waiting for them in the Philadelphia office. Now he introduced this practice in other towns having

newspapers, requesting that letters not claimed after three months
be forwarded to the general post office. This was the beginning of
the Dead Letter Office in America.

Postmasters throughout the colonies must have quickly realized
they worked now for a man who meant business. Franklin had forms
and instructions printed and sent them to postal officials from New
Hampshire to South Carolina. And they responded. The mails, for
the first time, wrote Franklin's biographer, Carl Van Doren, "were
made to travel night and day from Philadelphia to New York and
back, and later the same service was extended to Boston. . . . Soon
a letter could get to Boston and bring a reply to Philadelphia in
three weeks."

The Revolution did not end Franklin's interest. Appointed by
Congress in 1775 as chairman of a committee to establish a postal
system for the United States, he brought in their report and was
elected Postmaster General at a salary of £1,000 a year, which
"he gave for the relief of wounded soldiers."

Mr. Van Doren thought that "the present United States Post
Office descends in unbroken line from the system Franklin planned
for the Continental Congress." When, in 1847, the first American
postage stamps came into use, the denominations issued bore the
likenesses of Washington (ten cents), and of Franklin (five cents).

Chapter 2

Time & Change: A Panorama

AT TIMES before the railways came, it was said of people who lived almost anywhere along the Boston Post Road that they had seen *everything*.

This route from New York to Boston was the first post road on the American continent. It was so designated in 1673, and was also known variously in its early years as the King's Highway, or simply as The Great Road. As an official post road, however, it gradually took on new importance and, only a little later, after Benjamin Franklin became deputy Postmaster General for the Colonies, the Boston road gained immense prestige by reason of its being lined with well-cut milestones.

And thus, though the flattering tag about the sophistication of Post Road dwellers was much exaggerated, they did live on the main highway connecting two of America's bigger towns of the period. They had, in all truth, seen a great deal. By the time Cornwallis surrendered at Yorktown, they had passed through three wars and rated King Philip a more terrible enemy than George III.

These people had seen, with their own eyes, the great personages of Europe as they passed from one to the other big city, stopping to spend the night at various taverns on the way. They were familiar, too, with peddlers, mountebanks, tramps, religious pilgrims, escaped convicts, drovers, bootmakers, dealers in potash and pearlash, and uncounted emigrants, both Yankees and foreigners, to the West. Many of these had entered or left New England by the Boston Post Road.

My interest in this highway started in its connection with the migrations of Yankees from their native home, and began more than forty years ago when I first became conscious of the many deserted hill farms and fading villages in Vermont, where I was born, in New Hampshire, where I went to school, and in the four other states where I have spent much time in research, both amateur and professional. I wanted to learn who these Yankee exiles were, where they lived, why they went away, and where they went. The old cellar holes, the orchards and fields being slowly throttled by the encroaching forest, moved me deeply. I had a pretty good idea of the great effort that had gone into the making of those farms and homes; the fact that they were being abandoned, after a century or more, seemed to me a great tragedy. (It still does, although the reasons for it were as inevitable as are the workings of any other of the processes of evolution, including those having to do with the changing life and times of the Boston Post Road.)

During 289 years since the first postrider mounted his horse, the route has been a panorama of change. It has witnessed the mails pass in saddlebags, in post chaises, in stagecoaches, in Rural Free Delivery buggies and automobiles, and in United States Post Office trucks so big that clerks sort letters en route.

Here and there, too, sizable strips of the original post road itself were sold or granted to form portions of the rights-of-way of railroads over which the Fast Mail and the Lightning Express smoked, whistled, and clicked off the miles from the Hudson River to Massachusetts Bay. It was by general usage called and is still known in both cities as the *Boston* Post Road.

Many New Yorkers and shore dwellers in Connecticut have come to believe that the original and only Boston Post Road and present US 1 are identical. This is not so. In order to clear this misunderstanding, let us pause a moment at the eastern terminus of the route, at Scollay Square in Boston, to look west down the road toward the Battery in New York City. There were three Boston Post Roads from Boston to New Haven, where they merged to become a single route to New York. Each had a distinctive name as far as New Haven: the original Boston Post Road reached New Haven by way of Worcester, Springfield and Hartford. This later became known as the Upper Road, and often as the *Old* Boston Road.

The Middle Road left Boston to cross Massachusetts, then went on into Connecticut on a line which, to cite an old stage register, touched at Dedham, Medway, Uxbridge, Douglas, Pomfret, and Coventry to Hartford; then to New Haven with way-stops at Wethersfield, Berlin, Meriden, Wallingford, and North Haven.

The Lower Road out of Boston proceeded through Dedham, Walpole, Attleboro, Providence, Warwick, Bristol, Newport, Westerly, and New London, to follow the shore, making stops at Saybrook, Guilford, and Branford to New Haven. The Lower Road also used an alternate route from Providence through Scituate and Coventry, Rhode Island, to Norwich and New London, Connecticut.

The Lower Road is doubtless responsible for the mistaken belief that the Boston Post Road and US 1 are identical for, having reached New Haven, the Lower, Middle, and Upper Roads became a single route along the shore to New York.

Yet, the fallacy regarding present US 1 as the one and only post road between New York and Boston was also practically guaranteed credence by an undated map entitled, "An Account of ye Post of ye Continent of Nth America as they were Regulated by ye Postmasters Genl of ye Post House," which was reproduced in a recent book.* It is unlikely that a more romantic piece of cartography has been perpetrated than this alleged view of "New England, New York, New Jersey, and Pennsylvania, . . . bound one to the other by a single path of communication, the first post road." The route is shown to run from Philadelphia to Portsmouth, New Hampshire, by way of New York, Guilford, Newport, Boston, Marblehead, and Salem.

It will give one an idea of this unusual map's oddities to know that the Hudson River rises in a truly enormous lake that is many miles east of Lake Champlain.

I might mention here that another widely held belief is that, in general, post roads and stagecoaches were used in the same era. I too had entertained this idea until certain historical facts forced its abandonment. For well over a century the mails between New York and Boston were carried in saddlebags. Only some fifty years elapsed between 1785, when the first government mail contract was awarded to a stage line, and 1838, when Congress declared *every* railroad to be an official post road, and authorized the postmaster general to make mail contracts with railroad companies, stipulating only that the rate paid should be "not more than 25 per cent over and above what similar carrying charges would cost in post coaches."

In 1838, few railroads were in operation, and their total mileage was small, yet the steamcars were to push ahead so fast and so ruthlessly that within another dozen years editorials in the daily press were observing that "no more melancholy example of an entire class of workmen is to be found in New England" than that of the stage drivers who had been released "because of the advance of the Iron Horse." Only a few, it seemed, were able "to adjust to the new times."

This was not true except in the Northeastern states. In the Far West, for instance, stage drivers had another forty years of grace

* *U.S. Mail,* by Postmaster General Arthur E. Summerfield as told to Charles Hurd, 1960.

before the rails made them victims of technological advance; and, by that time, most of the old-timers had gone over the hill.

During the 1840 period, or even earlier, die-hard conservatives had started bemoaning "the new and vulgar and dangerous mode of travel" by steamcars, and recalling—the varnish was barely dry on the trains—the romantic era of the stagecoach. To hear them talk, one would think that in coaching days transportation was perfect, that only Ladies and Gentlemen were abroad on the post roads. (The vulgar mass of travelers perhaps went by wagon, or even two-wheeled sulky, but I do not remember meeting them in the stagecoaches of novels.) Novelists studded the whole legend with elegant travelers, and with elegant symbols. The coaches also achieved a pseudo antiquity well beyond their actual years.

Although this book will later consider more closely the stagecoaches and the taverns for which they were responsible, it should be said here, without reservation, that these were the things that brought sudden change to the country villages and even hamlets all along the three Boston post roads. For a brief period, these waypoints knew an excitement, a prosperity and a measure of sophistication that many of them were never to know again. Then, they faded in the echo of the steamcars. Not all of them were to brighten, in mid-twentieth century, when trucks stole mail and express and freight from the rails, and buses and automobiles and planes took care of the passengers.

But, consider the Boston, say, of the mid-1830s, just before the Boston & Worcester railway sent out its very first brigade of cars, as trains were known. In that heyday of coach and tavern, more than 2,000 mail and passenger coaches rolled into and out of Boston every week.

There were five distinct lines to carry the Albany Mail by as many different routes—via Greenfield, Northampton, Springfield, Brattleboro, and another, to Albany *and* Phoenix, New York, the latter then considered, for some reason no longer clear, to rate with the capital city. There was also an Albany Accommodation.

There were Accommodation stages to Amherst, Bolton, to the

two Concords (Massachusetts and New Hampshire), to Dudley, Duxbury, Londonderry, Lancaster, Amesbury, Newport, New Bedford, Portsmouth, Providence, Taunton, Uxbridge, and Worcester. And many more.

Almost invariably, the first coaches of the day "set off," as Badger & Porter's Stage Register phrased it, at three o'clock in the morning—"while it was still night"—even in June. They began leaving Boyden's City Tavern and the Marlboro Hotel as the clock on the Old South Church started to peal the hour.

The departing vehicles took different routes through the sleeping city to pick up passengers who had registered at the General Stage Office, or in the Stage Book kept at appointed taverns, hotels, and lodging houses. Because at three of the clock in the Boston of 130 years ago there was little traffic, the big coach made its lumbering way through streets deserted and silent, as if locked under an enchantment.

It was still dark, except for the faint glow of the stage's running lights, as one by one the new passengers boarded. They could have little idea who their fellow passengers were for at least another hour or so.

As the coach moved on into Roxbury, regular patrons might see the low bulk of a granite marker and know they had reached the Parting Stone, and that here the post road out of Boston City separated into two routes. The left-hand road led south to Dedham and the Middle and Lower Post Roads. To the right was the way to Cambridge and the Upper Road. The latter was the original or Old Post Road to New York.

By the time either Dedham or Cambridge was reached, a shadowy dawn began to mitigate the night, and soon the returning life of the open country could be marked by glimmers in the farmhouses. First, perhaps, by a candle in the shed-chamber. Then, and because at six miles an hour any passenger who was wide awake could take in pretty much everything along the way, he might watch while the farmers and villagers of Massachusetts prepared for another day in field or woods, or in the little water-turned mills and factories making cotton cloth and soap and candles and boots and other useful things.

The coach proceeded and the panorama of the New England countryside continued to unfold. Though cooking stoves had of late been coming into use, the farmhouses, stoves or not, were still lit up by the great fireplaces that occupied the best part of a kitchen wall. Flames leaped under the pots and kettles. And soon enough a figure could be made out in the gloom, carrying a lantern and pails, heading for the barn. . . . It was five o'clock in both Middlesex and Norfolk counties. . . .

During these early morning hours as many as thirty coaches, both mail and passenger, might pass a stated point in what is now suburban Boston.

Breakfast for Upper Road travelers might be had in Sudbury; or in Medfield on the Middle Road; or in Walpole for those taking the Lower Road to Rhode Island and points along the eastern Connecticut shore. Wherever they broke their fast, it was likely to be a substantial meal, for the Eastern Stage Company, which had come to operate or control much of the mail-and-passenger coach business in Massachusetts, favored the better taverns and hotels on the three Boston post roads.

In that time, the first meal of the day was no light matter of coffee, fruit, and cold cereal. Travelers might read on the blackboard menu of fish and fowl, mutton and steak, along with eggs, johnny cake, hot cream-of-tartar biscuits, and all the butter and fresh cream anyone could wish. The taproom was ready to provide Small Drink, which meant cider, beer, or ale, as well as brandy and whiskey, and of course, the celebrated rum made in Medford near Boston.

The Old Post Road

Ahead of the Boston passengers for New York were approximately 250 miles by the Upper Road, 225 miles by the Middle, and 270 miles by the Lower.

At this period, 1835–1840, an authority on travel by stagecoach in New York and New England wrote, "The roads were hard, the bridges good, the relays of horses frequent, and it took only two days to go from Boston to New York." One may assume that travelers, whether by the Fast Mail, Regular Mail, or an Accommodation coach, expected to spend at least two nights in wayside inns before reaching New York.

Like the stage lines, the inns and taverns had almost reached their high point in New England. In 1841, the first steam train began to operate through service from Boston to Albany. Three years later, when the Hartford & Springfield railroad was opened, thus closing a gap between those cities and providing through service from Boston to New York, an observer commented sadly and accurately, that "now came the closing of the old inns and the desertion of the turnpikes and highways."

It was true. The brave, loud claims of the Eastern Stage Company, "New York in Two Days," were soon a mockery of public transportation. Coach horns no longer heralded arrival of the mails. Little by little, then much faster, the tavern flunkeys and stablemen found less to do, as did the drivers and, like the horses, were put out to pasture [or wherever it was that human beings and animals went to when the last stagecoach passed down the road and over the hill to Valhalla].

The fine great coaches, made in Concord, New Hampshire, either rusted where they stood—one of them in a Shrewsbury barnyard —or were sold west of the Mississippi. Rusted, too, were the door hinges of the big old public houses where Washington had slept, or LaFayette dined, or Webster had hoisted a dram or two. Bricks tumbled into fireplaces. Dust settled in the old bedchambers, to be disturbed only now and then when country boys and maidens came on trysts in the deserted echoing halls.

As the decades passed, most of the empty taverns, many of them dating from well before the first stagecoach, were destroyed by fire. The many windows of others fell victim to weather and boys with stones, and once this happened, the place almost invariably and immediately became a "haunted house." There was nothing like staring windows and a few swinging blinds to infest the once jolly old place with apparitions of ancient suicides, or maybe the ghost of a murdered innkeeper. By then, one of two things could happen. It would either be torn down, or, if fortunate, it would be taken in hand by a few God-given men or, more likely, God-given women, to be preserved, while less imaginative townsmen swore *they* should take care that no such superannuated eyesore would ever again burden the town.

Traffic on the Boston Post Road, however, was to revive more than a century later, when the United States Post Office began taking the mails away from the railroads, which had carried them for over a hundred years, and putting them into trucks.

Among the most recent changes along the Boston Post Road, which, including the Upper, Middle and Lower Roads, is about 680 miles long, are two, neither of great importance, but both quite obvious, at least to the eye of the returning native of New England.

One is the appearance of ranch-type homes. I saw them often, sometimes in new suburban districts, again along country roads where they seemed particularly incongruous amid the great old mellow elms, or near houses that have stood 150, or perhaps 200 years.

But the real shocker was what I shall evermore remember as The Flamingo Invasion. This has taken form, it seems to me, most suddenly and horribly, in the shape of plastic fowl known as "lawn decorations." They come in pairs, one 30 inches tall, the other 20 inches. They are the pinkest, whitest, leanest, coyest examples of *Phoenicopterus ruber* imaginable.

Not only that, but these pairs of exotic birds are now, in the

1960s, to be found on Yankee lawns all the way from the Connecticut and Rhode Island shores up through Massachusetts to Great Barrington, the Berkshires, Methuen and Newburyport; on the Maine shore to Bar Harbor; up the Connecticut River and its tributaries to the Province of Quebec. Though the Boston Post Road by no means reaches all of this territory, *I* reached it, only to find the two pink birds there ahead of me. The Post Road region could not begin to contain so fetching and foreign an adjunct to nature.

The plastic flamingoes, which a friend invariably referred to in an unprintable manner as "Pokes," were sighted within 300 feet of the Wayside Inn. Another pair looked as if about to walk across Lexington Green; still another shivered in the White Mountains at a motel near the Great Stone Face.

I am still at a loss to explain these thousands of symbols that have nothing in common with New England. Are they some sort of status symbol? Were they bought in Florida by Yankees seeking escape from February? Or were they manufactured secretly in some ivy-grown old former textile mill in Massachusetts?

I neglected to find out. In any case, nothing quite so foreign had been seen since Phineas T. Barnum wintered his circus in Bridgeport, Connecticut. The once astute Yankees had been sold a bill of goods for the glory of Florida.

But where, one might ask, are the Texas boosters? Here in six populous states was obviously a vast market for "lawn decorations." What an opportunity for an honest, if revolting, dollar, in a plastic longhorn steer, to stand in the shade of uncounted thousands of sugar maples and English elms.

Chapter 3

Mrs. Knight
Takes the Road

SUCH ROADS as existed in New York and New England, when the first postman started to ride, had been made by "all able-bodied males between sixteen and sixty years" who were required to give one (or more) day's labor with their teams on the town ways; and another day's work or more toward a King's Highway, or Great Road, or what today would be the responsibility of county and state. The penalty for noncompliance was usually set at five shillings per day, an enormous sum.

Confusion was guaranteed by those missing links of roads between the towns. Although the law specified that they, too, were the responsibility of the adjacent towns, the town fathers were likely to devote more attention to the "ways" radiating from the village green to the last farm, than to worry about the wilderness beyond. For example, well into the eighteenth century, travelers heading east out of Willimantic, Connecticut, by the so-called King's Highway, found a dead end at Plainfield. The "able-bodied men between sixteen and sixty" had tired of road building at the very edge of the village, leaving a hiatus of several miles. And right on the Upper Post Road, in Brookfield, Massachusetts, the road builders had left an immense area of wind-thrown forest to make a jungle that was a terror to the postriders.

Getting any sort of a through road in Connecticut was particularly difficult, according to historian W. Storrs Lee, who declared that the King's Highway in that colony "was an insult to its proud title." Topography was to blame. The long ridges running from Massachusetts to Long Island Sound discouraged east and west roads. Except in the wide valleys of the Connecticut and perhaps two other rivers, the glacial remains of boulders, rocks, and outcropping ledges stood in the way. (Little wonder that today's tourists marvel at stone fences which mark Connecticut from border to border.) In addition to the geologic aspects of topography were virgin trees of 4- and 5-foot diameter that blocked progress. Clearing two such trees could well occupy a team of road builders a full day.

"What," asks Mr. Lee, "made the Connecticut settlers so ornery?" He explains that "Bad roads discouraged intercourse, lack of intercourse increased isolation, isolation developed independence and a lack of cooperation, which in turn caused the roads to suffer."

Somehow or other, the three eastern sections of the Boston Post Road—the Upper, Middle, and Lower—got built through Massachusetts, Rhode Island, and Connecticut, to meet and merge at New Haven. For more than a century, or until the stagecoaches came, they supplied the route over which the mails were carried by hard-riding horsemen between the two terminal cities.

Mrs. Knight Takes the Road

It will be recalled that among the duties which the postriders were to perform was that of guiding such travelers as wished to accompany them. It turned out, in 1704, that one of these travelers was Sarah Kemble Knight, a Boston schoolmistress and woman of affairs, who needed to go to New Haven, and who left one of the earliest records of what travel to New York by the Lower Road was like. She was nearly forty at the time, clearly a woman of perception, humor, and tolerance. On October 2, Mrs. Knight rode horseback to Dedham where she expected to meet the postrider. He failed to appear. Hearing that he had stopped some 12 miles short of the village, she got a guide, a local character called John, who charged her half a piece of eight plus a dram, to take her on to where the driver was staying. Here she remained the night, then set out with the postman at about eight in the morning, to stop the second night at a "Mr. Haven's," probably in Rhode Island.

Though the bed was not so hard as the one in Dedham, she got no sleep because a couple of drunks were holding an all-night debate on a subject that seemed to them of vast importance: the significance of the name "Narragansett." At last, "I set my candle on a chest and, sitting up, composed my resentment in the following manner:

> *"I ask thy aid, O potent Rum!*
> *To charm these wrangling topers dumb. . . ."*

Next morning about four, she was roused and set out in company with the postrider and another man who "put upon very furiously, so that I could not keep up with them only as now and then they would stop until they saw me." These churls kept up the game for some thirty miles. The third night was spent at or near Kingston, the fourth night at New London where, after a frightening passage on a wildly bounding ferryboat, Mrs. Knight was welcomed at the home of the Reverend Gurdon Saltonstall, the eminent Congregational minister, and one of the founders of Yale College, who was soon (1707) to become governor of Connecticut. "Here," Mrs. Knight confided to her journal, "I was very handsomely and plentifully treated and lodged . . . by this most affable, courteous, generous, and best of men."

Next morning, the kindly parson would not permit his guest to depart without a guide, but procured a young gentleman of the town who accompanied her on the way to New Haven. "The roads all along this way are very bad, encumbered with rocks and mountainous passages, which were very disagreeable to my carcass . . . and once in going over a bridge, my horse stumbled and very narrowly 'scaped falling over into the water. . . . But through God's goodness I met with no harm. . . ." She was now in New Haven, five days and four nights from Boston.

Mrs. Knight remained in New Haven, on business, until early morning of December 6, when she set out for New York, passing the Stratford Ferry about 11 A.M., and going on to stay the night at Fairfield. About noon next day they rode through "Norrowalk [*sic*]," and by 9 P.M. came to Rye, "walking and leading our horses near a mile together, up a prodigious high hill." The food—a fricassee—was so extraordinarily bad, Mrs. Knight hastened to bed supperless. Though most weary, she found the bed as hard as it was noisy from rustling husks, and during the night, the chambermaid came into the room "to make a bed for the men who, when they lay down, complained their legs lay out of it by reason of its shortness."

Mrs. Knight had gone to bed supperless, and she did not close her eyes the night. At three, she arose to sit by the fire till daylight, then she took off, without even inquiring about food, for New Rochelle where "we had a good breakfast." And, on the strength of that, at about an hour before sunset "we came to York." Not counting her stop of several days in New Haven, she had spent seven days and six nights between Boston and New York.

Mrs. Knight realized that her journey was an "unheard of thing for an unaccompanied woman to do." But she was as unconventional as she was able. Not long after her return to Boston, she sold her house there and moved to Connecticut where she speculated in lands, operated properties in New London and Norwich, ran a house of public entertainment, and in 1718 was fined for selling

Mrs. Knight Takes the Road

rum to Indians. These unconventional activities did not, however, "lessen her public repute." She left an estate of £1,800. Her diary was not published until nearly a century after she died at the age of sixty-one, in New London.

By the time Mrs. Knight, accompanied by the mail carrier, made her pioneer journey, the postriders between Boston and New York formed a fraternity that had developed certain habits of thought and action which were in conflict with their sworn duty to act always for the good of the public. Though they were obligated to guide travelers free of charge, they never refused the gratuities of which the astute Mrs. Knight speaks again and again.

The postrider was also subject to many other regulations which in time seemed to be a burden, possibly even an imposition, too great for man to bear. Thus, he began to pocket the charges on letters he picked up and delivered along his route. This naturally let him see the possibilities of his occupation, and before long he was carrying on various transactions for his own benefit. Many a rider acted as virtual agent in buying and selling bank notes and lottery tickets, a sort of customer's man for speculators. They performed shopping services in the cities for villagers, and collected commissions from both customers and merchants.

Several of the more alert postriders quit their jobs to start their own express services to carry merchandise. They were strictly forbidden to carry letters subject to the post. But because their deliveries were almost certain to be quicker than by the regular post, they were swamped with what we call first-class matter. And until widespread abuse put a stop to it, private express riders seldom went forth without as many "kite-tails" as they could carry. These were bundles of straw or paper wrapped around the forbidden letters.

How the postrider met his obligation "to watch keenly for all fugitive servants and deserters" is not clear, and for all one knows it may be a regulation today, though the fugitives are likely to be

23

post-office robbers, as witness the bulletin boards with the WANTED circulars.

Postriders were expected to average from thirty to fifty miles daily in the summer, and considerably less in the wintertime. And there must have been some allowance made as between the men whose regular route was from New York City to, say, New Haven or elsewhere along the Lower Road in Connecticut, and those who rode the Upper Road between Springfield and Boston. Especially in winter.

At least three riders were noted for their long service. All happened to live in Stratford, Connecticut, and all became rather celebrated personalities in their old age. One was Deacon Peet, thirty-two years aboard a post horse. The others were the Hurd brothers, Andrew, with fifty years as a rider, and Ebenezer, with forty-eight years. Ebenezer was believed to have carried to New York the news of Concord and Lexington, and was remembered also for his cry when he approached a turnpike: "Open the gate for the King's Post!"

How the public and even the post office condoned irregularities may be gauged by the high repute of Ebenezer Hurd. He was known to have never failed to collect all way-postage on letters for his own pocket, and to have carried on a sizable business in what could be termed express, or even freight. At least once he was detected, by a Royal post-office inspector, "calmly waiting for a pair of oxen that he was to transfer for a customer."

More widely known than these riders was Levi Pease, often called the Stagecoach King. He, more than any other one man, brought an end of the period of the postrider and put the post office on wheels. He was what the professors mean when they refer to a seminal character.

Chapter 4

Levi Pease:
The Stagecoach King

THOUGH FORGOTTEN NOW, Levi Pease was hailed in New York and much of New England as the Stagecoach King. If the title seems to brag a little too much, Pease surely did a lot toward introducing to the public the vehicle in which few had ridden until then. Unlike Henry Ford, Pease neither made nor sold carriages of any sort, yet he perhaps more than any other one man was responsible for the era named for the stagecoach.

Born in 1740 at Enfield, Connecticut, on the Upper Boston Post Road, he was working as a blacksmith when he enlisted in the army at the outbreak of the Revolution, and served throughout the fighting. It was here he developed the talents that were to fit him for the occupation he was to follow with such success at war's end. To begin with, Private Pease was found "so tactful, shrewd, and reliable" by his officers that he was often chosen as a dispatch rider. He became a favorite with General Jeremiah Wadsworth, who trusted him to buy horses and stores for the commissary department, and he went along with his chief when Wadsworth was ordered to supply the French troops also. It was Pease who bought the horses to move the French artillery out of Newport, and he stayed with the French until the end of the war. He was "much esteemed" by LaFayette.

By the time the smoke of Yorktown had cleared, ex-soldier Pease apparently knew what he wanted, and that was to establish a line of stagecoaches. Looking back, it is almost as if the stagecoach era had been waiting for Levi Pease to come along—a man of energy, persistence, and foresight, who would lay imaginative hands on this elegant vehicle of the wealthy few, and turn it into the common wheeled carrier of the mass of American people, and their newspapers and letters. Pease accomplished more. As a not wholly disinterested observer, he did what he could to encourage better roads and highways. Among his efforts was a long campaign to secure what appears to have been the first charter for a turnpike granted by the Massachusetts General Court.

But before he even bought a stagecoach, Levi Pease, who had traveled over much of southern New England, knew where he meant to begin business: It was a line from Boston to Hartford by the Upper Boston Post Road. Lacking ready cash, he called on an old friend, Reuben Sykes, broaching the subject of a partnership. Both men had had at least a brief stretch of driving a stage wagon in Connecticut; and both may have served as postriders. Sykes had a little money. He also liked the idea of partnership with Pease. They soon secured "two convenient wagons," and opened for business, simultaneously from both ends of the line, on the morning of October 20, 1783.

Note that the vehicles were called wagons, not coaches. A stage wagon was a rectangular box mounted on springs, containing four seats to accommodate eleven passengers and the driver. It had a top with side curtains. There were no backs to the seats. The rear seat was much preferred by reason of the passengers' being able to lean against the back of the wagon. There were no side entrances. One had to climb over the passengers in front. Although similar stage wagons were still to be used for many years more, the stagecoach for passengers and mail soon took the conventional form that lasted till the railroads came.

On that first day of Pease & Sykes' stage operations, Captain Pease drove westward, stopping the first night at Northboro, passing through Worcester the next day, and stopping the second night at Rice's Tavern in Brookfield. The third day took him through Palmer, to by-pass Springfield, and to spend the third night in Somers, Connecticut. Hartford was reached on the fourth day. The early runs, both ways, were terribly disappointing. Neither stage was filled. Occasionally they went out empty and did not pick up a fare on the way.

Pease & Sykes did not lose faith, but they introduced a few changes. Pease made arrangements to leave Boston from the popular Lion Inn, in what was then Marlborough (Washington) Street, and to stop the night at Farrar's Tavern, Shrewsbury. The second night he stopped at Spencer, where he exchanged passengers with Sykes, who returned to Hartford by way of Springfield. Pease returned to Boston. A few hours were saved. And before the first year was done, Worcester was reached in one day from Boston, passengers had increased at both terminals, and Pease had bought an inn on Tremont Street, facing the Boston Common. The fare was holding steady at four pence a mile, or about ten dollars, Boston to Hartford.

Before the year was out, Sykes had followed his partner's lead by opening a tavern, in Wilbraham, just east of Springfield, Massachusetts. Pease had been working toward extending their line through to New York City, and late in 1784 he added two partners, Jacob

27

Brown, with a tavern in New Haven, and Talmage Hall, of New York, who took over the Roger Morris mansion on Harlem Heights for a tavern, and with it the immense Morris stables. Both Brown and Hall were expert horsemen. They were to drive the partnership's stages between Hartford and New York.

Things were looking much better. Pease, who was determined to nail down the Pease & Sykes line before some come-lately could interfere, petitioned the Massachusetts General Court to grant him exclusive privilege to carry travelers from Boston to Hartford by stage. Whether or not this bill passed is not clear, nor does it matter: Pease & Sykes continued to carry a majority of the increasing number of travelers between Hartford and Boston.

Although the mails were still carried by postriders, the alert Pease believed they could be carried much more cheaply in light coaches, and almost as fast. When in 1785 the government got around to it, Pease & Sykes were awarded the first contract to carry mail in the United States. It is of record at Worcester that the first contract mail passed through that city on January 7, 1786.

At this time Pease announced in the *Massachusetts Spy* that now, in order to make his line "the cheapest" as well as the "most expeditious," the fare had been lowered from four pence to three pence a mile, and that passengers might carry fourteen pounds of baggage. In the same issue of the paper, Pease was quoted as saying that the through line, Boston to New York, would make the trip by mail coach in five and a half days, in winter, and four days in summer. He informed the public that the through mail-coach stages set out "from the home of Levi Pease, at the Sign of the New York Stage, opposite the Mall, in Boston," adding that "Said Pease keeps good lodging etc. for gentlemen travellers, and stabling for horses."

Yet, this first stage line in New England, with the first mail contract in the United States, was no stronger than its weakest link—Talmage Hall, one of the original four partners in the Pease & Sykes line. Talmage Hall appears to have had intimations of greatness as a sort of stage-line mogul. After joining the Pease combination, he set out to corner the line to Albany, and lost all his money in the effort. He lost not only the Morris mansion, the stables, the coaches and the horses, but also owed numerous bills in regard to the Pease Line. Pease hastened to New York when he learned of the crash, to find the entire New York end of the line in shambles. How he re-established the stage service as quickly as he did is not clear, but within a short time the Pease Line was again operating with regularity.

Perhaps the sudden collapse of one of his partners made Pease reflect on the chance of "irregularities" of his employees, the drivers. They were known to take advantage of the free and easy way of charging—they simply pocketed the money collected for fares, express packages, and letters. In any event, it was soon after the Talmage Hall affair that Pease virtually invented a new and important job in the stagecoaching business.

On each through stage between New York and Boston, and return, he installed what he called a conductor. He was to ride from one end of the line to the other. Here, almost fifty years before the first railroad was built, was the fellow who was to take charge of the "train of cars" originally called a brigade. One may hope that Pease's conductors, too, were garbed in blue with brass buttons.

Before Pease's innovation, the stage driver, almost invariably called Captain, was, like his sea-going prototype, responsible for his coach, horses, passengers, and mail—in short, everything. But now he was to be relieved of certain duties, even forbidden to perform them. The conductor would collect and issue tickets en route. He was also prepared to conduct what Pease described as "private business"; he would accept bundles, money, lottery tickets, newspapers, and such. In the press, Pease let it be known that his company warranted security for his conductors; he had bonded them.

It seems probable that the appearance of conductors brought several changes in stage operation. Pease and Sykes were obviously out for what could be called the express business. They meant, also, to put a stop to leaks due to free-loading passengers, whose custom had been to slip the driver a little something for a ride. Though the driver doubtless lost some of his importance, he was still the man who "made the stage go," and, if the reminiscences of travelers are to be trusted, he retained no little of his stature as the captain—the man with the reins and the whip who could put her through no matter the way and the weather, and who, after all, had control over the safety of his passengers.

Levi Pease, who had been awarded the first United States Post Office contract to carry mail, soon found the mail business to be so highly rewarding to the Pease & Sykes Line that it permitted him to run stages even when passengers were few. In Concord, New Hampshire, he prevailed on the legislature to grant him an exclusive right to operate stages between Boston and Haverill and Hanover, then he bid for the mail contract and got it. Two years later, he underbid other lines and won the contract to carry mail between Boston and Portsmouth.

By now several smaller stage lines were operating out of Boston, and many more had been started in other cities all over Eastern United States. It was Levi Pease who now contributed an idea that was to benefit them all. He proposed that all staging centers have a General Ticket Office to serve all lines in the district, and persuaded other Boston operators to join him in establishing such an office. Tickets to all points could be purchased here, even though in those early days each stage line had its own depot, often a tavern.

Pease's General Ticket Office idea was quickly adopted elsewhere, and was copied later by the railroads. So, too, was his next innovation—the first limited service of the coaching era. "The stage-carriages of this new line," he announced in his favorite newspaper, the *Massachusetts Spy,* "will be small, genteel, and easy, in which but four passengers will be admitted."

Though the word, "limited," had reference to the number of passengers rather than to the number of stops, the service really amounted to "limited" in that sense too, if for no other reason than that the coach could accommodate only four persons; and thus no time was lost on the road by loading and unloading way passengers. The limited coaches made much better time than the regular ones, and they cost more, a sort of extra-fare ride in the days before railroads. Did these "small, genteel, and easy" coaches also develop a snob appeal, as did fancy and swift trains later?

In any event, the Post Office Department must have been im-

Levi Pease: The Stagecoach King

pressed by the energy and ingenuity and judgment of Levi Pease, for in the last year of the old century, Postmaster General Habersham wrote to ask if Mr. Pease would take over a bad situation, and solve it. Because of poor service by mail contractors on the Philadelphia–Baltimore run, Habersham had lost patience to such an extent he planned to remove them and start a Federal post-office line of stages; in short, put the government itself into the mail-coach business. He wanted to know if Mr. Pease would come to Philadelphia and take complete charge of "setting the business in motion."

Mr. Pease would, and he did. After consulting with Habersham and other post-office officials, the Stagecoach King of New York and New England first designed a mail coach, and had the requisite number made under his direction, and selected the colors to be used. The body was to be green, "formed of Prussian blue and yellow ochre," he specified. The running parts were "to be of Red lead, mixed to approach vermillion as near as may be." There was to be an octagon black panel on the back of the body. And "lettered on the doors in Roman Capitals, with patent yellow," was to appear United States Mail Stages, and "over those words a Spread Eagle of a size and color to suit."

Such was the first government mail stage. Pease went ahead to take charge of "setting the business in motion" and ran things to the satisfaction of the Postmaster General. The United States Post Office continued to operate one or more lines for another ten years. (Chiefly, wrote an observer, as a threat—a club "to beat dishonest or incompetent mail contractors.")

Meanwhile, Pease returned to Massachusetts where he sold his tavern on the Mall in Boston, moved his family to Shrewsbury, on the Upper Post Road near Worcester, and bought the old Farrar Tavern, operated many years by the late Major John Farrar. Although at about this period, Pease seems to have made his original partner, Reuben Sykes, fifteen years his junior, a sort of general manager of the business, Pease continued active in the company, which was still in a flourishing condition.

Indeed, the Pease & Sykes combine on the Boston Post Road

had grown from four to fifteen proprietors; and the mail business had become so important that the directors called a meeting to settle the complicated problem of how best to share the income from it. They agreed that "the Mail pay should be equally divided among the whole number of proprietors according to the number of miles in Mail carried by each proprietor."

The proprietors had to be alert about competition, for even if a competing line had no mail contract, it might try getting passenger business by trimming the fare. This may have been the reason that in 1804, with Levi Pease in the chair, the Pease & Sykes directors voted to slash the Boston–New York fare by $6, doubtless to take care of an outfit which was seeking passengers by the Middle Road.

The time of departure and arrival of stages was naturally of utmost importance, and in 1805 the meeting of the Boston Post Road combination's proprietors, "held at the dwelling house of Ezekiel Lovejoy, Stratford, Connecticut," went carefully through the proposed schedule for April to October, referred to as The Summer Establishment, before signing. There were sixteen regular stops scheduled, each way, between Sudbury, Massachusetts, and East Chester, New York.

Not long before he sold his interest in the stage line to Reuben Sykes, Pease had the satisfaction of seeing still one more of his efforts come to fruition. This was in 1808, when the Commonwealth at last granted, after twenty-two years, the first charter to a turnpike in Massachusetts. The Old Bay State had been singularly backward in recognizing the "modern" type of highway. Connecticut had laid a turnpike as long before as 1792, and had since built another dozen pikes. Even Rhode Island had a turnpike. Back in 1796, Levi Pease's name had appeared at the head of "thirty-one solid citizens as incorporators" of this first Massachusetts pike. Now it was laid from Boston to Worcester, by way of Shrewsbury. (One notes that Shrewsbury was the town where Pease had bought the Farrar Tavern, and moved his family, in preparation for his own retirement.)

Levi Pease: The Stagecoach King

Before he retired to play landlord in his Shrewsbury tavern, proprietor-director Pease acted, in company with his board, to add a notable flourish to coaches of the Boston and New York Mail Stage Line: "It was voted that our Drivers shall be furnished with Horns or Trumpets that shall be blown on approach of the Stage at any Post Office, and the places where they Dine, Breakfast etc., etc., and if any Driver refuses to comply, he must be dismissed by his employer."

Whether the *"must* be dismissed" has anything to do with post-office regulations for mail stages, or if it is merely a natural liking for a little drama, the stage-drivers' trumpet or horn seems to have become an integral piece of the stagecoach legend before the Stagecoach King retired. It was said of Pease that in his retirement, he "often drove a coach until he was too feeble to do so."

Levi Pease died in 1824, aged eighty-four. Since his first through mail coach arrived in New York, the time for carrying the New York and Boston mails had been reduced from six days to thirty-six hours.

Chapter 5

Turnpikes

IT IS PROBABLE that when the Commonwealth of Massachusetts at last broke down and chartered, in 1808, the first turnpike in the state, Levi Pease and associates, its chief sponsors, believed that they were in the wave of the future. Modern times had arrived. Twelve years had elapsed since Pease had written the original turnpike petition.

By 1808, however, the building of new turnpikes was already coming to an end in Connecticut, New York, Pennsylvania, and several other states. Though a few continued in the 1840s, and one, the Hartford and Albany, collected 5 per cent for its stockholders until 1872 when it went out of business, the private pike era faded rapidly when the steamcars started operating. Even before then, the canal-building craze had taken the bloom from many a pike.

Just what was a turnpike? It was first of all a private toll road operating under a charter. No less than 135 turnpike corporations had been chartered in the New England states during the decade ending in 1806. They totaled some 3,000 miles. The turnpike was secondarily an "improved road." Just what that meant was an abstract matter, although boulders were sure to have been removed, and boggy places topped with gravel.

Turnpikes were begun like any public road. Oxen urged by two drivers dragged a plow, one man holding the handles, the other standing on the beam. This machine moved along the margins of the road, turning every fifty yards. The loose earth was then moved to the center by a stone-drag, a sort of leveling box drawn by oxen. On the steeper hills a succession of low earth ridges was left across the road—called "thankyou marms," according to Historian Kirkland—to divert rainwater to the ditches. The biggest boulders had already been dug up and rolled off into the bushes beside the road. The final touch was to dump gravel into the swampy places, and perhaps to add a culvert here and there. Then the gates were placed. The gate was the turnpike's reason for being. On the longer pikes these were erected every 10 miles.

Turnpikes varied from 3 to about 50 miles. Each pike had its name and its individual charges. One of the best, and among the earliest, was that between Norwich and New London, Connecticut, which was financed by a lottery drawn in 1789. And, until 1849, "every merchant and traveler along that route *bought* his right of way."

The cost of turnpike construction in Massachusetts seems to have been inordinately high. Either that or the Connecticut people were sharp buyers. The splendid Hartford and New Haven was laid for a mere $2,280 per mile; but the Salem–Boston job in Massachusetts came to $14,600, and the Newburyport–Boston $11,730 per mile. The average turnpike cost in the Bay State was $4,500 per mile.

The charges for use of the pikes have been reported so variously that it seems best to cite an act of the Massachusetts General Court of 1805 setting the official tolls there: For a coach, chariot, phaeton, or other four-wheel spring carriages, drawn by two horses, 25¢; two-horse wagons, 10¢; cart or wagon drawn by a pair of oxen, 10¢;

man and horse, 4¢; sleigh or sled, 2 horses, or 2 oxen, 8¢; horses, mules, neat cattle, led or driven, each 1¢; sheep or swine, by the dozen, 3¢.

This same act also forbade collection of tolls "from persons going to or from a church or grist mill, on military duty or on journeys within the town where the gate is located." Turnpikes were authorized to give rebates by commuting toll payments to a fixed, agreed sum. This arrangement was usual with stage companies, as were similar agreements in connection with tolls on bridges and ferries.

We come now to the most unpopular man connected with a turnpike—the toll-gate keeper. To begin with, there was a distaste for turnpikes almost inherent in Americans. This was partly a matter of democratic principles, and partly a commentary on the physical character of the pikes themselves. Gradually, as time wore away their sense of newness, or novelty, and travelers took a second and clear look at the pikes, they began to find fault with what they saw. A petition to the Massachusetts General Court in 1823, when the pike honeymoon was almost done, stated the case brutally: "In this age and in this land of Liberty, turnpike gates are everywhere considered a nuisance and are vexations to travelers . . . as are the turnpike roads themselves, which are generally the poorest roads over which the traveler passes from one part of the country to another."

This seems somewhat unfair. It does not acknowledge any contribution whatever, yet the pikes, poor though they might have been, were a decided improvement over the public roads. During a decade early in the nineteenth century, the number of conveyances multiplied three times, a much faster growth than that of the population. And only a little later, an estimate of the number of private vehicles, moving annually between Worcester and Boston, set the figure at 32,400. Indeed, as historian Kirkland pointed out, "the railroad had scarcely passed its cold hand upon this manner of travel" before the devotees of the glorious stagecoach, and of the horse-and-buggy, started to celebrate their virtues.

Turnpikes

Getting back to that man at the toll-gate, the poor fellow represented, in the eyes of the public, the visible, greedy, and unconscionable turnpike corporation. Subject to all the human frailties that accompany a boring, underpaid job, for which there could be no foolproof check or audit, was he not tempted to pass close friends without charge? Was he proof against mistakes of counting sheep and cattle passing through? Was he to remain sweet and reasonable when contending with short-tempered or merely smart-aleck patrons who "disapproved on principle" of turnpikes?

Then, there were the traders, the bargainers, who wanted special rates, and the out-and-out beats who tried to slip through the dark. Worst of all, there were those supporters of anarchy who used the Shunpike, which made a forbidden loop around the barrier.

The gate keeper was popular with nobody. Was there—many such a one must have wondered—was there no Balm in Gilead?

There was at least one gate keeper whose plight must have touched the otherwise stony heart of the superintendent of the Middlesex pike in Connecticut. He was Robert Rankin, who kept the Saybrook gate. Regulations obligated him to remain at his post until 9 P.M., until his superior, noting that Rankin obviously "valued an earlier bedtime hour," and that customers had got into the habit of waiting for him to retire before they came to the gate, ruled that Rankin could pocket anything collected after nine o'clock. It had an immediate effect on traffic at the Saybrook gate of the Middlesex pike.

One of the early indications that the turnpike era had passed its meridian could be seen as first one, then another established concern began to petition legislatures to release them from their obligations, or "negociated with county authorities to transform their pikes into public roads." Several old pikes merely tore down the gates and let the public enter as they would. These efforts mark an urgency to be shut of obligations almost as great as those made by promoters when the turnpike building fad was new and seemed to promise blinding wealth, to those who got in on the ground floor.

Historians seem agreed that the railroads alone did not put them out of business; they quit because a majority of them were not making money.

This brings up still another reason that turnpikes were resented; and it is the same reason that modern throughways, which are often called turnpikes, or toll-roads, caused no little resentment when the State faced the Individual in matters pertaining to condemnation proceedings. The nineteen-forties and fifties have been filled with such contentions. If a man of, say, 1800, or 1810, could have read our newspapers of recent years, surely he would never doubt the statement that "history repeats itself."

Here is the manner by which most turnpikes came into being: The turnpike corporation was granted a charter, then it surveyed the route. The towns through which it passed were then required to purchase the land for the corporation and turn over a clear title. And the courts, according to historian Storrs Lee, "almost always ruled in favor of the turnpike corporations."

Like the railroads in their flush days, the turnpikes were not only in a great hurry, but they were arrogant, and they trod hard on a public that was unequal to fighting the lawyers who shouted, threatened, and, if need be, pleaded the public weal. And so today do the catchpolls of the all-powerful State. Few of us cannot recall an individual who sought to contend against a throughway, in Connecticut or Oregon or elsewhere, even to armed resistance, but eventually he went down a victim of the *newer* turnpike fad, which for all I know may be just that, a fad, an illusion of Progress . . .

Back in 1800 or so, the turnpike surveyors held fast to the proposition about a straight line. They disregarded hills, swamps, and private homes. Item: The Hartford and New Haven cut so close to the residence of Samuel Yale in Meriden, Connecticut, that the house stood like a cliff above the roadway—naked, alone, and so melancholy a prospect that citizens bought and moved it out of sight. The damages paid to Mr. Yale by the turnpike corporation came to exactly fifty-five dollars and no cents.

The Colchester and Chatham surveyors were such determined

Turnpikes

anti-deviationists that, before a spade was turned, they located a high point between two villages where they could see two church spires, took a compass reading, then cut an unbending path between them.

The engineers of Waterbury sent their pike plunging directly through a cemetery at Salem Bridge, where graves were opened and bones scattered carelessly, much to public scandal. But the citizens of Stamford, Connecticut, where something similar had happened, rose in wrath. After watching the first day's grading operations in their cemetery, says an old account, "large numbers of citizens with many yokes of oxen gathered in the early darkness and labored all night, hauling boulders into the opening at each end and blocking the entrances." Although the turnpike corporation prevailed in the end, many citizens were so wrought up by the invasion of their sacred precincts that they never after would pass over that portion of the road.

During the war of 1812, when most American ships were locked in port, through embargo, both turnpikes and the public roads were often hard put to carry the long cavalcades of freight in Conestoga wagons. They crept over the pikes and highways from Maine to South Carolina often with military escort. "Like treasure-laden ships from afar," one who saw them remembered, "they were enveloped with mystery." They carried no identification, nothing to show whence they came or where they were going. With the jingling of many bells as accompaniment, each wagon drawn by eight and even ten horses encased in heavy harness, these caravans passed through town and village, day after day, to the marvel of the inhabitants. After sundown, one heard their rumble in the night, and could reflect that though this was "Mr. Madison's war," and not their own, the troops were to be fed with Yankee pork and beans, and equipped with Yankee muskets made by Eli Whitney in Whitney-ville, near New Haven on the Lower Post Road. (Mr. Whitney was already famous as the cotton gin man.)

The Old Post Road

There was still time, before the turnpike fad petered out, for another kind of experimental highway. This was the plank road. In Connecticut alone, some twenty companies were organized and granted charters for this purpose, one of which was the 34-mile stretch between Danbury and Westport. Optimistic followers of fads termed this white-pine highway "The Perfect Road," and made much of the fact that a noted trotter of midcentury, Flora Temple, had made "two-forty on a plank road," hence plank was the answer for the ultimate road base. It turned out, however, that white-pine planks as a road base had a life expectancy of less than seven years, and that in some cases, even before the charters had been carried out, "the planks at the far end had patently started to rot."

Let them rot. The turnpikes, too, were to rot when the railroads started to roll. Yet by 1825, New York, Connecticut, and Massachusetts had started to build public roads as never before. In Middlesex County, Massachusetts, alone, more than one hundred new roads were established. This revival was due in some part to the fact that all counties in the Commonwealth now elected a board of three road commissioners, which had taken over the functions formerly exercised by county courts. It was now the responsibility of the commissioners to say which roads were to be "of general use and importance to the public."

For all the improvements, however, made by the network of turnpikes and plank roads, such roads as were of "general use and importance" after the locomotive started to work, were those constructed on the novel doctrine of John Loudon McAdam, the Scots engineer, who declared that the proper roadbed was to be of finely crushed rock to which bitumen was added.

Being no engineer, I haven't the least idea of the chemistry that provides the surface of the modern turnpikes, the so-called throughways, which are seeking of late to relieve congestion of the common highways. I do know that on all such super roads, like the Connecticut and the Massachusetts turnpikes, you never know at

Turnpikes

a given moment just where you are. The best you can do is to keep one eye on the road map, and with the other watch for the exit numbers.

Anyhow, throughways, no matter what they are named, do not really run through Connecticut, or Massachusetts, or any other state. They operate in a sort of Never-Never Land of Round Rivers, Mixed Meridians, False Creeks, and Big Rock Candy Mountains. For many miles you pass through a countryside as strange to you as a Gobi Desert, or the canal country of Mars. Then, rising suddenly, from out of the ground, will appear an improbable mass of buildings, still unrecognizable, still nameless, until an exit sign blocks your vision to say, perhaps, HAMDEN, ¼ MILE.

You may have lived in Hamden twenty years, or fifty years, but during that time have never approached it except on foot, by railroad, by common highway, or from the air. It is probable that never before had you seen Hamden's church spire, or Hamden's water tower, or the smoking stacks of its biggest factory, from this strange new angle presented by the throughway. Yet, there in front of your eyes the exit warning says you are approaching neither Seattle, nor Gastonia, nor Albuquerque, but are already within the town limits of Hamden. It is startling.

Possibly it is the compelling speed on the new turnpikes that numbs the senses, the panoramic blur of the swiftly passing scene, as if the way were bordered each side with an endless picket fence.

Whether or not the new throughways will have any effect on the "congestion" of highways is in the realm of prophecy, but they "get you there" more quickly; and that, after all, seems to be the idea since long before John McAdam was born.

Chapter 6

The Stagecoach

THE PERFECTIONISTS who devised America's most romantic piece of rolling stock were Lewis Downing and Stephen Abbot. This was none other than the classic Concord Coach built in the New Hampshire town from which the celebrated vehicle took its name. Coupled with the "Patent Repeating Firearm" made by Samuel Colt in Hartford, Connecticut, the gun-coach combination so permeated the Old West that no romance of the time and place, either in book or film, is complete without them. They are instantly recognizable to millions who know nothing about them save that the one was used to hold up and rob the other.

The two young men of Concord did not invent the stagecoach, which came from old England. Since 1813, when Downing opened a wheelwright's shop in Concord, he had been repairing sleds and plows of the village, and making a few chaises and wagons. A dozen years later, when the stage business was coming into full flower, Downing felt it was time to build a passenger-and-mail coach; and, needing expert advice, sent to Salem, Massachusetts, for help. Help appeared in the person of J. Stephen Abbot. The coach was built, promptly sold, and was soon rolling, probably on the Upper Post Road out of Boston. It was the first of some three thousand made by Abbot and Downing.

This first stagecoach of the Concord brand was not yet perfect, but it was gradually to achieve perfection before the Western stagecoach kings like Wells Fargo & Company, Russell, Majors, & Waddell, Adams & Company, and Ben Holladay demanded perfection, and even in time for Ginery Twichell, the noted New England operator. But meanwhile, stagecoaches were known less for comfort or even safety to passengers than they were infamous for a number of things, including departure before dawn, too many tippling and reckless drivers, worn-out vehicles, shoddy harness and equipment, and consequent delays that made mockery of the stage line's claims for punctuality.

The wittily observant Josiah Quincy noted a number of shortcomings when he boarded one of Levi Pease's early stagecoaches to New York in 1785. "The journey took up a week," he wrote, "which in that day was considered a record of wonderful expedition. The carriages were old and worn. The harness was made of ropes. One pair of horses carried the stage 18 miles. We generally reached our resting place for the night, if no accident intervened, at 10 o'clock; and, after a frugal supper went to bed with a notice that we should be called at 3 next morning, which generally proved to be half-past two.

"Then, whether it snowed or rained, the traveler must rise and make ready by the help of a horn-lantern and a farthing candle, and proceed on his way over bad roads, sometimes with a driver showing no doubtful symptoms of drunkenness, which good hearted passengers never failed to improve at every stopping place by urging upon him another glass of toddy.

"Thus we traveled 10 miles a stage, sometimes obliged to get out and help the coachman lift the coach out of a quagmire or rut, wondering at the ease as well as the expedition of our journey."

Other travelers of the time mentioned the constant necessity of trimming and balancing the stage—all the passengers leaning to one side to prevent it from overturning in deep ruts: "Now, gentlemen, to the right, please. . . ."

As late as 1829 many coaches did not carry outside passengers. Captain Basil Hall, a visiting Englishman, remarked that "indeed it would try one's nerves as well as the dexterity of the most expert harlequin that ever preserved his balance, not to be speedily pitched to the ground from the top of an American coach, on almost any road I traveled over in that country." In that time the stages were fitted with leather curtains, not panels. There was only one door. Nine passengers sat three to a seat, the middle being a movable bench, with a leather band to support their backs. "It was terribly hard on the back."

Native or foreigner, no traveler failed to remark the early morning departure. Captain Hall wrote that "the nominal hour of starting was five in the morning, but as everything in America comes sooner than one expects, a great tall man walked into the room at ten minutes before four o'clock, to say it wanted half an hour of five; and presently we heard the rumbling of the stage coming to the door upwards of thirty minutes before the time specified. . . ."

Charles Sumner, heading out of Boston in 1834, had to be at the stage office at half past three in the morning: "The way was very dark, and though I rode with the driver, it was some time before I discovered he had six horses. . . ." And Longfellow, on his first acquaintance in 1840 with the Wayside Inn he was to make famous, found that "the stage left Boston about three in the morning, reaching Howe's Tavern at Sudbury for breakfast, a considerable portion of the route being travelled in total darkness, and without your having the least idea who your companions might be."

That the design, weight, and general quality of the average stagecoach had made these early departures necessary quickly became apparent when the vastly better Concord product—or a reasonably good imitation—came into use. By then, according to Stephen Jenkins, the historian, "only two horses were considered enough" instead of four (except that a third might be added in bad weather); and when, for the first time, the Boston–New York run was accomplished within twenty-four hours, "bells were rung and bonfires blazed all along the route." Doubtless there were other factors contributing to this notable advance, but unquestionably Abbot and Downing of Concord had much to do with it.

By the time the first Concord-made coach started operating on the Upper Road out of Boston, in 1826, Lewis Downing knew that in Stephen Abbot he had discovered an artisan after his own honest heart. The two young men formed a partnership that lasted until the stagecoach business had been buried beneath two layers of newer vehicles—the steamcars and the automobiles. Abbot and Downing strengthened the coach even as they made it lighter, and in fact so modified the whole as to have a just claim for inventing the *American* stagecoach.

By 1840 or thereabouts, the making of coaches at Abbott–Downing had become a dynamic religion. Downing himself constantly ranged the shop, seeing everything, saying little; but when he noted a piece of faulty work, he merely picked up a hammer or sledge to smash or otherwise ruin it so it must be done over. The care began in the forest, where either an Abbot or a Downing selected the best trees of white ash and oak. The elm for the hubs received the same treatment. The panels of prime basswood were curved by clamping their edges around a form, then placing them in front of an open fire, where they were intermittently moistened until properly shaped. When an axle was ready for the thread, four stout men took hold of four levers of a die and walked in a circle until the thread was made. Abbot and Downing held to a firm belief that, though Time might be, as some said, Money, it was of infinitely less value than quality.

The Concord Coach not only became stronger as it became

lighter; it also grew more decorative. From England the firm imported John Burgum, whose talents with bright colors were so apparent that he was made "chief ornamenter," and for decades he and his stable of artists made every Concord Coach a thing of beauty, or at least something that could not easily be ignored.

The Gold Rush of Forty-Nine to California carried two Concord Coaches to San Francisco, the first of many in which Adams, Wells Fargo, and other express companies moved the mails and passengers to the diggings and toted back gold from Hangtown, Bottle Springs, Angels Camp, and such places, a shotgun guard on the seat beside the driver. In the Pikes Peak Rush a decade later, it was to be Abbot–Downing all over again. And it was the same when the Comstock Lode began to pay off in bars of solid silver. Moreover, until long after the completion of the first two transcontinental railroads, Concord Coaches continued to travel the West. What appears to have been the last stick-up of a Concord took place as recently as 1893.

For all the boom in the West, the Atlantic seaboard wanted Concords too. Ginery Twichell was buying them as early as 1838 for his several New England lines; and later the great Eastern Stage Company of Massachusetts and New York had many of them running on its seventy-seven lines. (It was still important to have coaches named, and two favorite names of the time appear to have been *Thunderbolt* and *Thoroughbred*.)

The new stylish resorts in the White Mountains and the Berkshire areas, to say nothing of Lake George and the vast hotels at and near Saratoga, demanded Concord Coaches, with specified colors. New York City's Astor, Brevoort, and Fifth Avenue hotels wanted rigs. Most hotelkeepers were explicit about door panel decorations. Southerners often wanted a likeness of Stephen A. Douglas. In the North and West, Webster, Pierce, J. Q. Adams, and Fremont were favored; and there were partisans of pretty females, like actresses Mary Anderson and Fanny Davenport. Landscapes were favorites in the Far West, and the favored body colors were red and green, with bright canary for the running parts and scrollwork in gold leaf.

The marvelous lasting qualities of Concord Coaches became legend in the West. Once when the Downieville stage of Adams and Company on the Mother Lode went off a narrow cliff and rolled a good hundred feet among the boulders, nothing at all was broken, though the vivid scenes on the panels were scratched up. Again, a Wells Fargo rig went off a steep pitch, the horses with it, to roll over and over a distance of 300 feet down into roaring-full Greenhorn Creek. The front wheels became detached, the door paintings were partly obliterated. All else, everything, including passengers, driver, horses, even the harnesses, survived intact. Concords simply could not be broken, or smashed.

Possibly the peak for Abbot and Downing came as long ago as April 15, 1868. On that great day an entire trainload of their master work went out of Concord—a long, glittering procession of flashing vermilions and yellows, consigned to Wells Fargo & Company, Omaha and Salt Lake City. Most fortunately, some local photographer was alert on that tremendous day, his big awkward camera set up in a field along the Boston & Concord Railroad tracks. There he caught the locomotive *Pembroke* hauling the train of fifteen long platform cars on each of which rested two of Abbot and Downing's special Western jobs. John Burgum, master decorator, was stirred mightily by the noble sight; later, with the photograph in front of him, he took paints in hand and immortalized, in true and vivid colors and in one enormously long painting, this climax of his career as artist-in-residence at Abbot–Downing.

Even then, on its great day in 1868, the railroads had so encroached on Abbot and Downing's business that the writing on the wall was clear enough: the stagecoach, even a Concord stagecoach, was done. One after the other the fires in the forges were banked. The stout old firm attempted to enter the new age by building fire engines, then motor trucks. But their hearts were not in it. They had made things *by hand*. The motor business in America had no place for such artisans. Although there seems never to have been a formal shutdown of the works, the last Abbot and Downing employee got his gold-headed cane, the symbol of retirement for more than four hundred employees, in 1928.

During the summer of 1961, when I was engaged in ranging the Old Boston Post Road, I took time to run north to Concord, just to see the celebrated works that had built not only a stagecoach, but a legend. Almost nothing remained to indicate that the classic symbol of the Old West had been designed and made here beside the Merrimack River. Even the huge old depot of the Boston & Maine, which for more years than I could remember had displayed a Concord Coach, had been torn down. The passenger steamcars, too, seemed to be well on their way to oblivion.

Chapter 7

The Stage Driver

MANY OF THE EARLY stage drivers came from the ranks of the postriders. Already familiar with horseflesh, and familiar with the post routes, well weathered and hardy, riders were easily converted to drivers.

Good drivers had a high idea of the dignity and importance of their new calling. Almost from the first they were saluted as captain, and they meant that their passengers should not forget *who* was in charge of the dry-land ship.

Black Ben Jarvis, long a fixture on the Boston and Hartford run, was perhaps typical. Once, a rather pompous fellow bustled up to him at the stage office. "I and my people," he demanded, "want to go with Black Ben. Are you the fellow they call Black Ben?" Captain Jarvis looked the passenger dead in the eye. "Blackguards call me Black Ben," he said, "but gentlemen call me Mr. Jarvis."

The Old Post Road

And Little Jack Mendum, a veteran of the Eastern Stage Company, put it on the line for a fussy passenger who was hungry and wanted to get to the next stop. "Mister," Captain Mendum told him, "when I drive this coach I am the whole United States of America."

Like the railroad conductors a bit later, these coach drivers tended to become autocrats; and most of them loved the life. There was Harrison Bryant, old-timer on the Upper Post Road, who, having inherited the family farm in Athol, Massachusetts, thought he had said good-by to the cold, the exposure, and long hours, and "settled down to an existence of sheltered prosperity." But then, on his third day as a farmer, the driver of a passing stage gave Bryant a hearty greeting as he snapped his whip. Almost immediately farmer Bryant "walked somberly across the field to his new home, packed his carpetbag, and went to the local stage office." Two days later he swept down the same road snapping *his* whip, leaving the miles behind him. Before he quit for good, Bryant calculated he had driven a stage more than 135,000 miles. By the end of the stagecoach era, there were two- and even three-generation families of stage drivers.

When rigged out in his regulation working clothes, the stage driver was an imposing sight. With his big bell-crowned beaver hat, a vast greatcoat and calfskin boots, he *knew* he was somebody. In what drivers generally conceded to be *real* weather, which started somewhere between ten and twenty below zero, the captain might replace certain items of his usual "summer" garb by putting on a coat of fur or buffalo hide and handknit stockings made in Canada, which came up nearly to the thighs and were invariably bright red, believed to be warmer than any other color. The final winter touch was a sash of knit wool, or even of silk with tassels, wrapped around the waist and tied on the left side. This was the *ceinture flèche* of the French *habitant*. It, too, was of brightest red, and added no little dash to the man on the box.

Summer or winter, his whip was the badge of his calling. This came in time to be a standard 5 feet 1½ inches from butt to holder, and 12 feet 5 inches from holder to the end of the lash. The better drivers used the whip sparingly, though any of them enjoyed showing off by making the long lash crack like the report of a rifle.

Like the postrider before him, the stagecoach driver was supposed to build good will with the public, and to be especially attentive to women, children, and the aged. Drivers were commonly permitted to carry on a business, mostly of errands done in the cities for country people. The driver's "office" was the big, bell-crowned hat that he wore in summer, into which he stuffed papers, documents, valuables. But for some reason or other, after many lines merged to form the Eastern Stage Company, one of that corporation's first regulations said that "no driver shall carry anything except in his pocket."

One observer wrote that many drivers did "handsomely well" with this pocket business, supplementing their usual wages which ran from $22.50 to $28 a month, plus room and board while on the road.

In regard to tipping, there is considerable conflict in the memories of travelers by stagecoach. Though one long-retired veteran said that drivers "never countenanced the acceptance of gratuities from passengers," one need not be cynical to doubt this statement.

The same is true about the temperance of the fraternity. Josiah Quincy wrote of riding at times with a driver who "showed no doubtful symptoms of drunkenness." But many years later, an official of the Eastern Stage Company told an inquirer that intemperance had been forbidden, *successfully*, to their drivers, and explained matters: "You were saying that passengers in your section were uneasy and often had fears for their safety while riding with your drivers. . . . Here all that is reversed. In former years the travelers used every precaution to keep the drivers sober, but now the drivers by their example try to keep the passengers sober." This statement may well have had substance, for at this period the railroads had started to crack down on drinking if only for the sake of punctuality of trains. Time, for the first time in history, became an important measure in the lives of most Americans. Even so ordinarily detached a man as Henry David Thoreau, in his cabin in the woods of Walden Pond, had noticed the difference. "They come and go," he wrote of the trains that passed his pond, "with such regularity and precision, and their whistle can be heard so far, that the farmers set their clocks by them, and thus one well-regulated institution regulates a whole country." And he wondered if men had not improved in punctuality since the railroad was invented. "Do they not talk and think faster in the depot," he asked, "than they did in the stage-office?"

Temperate or not, neither the riders of post horses nor stagecoach drivers on the Boston Post Road had to face the dangers of highwaymen. Not in the 289 years of the road's history was horseman or stage stopped for the purposes of robbery. This is a considerable statement, as sweeping as it was regrettable to the writer of this book. I had taken for granted that the old Boston Post Road had experienced, at least in the era of the United States Mail Coach, a few of the stand-and-deliver robberies that were common in the Old West.* But no; sixty-odd years ago, when so careful a researcher as Alice Morse Earle was writing about stagecoaches in New England, she could discover but two authentic robberies, and these were not stick-ups. They were inside jobs. "One was the stage driver himself, of a large sum of money that had been entrusted to him; and it was his wife who stole it. The other theft was of a bonnet."

Mrs. Earle observed that this record was not for lack of rogues, as witness the periodic robberies of Yankee banks and individuals. It was rather that in New England men started early to use drafts and bills of exchange, which were not easily negotiable if at all, whereas "travelers in Old England persisted in carrying gold and banknotes" and Western Americans largely used gold and silver currency, and there were also for many years the shipments of gold dust and silver bullion in the stages. Mrs. Earle said she re-

---

* When this dismal fact became known to one of my teenage daughters, well versed in the TV school of Westerns, she remarked: "Daddy, I guess you picked the wrong road to write about."

gretted "there were no knights of the road like Dick Turpin and such," for she would have enjoyed knowing they had "held up Benjamin Franklin and John Adams." Rather than citing Dick Turpin, Mrs. Earle could better have mentioned him who operated on Wells Fargo under style of Black Bart and left a tradition still unmatched in the Far West. (His name may or may not have been Charles E. Boles.)

If many former postriders were quick to exchange their saddle-bags for the driver's seat of a mail coach, here and there a driver was happy to set up as an operator of his own line, almost always with a post-office contract in his pocket. Levi Pease was notable among these ambitious men. Another was Chester W. Chapin, who drove a stage between Springfield and Hartford. Another was Benjamin Pierce who became known as the Stagecoach King of the Northern Lines.

And then there was the remarkable Ginery Twichell, the "Very Napoleon of Stage Lines" who before he went on to Congress and the presidency of railroads had "flashed like a brilliant comet through the stage-driving world of New England." As a girl herself Mrs. Earle once saw the great man in the flesh. It may have been in 1867, in Worcester, in front of the former Central Hotel, which had been Twichell's stage headquarters. The young girl hung out a window and was stirred by what she saw:

"A great stagecoach with six horses which stood, reeking, foaming, pawing . . . and a dignified, self-contained old man [he was actually fifty-six] ruddy of face, dressed in a heavy overcoat and tall silk hat, erect on the driver's seat, reins in hand—and suddenly Ginery Twichell and his six horses were off in a rattle of wheels and blowing of horns and cheers of the crowd. . . . It was an anniversary of some memorable event and Congressman Twichell celebrated it by driving once more over his old-time coaching route amid the cheers and admiration of all beholders."

Driving up the Post Road to Boston on this occasion, Mr. Twichell was hailed by the press for special achievements with a coach in times past. Back in 1840, for instance, and "by request of the citizens of Barre, Massachusetts, seats were added to the top of the stage, so that a party of thirty-two persons could be accommodated, twelve inside, twenty outside." But this was modest compared to what Stage Driver Twichell could do when in top form. "The largest load ever carried was a party of sixty-two young ladies of Worcester who, uniformly dressed, were driven on a blackberry excursion into the suburbs by Mr. Twichell himself, eight matched horses being required for the occasion."

None of Twichell's feats with a stagecoach, however, great as they were, could match a ride he made on horseback on the cold and stormy twenty-third of January, 1849. This tremendous event was to make him practically immortal through the medium of lithography as "The Unrivaled Express Rider."

Chapter 8

The Saga of Ginery Twichell

THE LIFE SPAN of Ginery Twichell, born 1811, died 1883, was little more than of biblical measure, yet it witnessed the rise and golden age of the stagecoach and its virtual disappearance in New England. It seems likely that he was the only man, starting life as a common stage driver, whose funeral procession was a special train of the Boston & Albany Railroad, of which he was a director, from Brookline, Massachusetts, to Worcester.

Twichell's career was extraordinary. A sort of obituary booklet, printed at the time of his death, merely hit the conventional highlights in its title:

A Sketch of the Life of Ginery Twichell, in Early Life A Stage-Driver, For Many Years Proprietor and Manager of the Largest and Most Important Lines of Stage-Coaches in New England, Afterwards President of the Boston & Worces-

55

The Old Post Road

ter; Atchison, Topeka & Santa Fe; Boston, Barre & Gardner; and Hoosac Tunnel and Western Railroad Companies, and Member of the 40th, 41st, and 42d Congresses of the United States.

Member of Congress? Listen, stranger, Ginery Twichell was the man who rode a blizzard from Worcester to Hartford, 66 miles, three hours and twenty minutes, and thus rode into song and story and picture and legend.

President of railroads? Mister, Ginery Twichell, a bagful of mail on his back, put on snowshoes and walked 17 miles from Worcester to Coldbrook, Massachusetts, in five hours. In a blinding snowstorm.

There was, however, nothing wintry about his personality and character. Indeed, one of his strongest points, said one who knew him well, was that he was not only affable, but he "could make friends and *hold* them." Old Henry Miner, possibly the sole surviving stage driver of Twichell's lines, recalled years later that "he was a shrewd, quiet, persevering man of few words and those to the point. His voice was clear and low, never raised to horses or men." He seems to have had one nervous habit, that of rubbing his hands rapidly when in earnest conversation. Though quite florid of face, he "was strictly temperate."

Born at Athol, in the back reaches of Worcester County and far from the Boston Post Road, young Ginery quit school at sixteen, worked in a local mill, clerked in a store, and was hired to help Josiah Stockwell, a farmer who also operated a stage wagon to carry passengers, the mails, and the weekly newspapers from Worcester into the northern part of the county. One thing led to another, and in 1832, when he turned twenty-one, Ginery moved to Worcester, where he bought the route and business of Stockwell, whose son was proprietor of the Central Hotel, one of Worcester's best-known taverns of the time.

"Mr. Twichell," wrote his obituarist, "was thus put in competition with another line running over the same route which had the advantage of larger resources and patronage." What happened next may have been softened by the genteel conventions of obituary writing of the day. "By patience and kindness, not only to his patrons, but also to his rivals and competitors in business Mr. Twichell, by the strictest fidelity to all the trusts committed to him, by cheerfulness and imperturbable good humor, by firm adherence to the determination early formed to abstain from all intoxicating drinks, by wise economy in the conduct of his business, and finally, by thus conciliating and winning the public patronage exclusively to himself, drove his rivals from the field." (The use of "drive" here indicates something other than "patience and kindness" to Ginery's competitors. But never mind.)

One has no doubt but that Twichell was kind, patient, cheerful, sober, wise, generous, as well as dedicated to the proposition that "character and ability, tested and manifested, alone challenge and secure public confidence." And although it is not mentioned in "A Sketch of the Life of Ginery Twichell," he must have observed that the most successful leaders in the stagecoach business had forged ahead by getting a contract for carrying the mails. For instance, the great Levi Pease had operated on rather short rations until he came back from a trip to Philadelphia with a contract from the post office in his pocket. This secured for him not only "his proportion of mileage on the Boston–New York City run, but $1,600 to boot." The passengers in the mail coach were pure velvet.

Ginery Twichell soon expanded his Worcester–Athol line to reach Keene, New Hampshire, bought horses and coaches to open branch lines, one to Brattleboro, Vermont, another to Greenfield, Massachusetts. And now he went to see the post-office man at headquarters, which by then was in Washington, and returned to Worcester with not one but "several contracts."

At about the same time, the long-expected railroad from Boston was opened to Worcester, and Mr. Twichell's expanding lines felt an immediate upsurge of business. He purchased more horses, hired more drivers, and bought a few more stagecoaches. Unlike many operators of stage lines, who fought the new railroads, Twichell did everything possible to aid both passenger and freight business of the Boston & Worcester. During the brief but hot struggle for dominance between the canal builders and the rails, he was heart and soul for the latter, fitting stage schedules to those of the Boston & Worcester and the new Norwich & Worcester, which, under various names including the Boston, Hartford, & Erie, was planning to reach the Sound at New London and a steamboat line to New York City controlled by Commodore Vanderbilt.

Until this road could be extended from Norwich to Allyn's Point, 8 miles south on the Thames River, passengers and freight must be moved, when the river was frozen, by such conveyances as the railroad and steamship companies could obtain from the surrounding companies. "It was an arrangement," says an old account, "attended with considerable confusion, for the owners of the teams shirked responsibility and quarreled among themselves, much to annoyance of the patrons and managers of the line." Commodore Vanderbilt was not a manager to suffer annoyance long, and at his "urgent solicitation, Mr. Twichell assumed the responsibility" of the problem.

Building a vast stable near Allyn's Point, Twichell stocked this new venture with ten stagecoaches and one baggage wagon of four horses each for passengers, and ten long wagons of four horses each for freight. Whether fifty or two hundred passengers, he was prepared. The transfer of 8 miles was to be made always at night— freight moved by day—and it worked wonderfully well for the two winter seasons that elapsed before the rail line closed the gap.

Because Ginery Twichell was a man of imagination, his men and coaches were conspicuously numbered, and moved in consecutive order, "starting on signal, without a word being heard by passengers, and each coach keeping an equal distance from the one preceding." Such unusual precision was considered a marvel at the time. Not a passenger was left behind or injured during the two seasons. Commodore Vanderbilt "bestowed great commendation upon Mr. Twichell who" at this period seems also to have been breveted "General" by acclamation of passengers, a title which accompanied him ever after, though it was nowhere nearly so distinctive as his own name.

Ginery Twichell's name became widely known in 1840, the first year he conducted the transfer line from Norwich to Allyn's Point, when Major Houghton, proprietor of the Boston *Atlas,* decided to astonish all other newspapers in New England by publishing the election returns of Massachusetts on the *morning after election day.* The enterprising Houghton approached Twichell, who naturally knew a great deal about roads and towns in the state, especially the many towns which, in 1840, were not served by a railroad. Yes, said Twichell, it could be done.

And it *was* done. Twichell accomplished the feat, accounted generally as impossible, by engaging messengers from "every town in the state," with relays of horses when needed, to bring the returns "to a central point." It must have been quite a day for him. Having himself voted early in Worcester, he rode to Greenfield, 55 miles, where he was to receive in person returns from the "four western counties" of the state. But several of these riders were delayed by bad weather, and he was unable to leave Greenfield until two hours after the appointed time.

He tore out of Greenfield "in the face of an easterly storm," but with fresh horses ready and waiting at selected places along the route, he thought he would make Worcester in time to catch the Boston & Worcester train. The Boston & Worcester, however, waited for no man, and Ginery arrived at the depot "ten minutes after the locomotive engine had left." He paused only long enough for a fresh horse, then pushed forward 45 miles farther, reaching Boston "in season to have his despatches appear in the morning *Atlas.*"

"Such enterprise," wrote an observer, "in collecting news was unequaled in those days." Apparently, the *Atlas* was happy with the results, for it continued the practice until telegraph and railroads presently were equal to the task. Twichell must have enjoyed the experience, for he seems to have made something of an avocation of riding dispatch, or express, when chance offered. And then, in January, 1846, came the tremendous effort that gave him celebrity, plus the immortality of lithography in fullest color.

The Old Post Road

The business had its inception in the frantic competition among the leading newspapers of New York City. All were eager to secure certain dispatches that were expected to arrive at Boston by foreign steamships in January; but only James Gordon Bennett (the elder) of the *Herald* had taken pains to make certain that, no matter when the ship docked in Boston, the dispatch for his paper, and only his paper, should go by special train to Norwich, Connecticut, thence by boat to Long Island, and across the island by special rider to New York. The *Tribune* and other New York papers, along with those of Philadelphia, were excluded by Bennett's orders from participating in his arrangements with the railroads and steamboat companies involved.

It is probable that rumors of the *Herald's* plans for a special and exclusive train on the Boston & Worcester, with which Ginery Twichell was so closely connected, had leaked. In any event, now came the *Tribune* of New York—whose Horace Greeley was long familiar with Bennett's brass-knuckles style—to ask "General" Ginery Twichell, the superb horseman and gatherer of election returns, if he would undertake to beat the *Herald's* dispatch to New York City, fetching with him the dispatches for the *Tribune* and the other "excluded" newspapers.

Ginery Twichell said he would undertake to do as much, and set about his plans. Knowing full well that to beat the combination of steamcars and steamboats he must ride horseback at least two-thirds of the distance from Boston to New York, he made arrangements that the best relay horses possible, and reliable stablemen, should be stationed at proper distances between Worcester and Hartford, and between New Haven and New York. There was at least one other arrangement we can feel reasonably sure he made: to change into the *buckskin* underwear he always favored when faced with a long ride in cold weather.* And just before he left to await arrival of the Cunarder in Boston, which was then that famous line's American port, he ordered a special train—it was only a

---

* In an effort to preclude queries about these underclothes, I am quoting Henry S. Miner who, in 1900, was reputed to be the "last surviving driver on Ginery Twichell's stagecoach line." See Alice Morse Earle in Bibliography.

locomotive—to have steam up, ready to leave for Worcester when the fifteen minutes demanded by the *Herald's* contract should have expired.

The great day came and Twichell, the dispatches bound to his belt, was away to Worcester by locomotive of the Boston & Worcester Railroad. There had been a heavy snowfall, and when he left Worcester, by Boston Post Road, he faced 66 miles and ten changes of horse before he hove into Hartford in what experts of the day conceded to be the "remarkably short time of three hours and twenty minutes." From Hartford to New Haven he moved the 36 miles by railroad. From New Haven to New York it was horses again for 76 miles. Ginery Twichell turned over the dispatches for the *Tribune* and other papers of the group before the Long Island rider had arrived with the most exclusive dispatch for Mr. James Gordon Bennett of the New York *Herald*. An old account has it that Ginery was *"considerably* ahead of the *Herald* couriers."

I cannot help but wonder if Ginery Twichell and Horace Greeley, two dedicated Yankees, happened to meet in the *Tribune's* office. Both young men were on their way upward to greater things, Greeley to become a candidate for the presidency of the United States. As for Twichell, apparently he was content to serve as Congressman, for his ambitions had to do with transportation and politics.

Within a year after his great ride, he was made superintendent of the Boston & Worcester, and in 1857 was elected president of that road, which office he held until the merger of the Boston & Worcester with the Western and other lines under style of the Boston & Albany, of which he was a director. Meanwhile, Boston & Worcester shares went from $78 to $160. "At the next meeting of the directors," wrote Twichell's obituarist, "Mr. Twichell was asked to retire from the Board for a moment . . . and a vote was passed directing the treasurer to place to his credit five thousand dollars in addition to his regular salary."

From this point on, railroad directorates and presidencies seemed to fall into his lap, the latter including those of the Atchison, Topeka, & Santa Fe, the Boston, Barre & Gardner, and the fearfully named Boston, Hoosac Tunnel & Western of New York. Although these events take Ginery Twichell beyond the orbit of stagecoaches, it is worth knowing that of his five brothers, four were tavern keepers: Sylvanus at Athol; Francis at Petersham and Templeton; Simeon F. at South Framingham; and Amarish at Northboro, all in Massachusetts, and all situated on stage lines operated or controlled by Ginery himself.

It is perhaps significant that pallbearers at his funeral, which, as noted, moved by railroad train from Brookline to Worcester, included ex-governors of states, a Postmaster General, eminent judges, and officials of railroads. Also "accompanying the remains to the grave" was the Reverend Edward Everett Hale, who officiated at the obsequies and who, not long since, had written for the *Atlantic Monthly* a short story entitled, "The Man Without a Country."

It was a notable send-off for him who, despite his achievements with railroads and stagecoaches, was to be remembered as "The Unrivaled Express Rider."

I have a black-and-white copy of this "large and beautiful engraving" which depicts Ginery Twichell on that great January 23 of 1846. He is shown ahorse, galloping through deep snow, just about to pass a snow-topped crossroads sign that indicates he has come from Worcester, 10 miles back, and is heading for Hartford, 50 miles to go. At a snowy farmhouse and barn in the background, two men are putting bridle and saddle on a relay horse, which seems alert and expectant. The rail-fences and the bare trees are topped with snow.

Around the rider's waist is a belt holding four or more dispatches. The rider's scarf billows out from his shoulders and neck. Both horse and rider are obviously leaning against a fierce wind. Far in the distance, across a wide field, is a train of cars, the big-stacked locomotive engine doing its best in the blizzard, smoke rolling backward. But Ginery and horse are still in the lead, and this, of course, tells the story.

The Saga of Ginery Twichell

The picture has all of the immediacy of the great age of lithography when the eye and imagination of the artist did what they would with the scene, no matter the facts. Facts were not permitted to clutter up and confuse a good story: And the good story in this case was that "horsepower had surpassed steam-power." It said so in as many words in the obituary of Ginery Twichell.

The irony makes the story even better. Twichell was in fact one of the outstanding railroad men in the country. Yet, forever after his ride in 1846, he was the great horseman: The Unrivaled Express Rider, a legend of the old Boston Post Road.

Chapter 9

The Taverns in the Towns

MANY A PIOUS YANKEE and many a Yankee rounder
have alike undergone a mild shock when they learned that
the earliest taverns in New England were licensed for two purposes:
one to provide common entertainment for strangers, the other to
promote the worship of God.

This fostering of religion was no matter of doctrine. It had to do
with simple heat, and so close was the relationship between meeting
house and tavern that the town fathers did everything possible to
have the one structure near the other. Thus, in 1651, the town of
Boston would grant one John Vyall liberty to keep a house of common entertainment, "provided he keeps it near the new Meeting
House." In that time, and for many years more, a fire never was
kindled in colonial meeting houses. To appreciate the discomfort
this entailed, one needs know only the normal January temperature

of Boston, Massachusetts, which ranges from maximum 37° to minimum 22°, with now and then a dive to —19°.

One should consider, too, that going to meeting in that time and place, be it January or July, was something to give a Spartan pause. A sermon was no light discourse. It was two solid hours of hypostatic density. Then, after a brief nooning for refreshment, came another two hours of substantial heavy matter from the pulpit.

Because it was a period of virtually compelled, if not quite devoted attendance, no few of the congregation had come many miles to meeting. That they should find a cheerful, or at least warm place to thaw out between the cold drive and the chilly service, may have been a piece of good public relations on the part of the clergy.

Thus did publican and preacher come hand and hand down through two centuries, exchanging comfort of the body for certainty of the soul.

The relationship between the church and tavern was so close that, as was the case in Fitchburg in colonial days, religious services were held in an ordinary tavern pending erection of a suitable meeting house. The same was true in Providence, Rhode Island, where in 1655 Goodman Mowry was licensed to keep a public house and was directed to "Sett out a convenient signe at ye most perspicuous place of ye saide house thereby to give notice to strangers that it is a house of entertainment." Mowry's Tavern not only survived when most of Providence was destroyed by fire in King Philip's War, but was the oldest tavern, and the oldest house, in the city when it was torn down in 1900, after 245 years.

There seemed to be nothing in the mores of our ancestors to prevent a meeting house being turned into a tavern, which happened to the so-called Great House in Charlestown, Massachusetts, the official residence of Governor Winthrop. In 1663 it was made a church, and later into the Three Cranes, an excellent tavern kept for many years by landlord Robert Leary and his descendants.

In the eyes of the Plymouth Pilgrims, strong drink was no enemy except when it interfered with duty. Their long-time governor, William Bradford, was scandalized to see soldiers "so steeld with drinke as their peeces were too heavie for them," yet the abuse of spirits was not his great worry. What caused him to fear and tremble was the breaking out of incontinence between unmarried persons and "married persons allso." But of spirits old Bradford amusingly recorded the ironic term still in use three hundred years later to describe the secret misappropriation of liquors in storage or transit. When tapped, a consignment of two hogsheads of mead was found to contain no more than six gallons, the remainder having "been drunke up under ye name of leackage and so lost."

Typical of the different attitude of the Massachusetts Bay Colony (Boston) was that one of the first protests against rum was that of Increase Mather who feared it would drown Christianity because its use tended to keep people from church by reason of reveling. By 1700 at latest, distilleries, however, were in operation in all the New England settlements to supply not only the multiplying taverns but the blackhearted business of the slave trade.

New York City was safely awash with drink from the first. By the time the Boston Post Road got its name, the road itself swarmed with taverns, two of the most noted being the Bull's Head in Bowery Lane, and the Dyckman at Kingsbridge. Tavern competition for the custom of travelers grew apace all along the Road from the Bull's Head to the Bunch of Grapes at the Boston end. Their number grew rapidly when the stagecoach became popular after the Revolution, and landlords were quick to appreciate the value of identification with the names of eminent men, and sign painters of considerable talent took to the road.

Throughout all the colonies the name of General Wolfe, the hero of the Battle of Quebec, was a great favorite till the Revolution, and even then it survived in many places, including Brooklyn, Connecticut, where the landlord, Israel Putnam, became something of a hero himself. The names of other new heroes, and of patriotic objects, were soon swinging on tavern signs. That of The Liberty Tree, the Patriot, the Independence, and even the United States taverns appeared. So did taverns named for John Hancock, Benjamin Franklin, and of course Washington. LaFayette became a name to conjure with. Only a little later Daniel Webster made the grade in New England.

A much older tavern, the Green Dragon in Boston which in 1775 was already long since green with verdigris and age, was celebrated in history as the meeting place where the "Mohawks" planned the Boston Tea Party. Esther Forbes, biographer of Paul Revere, wrote that on the front of this tavern hung a dragon hammered out of copper, and that the St. Andrews Lodge of Masons met in one of the rooms. Soon after the famous Tea Party, some local bard composed a ballad that became instantly popular:

> *Rally Mohawks! bring out your axes/ and tell King George we'll pay no taxes/ on his foreign tea./ His threats are vain, and vain to think/ to force our girls and wives to drink/ his vile Bohea. . . . Fighting Freedom's call!/ Then rally boys, and hasten on/ to meet our chiefs at the Green Dragon/.*

There is plenty of evidence that New England taverns were notorious, to Tories, as subversive places where plotters against the Crown agitated for liberty. John Adams tells of listening while several pub-crawlers of the period got well wound up in a country tavern on the Post Road. In 1774 when he was on a tour of the circuit courts of Massachusetts he . . .

> *. . . stopped one night at a Shrewsbury tavern about forty miles from Boston and, as I was cold and wet, I sat down at a good fire in the barroom to dry out my great-coat and saddle-bags, till a fire could be built in my chamber. There presently came in, one after the other, half a dozen, or half a score substantial yeomen of the neighborhood, who, sitting down to the fire after lighting their pipes, began a lively conversation. I sat in total silence to hear them.*

One of these lads started the ball rolling with the statement that "The people of Boston are distracted." (He may or may not have been one of the proficient *agents-provocateur* set in motion by Sam Adams, one of John's cousins, who has been called The Great

Agitator of the Revolution.) The remark touched off a discussion that grew more "treasonable" by the hour, and was still going strong when John Adams went to bed.

Although John Adams was probably given the "best room" in the tavern at Shrewsbury, the public houses of 1774 still lacked a good deal in taste and comfort. Usually, however, they had at least one chamber of modest pretension, heated, well furnished with a feather bed, and decorated, after about midcentury, with the imported "scenery wallpaper" that was becoming popular. The less said about the other rooms—and the landlord was likely to say nothing at all—the better it was for business. Save for the better taverns, whose superior furnishing and service were known to experienced travelers, the rooms were cubicles without even a window, often without a door, and surely not a fireplace; or they might be great, stark "shed-chambers" with from three to six or eight beds. The beds were commonly ample for one person, but they were expected to accommodate from two to four guests each.

In these virtual dormitories, those guests who went early to bed might anticipate being aroused several times during the night when the landlord appeared, candle in hand, to escort late arrivals to their exact lodgment. Lone female travelers, as witness the self-assured Mrs. Sarah Knight, complained about being bedded down in the same room with strange men.

In early stagecoach days, when Levi Pease, the famous stage operator, took over Major Farrar's tavern in Shrewsbury, where John Adams listened to the "substantial yeomen" discussing liberty, there was a large shed behind the house for freight wagons and mail coaches. Pease cut holes in the side of this barnlike structure, one above the other, so that the teamsters and stage drivers could climb up and down without disturbing guests in the tavern proper.

Tavern keepers amounted to being the official hosts certified by the civil authorities as greeters to the rest of the world, and licensed to feed and keep all who applied. They were likely to be men of local distinction, perhaps an officer of the militia, or of the town itself, say, a selectman, clerk, constable, or even a Crown surveyor, a tax collector, or customs man. If contemporaries are to be trusted, the tavern keeper tended to corpulence, as befitted one who ate well, drank when it suited him, and whose very occupation called for dignified calm rather than the frantic hustle of the ambitious businessman.

John Adams saw him as "happy and as big, as proud and as conceited as any nobleman in England, always good natured and lazy. Contemplation of his farm, his house, his sound judgment (as he thinks) and his great holiness, as well as that of his wife, keep him erect in his thoughts as a noble or a prince." Because of its source, this opinion may well be a gibe. But the tavern keeper had to set his own standards, for he had no advertising agents other than satisfied customers.

For decades on end, tavern keepers "performed a noble function, unique in the annals of hostelry," as historian Storrs Lee said of them. His tavern was the reception center, he the town greeter. The reputation of the town, among strangers, depended in large part on his treatment of those from beyond its borders. Whether they came by coach, shay, chariot, phaeton, wagon, cart, or on foot or horseback, it was his duty to take them in and make them comfortable. It seems probable that tavern keepers might be a shade more prompt and more courteous to obviously eminent people like governors, famous soldiers, and even churchmen, and others who came to the door in the lofty leisure of their own private coaches. So, too, were the tavern help. But this is no serious charge.

In view of the much later animosity of the clergy toward taverns and their keepers, this was due in large part to the evangelical preachers who began to foster a reform in habits which they persisted in calling the Temperance Movement but which, in reality, meant total abstinence from strong drink. In olden times, or before about 1840, New England's men of the cloth liked to hold the festivities attendant on ordinations in the local tavern; and there is record of one clerical group which ran up a tab—exclusive of rum and bitters

69

—for twenty bowls of stout punch, twelve bottles of wine, five mugs of flip, and two mugs and three bowls of toddy. It is obvious that these same jovial ecclesiastics also ran up a record for mass hangovers; although they were billed for twenty-four dinners, only three of them thought they wanted breakfast.

Until the village general store came of age, the tavern was a place of congregation second only to the church. A majority of the lodges of Freemasons met there during Revolutionary times and often much later. The common room of the tavern was the town's business exchange until it outgrew the place and called for a building of its own. It was also the dancehall, theater, convention auditorium, the lecture and concert hall. In many a village it was the courtroom, and a few taverns even had a strong room used as jail. No few of the early insurance companies of Connecticut take pride in the fact that their first office was in a tavern.

In Warwick, Rhode Island, the town ordered that public stocks and whipping post be erected near David Arnold's tavern. A public house in Cambridge periodically attracted immense crowds because in sight of it was the gallows tree. For many years, idiots, the mentally deranged, and all manner of paupers were sold at auction, often held at the local tavern, to the lowest bidder who would care for them.

In the course of time, tavern keepers found need to meet the competition of their fellows by staging turkey shoots, wrestling matches of the collar-and-elbow type, dogfights, cockfights, and bull-baiting shows. Landlord Sally Barton, who kept The George Tavern on Boston Neck, was noted for these displays and advertised regularly that her animals were never else than "Good Active Bulls and Strong Dogs."

An amazon named Hannah Fisher, who kept a tavern on the Boston Post Road near East Chester Creek, in Pelham Manor, New York, needed no special added feature to attract business. She herself was worth stopping to see, for she was not only a good-natured woman of large frame, but of "such great strength she could lift a barrel of cider and drink from the bunghole." Bunghole-drinking males are common in legend, but Hannah Fisher stands alone among them, so far as I am aware.

The long and dreary night that was to overtake the village tavern no less than the hotel barroom and the city saloon was the labor of thousands of devoted or fanatical men and women who insisted they were working for the cause of Temperance.

There is neither need here nor room to follow the antiliquor movement from its shadowy genesis to its stunning triumph on January 15, 1920, when the Eighteenth Amendment to the Constitution became effective, and the current dry forces announced the new era as follows: "It is here at last—dry America's first birthday. At one minute past twelve tomorrow morning a new nation will be born. . . . Tonight John Barleycorn makes his last will and testament. Now for an era of clear thinking and clean living! The Anti-Saloon League wishes every man, woman, and child a happy Dry Year."

The era of clear thinking and clean living turned out to be fourteen years of titanic farce, tragic and costly beyond calculation. The lid was on, and the several score of ancient village taverns along the Boston Post Road could do one of two things: close the taproom and watch the rest of the place become a haunted house, or operate between raids as a bootlegging joint. Meanwhile, the Post Road, and especially the Lower Road along the shores of four states, was cluttered with new traffic brought about by the results of Temperance, which by then was called Prohibition.

Prohibition brought a tremendous legendry and mythology new to the Boston Post Road. Much of it had to do with the transportation of booze. Let us let it lie. I heard enough of the stories to learn they followed the pattern common to the bootlegger hero and villain in much of the United States.

Chapter 10

Washington Was Here

W HEN I BEGAN research to write this book, there was no
thought that George Washington would make his appearance in it, other than casual mention of his arrival in Cambridge,
Massachusetts, on July 3, 1775, to take command of the American
troops on Cambridge Common, close by the old Boston Post Road.
But when I got down to the specialists in Post Road matters, it
became obvious that I must do much more than that; and lest I
lay myself open to the charge of being unfair to my native New
England, at least in regard to taverns, there had better be some account of President George Washington's inaugural tour of what
he termed "the Eastern States."

This first tour of the first chief executive of the United States
began on the rainy Thursday of October 15, 1789, when "Major
Jackson, Mr. Lear, and myself with six servants, which composed

my Retinue," dined at Kingsbridge, "in a tavern kept by one Hoyatt." They were now on the mainland, and had dinner and spent the night at Rye in the tavern kept by the Widow Haviland, whose husband, Dr. Ebenezer Haviland, was killed while serving as a surgeon in the Continental Army. The President wrote that the widow "keeps a very neat and decent inn." He also observed that the Post Road was rough and stony through East Chester, New Rochelle, and Mamaroneck.

Note that Rye had the first Washington-Slept-Here house on the road to Boston. Yet, hardly a month later, when Washington returned to New York, Dame Tamar Haviland, for that was the widow's name, had sold her tavern to Peter Quintard; and he, in turn, later sold it and there was a succession of landlords. Yet it was still noted for Washington's visit, and in 1824, when General LaFayette returned from France for *his* celebrated tour, he was given the same quarters previously occupied by "his beloved and illustrious commander." By then, the house was also a regular stopping place of the Boston stages. In 1903, the old tavern had come on tragic days, and its new owner was planning to demolish the building when "three patriotic gentlemen of Rye bought it, with the idea of converting it into a museum of colonial and other historic relics."

Fairfield had the honor of Washington's first overnight stop in New England. This was at the old Sun Tavern on the village green. The party moved on at sunrise, to breakfast at Stratford, to ferry the Housatonic River, and to spend the night at Clark's Tavern in Milford. On the authority of a local historian, it is obvious that Mr. Clark did not keep a very good house, for his distinguished guest, not much relishing his supper of boiled meat and potatoes, called for a bowl of bread and milk which "was brought to him with a *pewter* spoon that lacked a handle." Washington asked for a silver spoon, and was told that the house afforded none, whereupon the Federalist father of his country gave the servant a two-shilling piece and told her to go borrow one. This she did, at the local minister's, and "on the reputation thus established for him, Landlord Clark could soon afford silver spoons."

73

The Old Post Road

It was with good reason that Washington-Slept-Here taverns suddenly appeared in the wake of every tour made by the first President. On back roads as well as post roads, so wrote a skeptical historian much later, "still stand ancient houses in which Washington is alleged to have taken refreshment, or to have spent the night, or at least to have entered. . . . Nothing else brought lasting fame so quickly to an inn."

There is little need, however, for doubting the great American's presence. When traveling, he preferred taverns to private homes. For many years he kept a diary, and the entries for 1789 are impressive evidence not only of the punctiliousness with which he fulfilled all his engagements, but also something of a guide to taverns of the period, both good and otherwise.

And now, in 1789, as he and his party moved eastward on the Boston Post Road, the names of publicans often appear.

In New Haven, he writes of the "House of Mr. [Jacob] Brown, where I lodged, and who keeps a good Tavern." (On a previous stop in New Haven, when on his way to take command of the troops at Cambridge, Washington stayed at the house kept by Isaac Beers who, four years later, was killed by the British in his own tavern when the redcoats invaded New Haven.)

On the way to Hartford, neither Wallingford, where the party breakfasted, nor Middletown, where they dined, nor yet Wethersfield, could hold them overnight; they were met at Wethersfield by a detachment of the Hartford Light Horse, and escorted to Bull's Tavern, arriving in Hartford about sundown, and there they lodged. (No comment on Mr. Bull's house.) Next day, according to the President's diary, "by promise I was to have breakfasted with Mr. Ellsworth at Windsor, on my way to Springfield," but the morning being very wet "and the rain not ceasing till past ten o'clock, I did not set out until half after that hour." But Washington did call on Mr. Oliver Ellsworth, later Chief Justice of the United States, and "Stay'd near an hour," then went on to Springfield where, "while dinner was getting, I examined the Continental Stores at this place." Here he lodged at Zenas Parson's Tavern, "which is a good House."

Washington Was Here

In addition to the immediate fame brought to public houses by Washington's visits, there was another effect of much greater importance. This was that the fortunate tavern was "to have ten times the chance of preservation accorded to the ordinary old building." As was the case at Rye, New York, so at Springfield, Massachusetts, where in 1819, "a company of public-spirited townspeople purchased the main part of Parsons Tavern that was being razed," and moved it to "its last resting-place at the foot of Court Street." Apparently, too, David Hitchcock's Tavern in West Brookfield, Massachusetts, where Washington dined in 1789, survived to entertain another President, John Adams, in 1821, and it was also where LaFayette stopped in 1825. Mrs. Mary Caroline Crawford, the historian, wrote in 1907 that Hitchcock's was "one of the few taverns that entertained Washington which I can cordially recommend today to the wayfarer," but most of the rest of them "are not inns any longer and, such as they are, the least said the better." Possibly one of these was at Spencer, the house of one Jenks who, according to Washington, kept merely a "pretty good" tavern. Yet Mrs. Jenks told ever after that "the General at Breakfast remarked, 'Madam, your bread is very beautiful.'"

The presidential party was now approaching the Worcester–Boston orbit, and the taverns get spare mention in competition with the military groups and the various committees of "Respectable Citizens" which started to appear in Leicester and were in almost continuous attendance through Worcester, Marlboro, Weston, and Cambridge. It is known, however, that Washington dined at Williams Tavern, Marlboro; had lunch at the Howe Tavern, Sudbury; lodged at the Weston Tavern, Weston, kept by John Flagg, and so into Cambridge.

At Cambridge, across the Charles from Boston, began what was locally remembered as the "John Hancock Incident." It was really a series of incidents; because the Widow Ingersoll's lodging house is prominent in the business, and because the whole affair shows

The Old Post Road

Washington's ability to cut a pomposity down to size, it deserves mention in any account of the old Boston Post Road.

John Hancock, having signed the Declaration of Independence, had also been elected president of the Continental Congress. Not realizing his own limitations, says one of his biographers, Hancock "desired to be made commander-in-chief of the Army, but Congress promptly thwarted his ambitions by the appointment of Washington to that office; and he never forgave what he considered this slight to his ability and pretentions." And now in 1789, when General Washington was making his first visit as President to Boston, Governor Hancock of Massachusetts, was "indisposed."

On October 24, Washington and his official party arrived at ten o'clock in Cambridge, on time "according to appointment." Not only had Governor Hancock not put in an appearance, but neither had the company of militia troops selected to escort the distinguished visitor into Boston. An hour later the troops showed up, and so did the Lieutenant Governor, Mr. Samuel Adams, with the Executive Council. The procession moved across the Charles, then to the State House, which had been "most handsomely decorated" for the occasion. Boston was doing its best to welcome the man proclaimed by the banners, "To the Man Who Unites All Hearts" and "To Columbia's Favorite Son."

The visitor soon appeared on the State House (North) Balcony and "a vast concourse of people" let go with cheers. Then came an ode composed in the President's honor, "well sung by a band of select singers," and more cheers. Meanwhile "the Streets, the Doors, windows, and tops of the Houses were crowded with well dressed Ladies and Gentlemen."

Still no Governor. Whereupon, Washington later observed in his diary, "the procession being over, I was conducted by the Lieut. Govr and Council, accompanied by the Vice President [John Adams] to my lodgings at a Widow Ingersoll's, which is a very decent and good House." And that evening the good widow had not only the President for dinner, but the Vice President too.

On that night, Washington confided to his diary the reason he had chosen to dine privately in his lodging house: "Having engaged yesterday to take an informal dinner with the Govr [Hancock] today, but under a full persuasion that he would have waited upon me so soon as I should have arrived—I excused myself upon his not doing it, and informing me thro' his Secretary that he was too much indisposed to do it, being resolved to receive the visit. Dined at My Lodgings, where the Vice President favored me with his company."

Next day, a Sunday, Washington attended services in both the Episcopal and the Congregational churches. Between the two services he "received a visit from the Govr who assured me that indisposition alone prevented his doing it yesterday, and that he was still indisposed; but as it had been suggested that he expected to *receive* the visit from the President, which he knew was improper, he was resolved at all haz'ds to pay his Compliments today." In short, Hancock had been having second thoughts on the matter of protocol, yet his call had no effect on the President. "Dined at my lodgings with the Vice President," said the diary that night.

On Monday, the President had a full day. At ten he received visits from the clergy; at eleven he went to an Oratorio in King's Chapel. Then he received the official addresses of the Governor and Council, of the President of Harvard College, and of the Cincinnati of the State, followed by "a large and elegant Dinner at Faneuil Hall, given by the Govr and Council." (Hancock was warming up by the minute.) Yet Washington "spent the evening at my lodgings."

By this time, the Town of Boston was cognizant of the battle of protocol and, apparently to a man, was on the side of Washington. The citizens had been on hand to welcome the President, and so had the Governor's suite. When the Governor himself did not make an appearance, most everybody figured the pompous Hancock did not wish to recognize a superior personage—at least, not in Massachusetts. "Consequently," wrote a Bostonian, the Governor allowed the crowds, standing in the raw, chill weather, to contract what for many years was known as "the Washington Cold. . . . But Washington had as high a sense of personal dignity as did Hancock; he had also a much nicer appreciation of when it is improper to show personal pique."

Hence, Washington rode between the throngs massed on State Street, and past the State House, to "his cold dinner at Mrs. Ingersoll's on Tremont Street near what is now Scollay Square . . . and there he kept to his room, refusing flatly an invitation to dine with Hancock."

The "Hancock Incident" became widely known in the thirteen United States, and thus went into American history. Says the sketch of Washington (in the authoritative *Dictionary of American Biography*): ". . . his tour of the New England States was productive of little other than a warm welcome from the inhabitants and an unnecessary test of official strength between the President of the United States and Gov. John Hancock of Massachusetts, in which the latter came off second best, to the great glee of the citizens of Boston."

The presidential tour continued from Boston to touch at Marblehead, Salem, Ipswich, Newburyport, Andover, and on into New Hampshire, at Portsmouth and Exeter, none of which towns were on the Boston Post Road. It returned to Massachusetts by way of Haverill, Andover again, and Lexington, and to the Post Road at Watertown, where the "Widow Coolidge kept the tavern and a very indifferent one it is."

From Boston the President's party left town by Needham, Sherborn, and Holliston, none of which is now on the Middle Post Road which they reached at Milford and Mendon, to lodge the night of November 6 at a Mr. Taft's tavern, in Uxbridge. Washington must have found Mr. Taft's house and family of unusual charm, for only a couple of days later he wrote to Proprietor Taft:

Washington Was Here

Sir—Being informed that you have given my name to one of your sons, and called another after Mrs. Washington's family, and being, moreover, very much pleased with the modest and innocent looks of your two daughters, Patty and Polly, I do for these reasons send each of these girls a piece of chintz; and to Patty, who bears the name of Mrs. Washington, and who waited more upon us than Polly did, I send five guineas, with which she may buy herself any little ornaments she may want, or she may dispose of them in any other manner more agreeable to herself. As I do not give these things with a view to have it talked of, or even of its being known, the less there is said about it the better you will please me; but that I may be sure the chintz and money have got safe to hand let Patty, who I dare say is equal to it, write me a line informing me thereof, directed to "The President of the United States at New York." I wish you and your family well, and am your humble servant,

George Washington

What a stunner this letter must have been to the Tafts of Uxbridge tavern—father and sons, mother and daughters; and despite the President's expressed wish that the occasion not be talked of, one may be sure it was not kept secret. One may wonder, too, if these tavern-keeping Tafts of Uxbridge were not in the line of the twenty-seventh President of the United States, William Howard Taft, whose ancestors "on his father's side had dwelt in Massachusetts and Vermont since the seventeenth century," among whom were the Tafts and Torreys of Mendon, Massachusetts, scarce ten miles from Uxbridge on the Middle Post Road.

Beyond Uxbridge, however, the quality of the Post Road taverns seemed to have dropped. Washington said that Jacob's Inn, Thompson, Connecticut, was "not a good House" and has no comment to make on Colonel Grosvenor's house in Pomfret. In Ashford was Perkins Tavern, "which, by the bye, is not a good one." It was at Ashford, too, where the tithing man, a town-and-church officer whose chief duty, at this period, was to enforce observance of the

Sabbath, reminded the President, with less courtesy than stubbornness, that travel on Sunday was forbidden by Connecticut law. Washington had stopped at Ashford specifically because "my horses, after passing through such intolerable roads, wanted rest. . . ." Nevertheless, he also attended morning and evening services at the local meeting house where he heard "very lame discourses from a Mr. Pond."

Then, after passing through Hartford, Berlin, and Wallingford, with no comment on taverns, the party reached New Haven before sundown. Here Washington met Elbridge Gerry, the noted patriot-statesman (whose name was later given to "gerrymander"), from whom the President got the "first certain account of the health of Mrs. Washington." Next morning, the party set out at sunrise for Milford, where they breakfasted; baited (fed) their horses at Fairfield "and lodged 9 miles further at Maj. Marvin's." The tour was almost done, but on the way between Stamford and Rye, some of the horses turned lame, and the last night on the road the party lodged again at the Widow Haviland's in Rye, where the first night had been spent, though the place was now kept by Mr. Quintard.

On November 12, the President arrived "at my house in New York, where I found Mrs. Washington and the rest of the family all well. . . ." The tour "through the Eastern States" had occupied almost exactly one month.

It will have been noted that Rhode Island has not been mentioned. This was due to the fact that the citizens there had still not ratified the Constitution, and did not do so for another six months, or until May 29, 1790. In August of that year, President Washington dutifully visited Rhode Island, arriving at Newport and being welcomed by a salute from the fort. After being presented to the "most respectable citizens" of the place, he was wined and dined in the Town Hall. It was to be a brief visit: next morning at nine o'clock, a newspaper reported, "the President and his company embarked for Providence." Here he made his headquarters at the Golden Ball Inn, opposite the

State House, already famous because LaFayette had been entertained there in 1784.

Thus were the many tavern keepers of Rhode Island denied the incomparable inheritance of the Washington-Was-Here legend.

More than once the thought has occurred to me that in the far distant future, some ambitious student at a New England college, seeking a Ph.D., might tackle the subject of ancient taverns on the Boston Post Road; if so, he *could* come up with the thesis that although eminent men named Franklin and Webster and LaFayette and Washington all had had something or other to do with the public houses in the region, the major taverns were subsequently taken over by an otherwise unknown character named Duncan Hines.

Chapter 11

Scollay Square

IN THE HEYDAY of New England's stagecoach era, the busiest section of Boston centered around Mr. Scollay's Buildings and was known as Scollay Square. Here were many of the stage offices, including those of the famous Pease Line to New York, which had dominated traffic on the Boston Post Road since late eighteenth century.

Badger and Porter's Stage Register, the bible of the transportation business, listed, as early as 1826, no less than fifty-eight lines operating mail and passenger coaches out of Boston; and before the railways began running, more than 2,000 stage vehicles were rolling in and out of the city every week. Although a majority of them "Set Out From" Scollay Square, to use the contemporary term, incoming passengers might get off the stage at any of several regular stops after entering the city.

Scollay Square

When the horsecars came in, they, too, made their way through Scollay Square; and eventually the various railroads combined to build the North Station within the Scollay orbit. To bring matters down to the present, a stranger to Boston who does any casual strolling is pretty sure to find himself in Scollay Square. He does not need to plan it so. He may wish to avoid the place. But first thing he knows, there he is in the middle of the most fearsome maze of streets, dead ends, rookeries, and rabbit warrens in North America. It is a thing certainly of no beauty, but a wonder unique in cities of the United States.

It is not given to man, even a Bostonian, to describe in adequate terms the flavor of Scollay Square. A visitor might liken it to New York's Bowery. If he did, he would be no nearer the fact than if he likened it to the Place de la Concorde in Paris. True, it still musters a few employment offices, now fallen on hard times. It has garish penny arcades, two burlesque theaters, several gaudy movies, many saloons, flophouses, a tattooing parlor ("See Dad Upstairs"), and more often than not a drunk or two in the gutter.

But Scollay Square has something else; and this other element, this overlying flavor or characteristic, is the largely unseen yet powerful sense of old things, ancient things by American standards, many of them great and good things in the best sense, and as solidly American as Indian pudding and Medford rum. These press on Scollay Square from all sides, and Scollay has more sides than any other so-called square in the country, if not in the world.

Perhaps this indefinable feeling that inhabits Scollay lies in the realm of metaphysics, but it is as real as the cobblestones which have given kidney complaint to generations of drivers of coaches, herdics, and taxicabs. I am not prone to whimsy, and never in my youth happened to see the shade of Daniel Webster delivering a speech from the wrought-iron balcony of the Revere House of blessed memory. But if any reasonably sober man told me he had seen such a sight, I should readily believe him.

Scollay is also the place where more men have become lost than in the Maine woods. One sees them, roaming aimlessly in attempts to discover an outlet from the Square that will lead them to the Parker House or to the North Station, peering wild-eyed at street signs which apparently conflict and give the direct lie to one another until at last the lost stranger, no matter how determined, is driven to ask a policeman or a bootblack to lead him, shaken and twitching, to the sudden peace and quiet of King's Chapel Burying Ground, less than five rods from where he was standing when he gave up and demanded succor.

Scollay wasn't always thus. For fifty years it was a cow pasture. Then, before 1684, a schoolhouse was built "against Captain Samuel Sewall's house." In 1753, the school was enlarged, and Samuel Holbrook was made schoolmaster at an annual salary of £60. In 1790, the school was abandoned and William Scollay bought it and other houses nearby, living in one and renting the rest. These became known as Mr. Scollay's Buildings and were occupied for years by "barbers, braziers, lawyers, and the largest tea store in the city."

In 1816 this row of structures was torn down to make a new street, Cornhill, and the Scollays were paid an indemnity. By this time, brick buildings were rising along the crooked cowpaths, and the area was soon known as Scollay Square. Stages used it as a terminus. So, in turn, did horsecars, then the trolleys. Large hotels went up, the American House, the Quincy, the Crawford, the Revere. The latter was on Bowdoin Square, but today no man can say where Scollay leaves off and Bowdoin begins.

Today in Scollay Square one can walk a few rods in any direction and come face to face with history. Along Cornhill (to which "Street" is never appended) are secondhand bookshops. A few steps down Tremont, one immediately drops out of the present hurdy-gurdy of Scollay and is at squat, black, old King's Chapel, whose bell, by Paul Revere, has a deep, haunting voice, and in whose burying ground lie the remains of the Colonial Governors Winthrop and Endecott, and those of William Dawes, who rode that night with Revere but had no immortalizing agent like Longfellow. Across Tremont Street is the Old Granary Burying Ground, where sleep the so-called martyrs of the so-called Boston Massacre. Paul Revere himself sleeps here, and so does Samuel Adams, "The Great Agitator" of the Revolution.

Or, walk north a few steps from Scollay, and come to the plaque marking the site where lived one of Boston's most illustrious citizens, Charles Bulfinch, the architect. Great preaching has been heard in these parts, too, down Brattle Street where stood the Brattle Square Church, organized in 1665. Such men as Edward Everett and John G. Palfrey discoursed here. During the siege of Boston, a cannon ball heaved from Cambridge by Colonel Knox's artillery bedded in a side of this meeting house, and there it remained until the structure was razed.

One side of Scollay Square is Court Street, once Prison Lane where the colonial lockup stood and where, in 1699, Captain Kidd himself peered through the bars to watch the cows and city rustics. (Hawthorne described this jail in *The Scarlet Letter*.) Through this street hurried mobs in a vain attempt to rescue Anthony Burns, Negro, from the slave catchers, and Thomas Wentworth Higginson, Theodore Parker, Wendell Phillips, and others were arrested and charged with obstructing the process of the United States. For more years than men can remember the Ancient and Honorable Artillery Company paraded through Scollay from their headquarters in Faneuil Hall, from the cupola of which the famous grasshopper weather vane still marks the winds.

It was through Scollay that Dr. Parkman walked, "with his long, quick strides," on that fatal day in 1849, on his way to Harvard Medical School to see Professor John White Webster, who was later hanged for murder and went into history as the only murderer to perform while a member of Harvard College Faculty.

The character of Scollay Square changed slowly until 1903, when things sort of went to pieces. The bronze statue of Governor John Winthrop was removed from the Square because of congested traffic conditions plus work on the East Boston Tunnel. Pawnshops and employment offices moved in and there they remain along with passport photo shops, aromatic eating dives, two-pants clothing stores and other skidroad places—and noise. The noise comes from many things: the roughest cobblestones in all geology, bumping the trucks and drays and cabs which bounce in endless procession day and night; the rumble of subway trains; street hawkers and newsboys whose A's are broad and voices terrific; Salvation Army and other street evangels.

I mentioned that on the Square were two burlesque theaters. Now I fear that only too soon one of these, the Old Howard, will have been demolished. If this happens, it will be wanton destruction of a building that has stood 115 years and is as historic a structure as many another that Boston has preserved as a public service. Because Boston's Watch and Ward Society long ago certified the ancient playhouse variously as a "Social Cancer" and a "Sink of Sin," it has been closed for periods during recent years. But if readers will bear with an interpolation, a brief account of the storied old temple of the arts may not be out of place.

One August day, more than a year ago, I stood again, just off Scollay Square, to gaze at the medieval pile of granite that arches up so suddenly here on the "wrong side" of Beacon Hill. There is nothing phony about it. It is granite, 3 feet thick, the same stuff that went into Bunker Hill Monument. It was built in 1843, as a church for the disciples of William Miller, the Millenarian prophet, who planned to be inside it when Gabriel blew that horn and the Last Day arrived. It did not sound, so these Adventists leased their temple to a theatrical company.

For the next century and more the playhouse presented Sheridan, Shakespeare, opera, variety; then melodrama, minstrels, sword swallowers, fire eaters, human flies, and BURLESQUE in big letters, and with programs printed on mauve-tinted paper. Ever so slowly it degenerated, as did Scollay Square itself. No rural Yankee in my time, or my father's time, felt he had seen Boston until he had furtively witnessed a performance at what for decades had been known as the Old Howard. Its shows had gone into legend which

Scollay Square

was described by Professor John Fiske of Harvard as Anatomy I, II, III, and IV. No sailor in port went away without a visit to the Howard. Neither did any drummer, nor, for that matter, did any parson.

It was in this gothic arena that I first saw the Boston Strong Boy, John L. Sullivan, and with him, for good measure, were Dainty Violet Mascotte and her Thirty Merry Maids. I had come of age. All for fifty cents. By that time, too, the place had its famous slogan "Always Something Doing at the Old Howard 1 to 11," and had entered folklore with unprintable stories about the dancer in tights who was responsible for "Grandpa being killed in the Rush."

The Howard's troubles came in the 1930s, when it was closed for thirty days on account of "voluptuous dancing and profane dialogue." Whether or not the house reformed is an abstract matter, but it is of record that it reopened with a bill called "Scrambled Legs." Other closures bothered the house. So did labor controversies. Finally, it closed its doors, and rumors of wreckers and Urban Renewal took the wind.

There are, however, many citizens who favor restoration of the Howard Atheneum to its original 1846 elegance, to make it a sort of National Theater Museum, a proper place to house and display collections of theater materials, and in which period plays could be produced. According to Miss Gladys Lyons, of the Boston Development Authority, a movement is under way to raise money for this most desirable effort. I can hope there is a sufficient number of Bostonians with the imagination to realize that their city's major attractions to visitors are its associations with American history. The Howard belongs among them. It is unquestionably the oldest theater in the country built for the centuries, of which it has "used up" a mere 115 years.

Should the old playhouse disappear, it will be an unqualified shame. Is there in all Boston no voice equal to that of Dr. Holmes, who protested destruction of the frigate *Constitution* whose tattered ensign had so long waved on high? Even if, in its age, the Howard had fallen into disrepute, is that any reason to ignore its potential? Let it stand right where it is, within range of the deep, mellow peals of Paul Revere's masterpiece in the belfry of King's Chapel.*

There is one more item, and it concerns a small building which Boston today would give a good deal to have, had it not been destroyed long ago in some earlier phase of Urban Renewal.

On Scollay Square, down the preposterously named Franklin *Avenue*, which is exactly 9 feet 6 inches wide, there used to be the shop of the *New England Courant*, James Franklin, Proprietor, whose brother Ben was printer's devil before he went away to many other things, including office as the first Postmaster General of the United States.

* On June 20, 1961, fire gutted the ancient theater's interior. (OLD HOWARD EXITS IN BLAZE OF GLORY, said a headline.) In August, when I visited the ruins, with Miss Lyons and Mr. Dean L. Gitter, head of the group raising funds for restoration, they were doubtful of saving even the granite walls.

Interlude

They
Didn't Get
the
Railroad

The shadows grew longer. It was afternoon, late afternoon, in New England, and the old men who sat endlessly in the crossroads stores wondered aloud to each other: Why didn't their village Get The Railroad?

Fitchburg got the cars, didn't they? And look at her now! Growing like a weed, Mister. Yes, sir, and look at Waltham, she got the cars, too, and now they got a watch factory as big as all outdoors.

The shadows grew longer, and the old men at the crossroads talked on without end, talked for months and years, calculating time, warning of the growing dusk, crying night. Why *didn't* their village Get The Railroad?

Bridgeport was nowhere near so pretty a place, but Bridgeport sure knew what to do; they *paid* somebody more than 2,000 dollars to put the steam-cars into their town, and now she's booming. In another couple of years be almost as big as Hartford.

Once upon a time it had been enough if a town was a station on the Boston Post Road. That meant a tavern and a mighty big stable, too. Perhaps three taverns. But no longer. You had to have the railroad, either in hand or coming soon, after about

8 9

1840. Most of the effects of steam upon the United States were easily perceptible. For one thing, the forces of nature meant little to steam locomotion. It overcame wind and tide. It abolished the Mississippi River, until then a mighty fact. It abolished the Great American Desert. All that the Rockies meant to steam locomotion was a little more fire under the boiler.

Yet, steam turned out to be capricious. Was it not proving as much a master of what Americans liked to call their Destiny as it was its slave? It carried the individual wherever he would go; and it carried away whole communities who did not want to go anywhere at all. Either that, or it buried them where they were.

These ancient men at the crossroads realized that the old order of Post Road times was passing; in the backwashes of New England the passing of that order was seen more plainly than elsewhere, for here there was infinitely less to distract attention. You could see that these old cocked-hat fellows were now tragically few—these survivors who still wore small-clothes and hose and shoes with big buckles —the men who took snuff, who in spite of the new Locofoco matches still lighted their fires, and often their very pipes, with flint and steel, and were likely as not to be Deists, or worse. . . .

They talked on, these immensely ancient men, and they were listened to. Had they not *seen* with their own eyes Colonel Ethan Allen, or shaken the hand of Paul Revere? Had they not been with Old Put in Mr. Bunker's pasture at Charlestown? God save us, you *listened* to such men, for they came from a world as far removed from the present, for all practical purposes, as the times of Mordecai. They were believed somehow to have a wisdom not given to other sons of men.

In the name of the Great Jehovah and the Continental Congress they had performed prodigies. They had told the King's men, in their day, that if anybody wanted a war, then let it begin here and now. They had known, too, that if they did not beat the redcoats, then Molly Stark would sleep a widow.

Aye, you listened to men such as these, sitting with their canes in the crossroads stores, while a bluebottle fly beat again and again on the dusty window, and outside a horse stamped at the hitching post. They talked in an aroma of coffee and spice and tea and kerosene and tobacco. Some of these men had mellowed since Yorktown; others had merely dried and toughened, and these latter spat at the cold box stove and said they would be goddamned if they would lift a finger to Get The Railroad.

What did the steamcars do, save to set fire to barns and fields with their hellish sparks and wound or kill man and beast? Well, they were carrying away the younger generations of Yankees—man and maid together—to ungodly places called Ohio and Ioway and Californy. Well, let them go. They were a poor lot, anyway, who had long since deserted the ways of their fathers. It mattered little if what the *Hartford Courant* said *was* true; that 160,000 natives of Connecticut had gone away to the West. The same was probably true of Massachusetts; and still others were leaving Rhode Island and three more Yankee states.

Consider how the fine old stagecoach villages were mouldering even while you watched. The railroads were doing it. Every stray wolf seen or killed, or merely rumored, was evidence—wasn't it?— that the packs were returning from the Far North, where they had been driven in your grandfather's day. Every abandoned hill farm in six states showed that the wilderness was returning, and Chaos and Old Night were riding the wilderness. . . .

Dust blew in an open window. Outside, an unheard wind fluttered the leaves on the great old elms; and on the wind came the godless chatter of a mowing machine, a device direct from the Pit, which a few thoughtless men called an improvement over the honest hand scythe.

Indeed, cried the old men, the shadows were getting longer and darker. It was not noon any more. It might not be afternoon but maybe night, in the Yankee kingdom. Should the clock strike again, it might well strike thirteen. Time, you'd best believe, was running out.

Why, one read in the papers how curious professors were digging into strange mounds in the West, in Ohio, digging into lava beds in Italy, plumbing the earth in foreign parts, all for the sake of learning something of ancient peoples whom Time had buried deep and then forgotten. Better far they came to New England and paused at this or that cellar hole on what had been a hill farm.

Here, my good professors of archaeology, is a relic, a fossil, a memoir of a nigh extinct people—the hill farmers. Dig into it. You will find a spoon or two of pewter, perhaps a latch of hand-wrought iron and a bullet mold, a candle mold, a bee runner's trap. Those spikes came from a hatchel, used in preparing flax. Fossils, every one.

That great slab of pure granite was the doorstep; to move it a hair would call for a yoke of the oxen of Job and a goad like unto Shamgar's. That rotting hulk of cedar, mossgrown these many years, was once a noble trough, to hold water that was carried half a mile in logs bored end to end. . . .

The desolation that began in the hills spread to the rural lowlands and along the post roads, seeking out the places that Didn't Get The Railroad. The local industries which for generations had been supplying local needs—the tanneries, the sawmills, the gristmills, and such—felt it. Their vats moulded, their water wheels ground to a halt, while the untended dams gave way or filled with silt, and alder and willow grew high in the millrace.

The once bright clapboards of the old stage taverns weathered to a mellow patina, then started to molt like Plymouth Rocks in autumn, while moss climbed the shingled roofs from eaves to ridgepole, where a bent and mangled weathervane pointed, no matter the quarter of the wind, straight down to hell.

The crossroads stores hung on a while longer, though they faded by the year, and around their stoves, summer and winter, the newer old men talked on; and on the shelves mice nested and brought forth their young, and the spots of flies grew so thick they were no longer distinguishable from the paint, which had been last applied in the year John Quincy Adams died, which was 1848, and may God give peace to the great man's noble, if puckered, soul.

Time here at the crossroads did not stand still, nor did it move forward. It actually moved backward. On a wall in the store, perhaps near the molasses barrel, was still a sign, faded but perfectly legible, which announced the goings and comings of the splendid coaches of the Eastern Stage Company, whose wheels had long since ceased to roll. Time here, I tell you, moved backward. In the Town Hall was a poster, once a handsome thing in four colors, bidding Welcome to New England to the great and popular, if aged, General LaFayette. The First Selectman had tacked it on that wall in the summer of 1824.

Elsewhere, Time seemed to move on. In Boston, Prophet William Miller said that Time was not only running on, it was running out. The end was nigh. The Last Days were here. When people ignored him, Miller stood forth again and gave cry: *Behold the Bridegroom cometh, go ye out to meet him!*

He was right, almost. In 1861 came the very Apocalypse, four bloody years of it; when it was over, the Yankees began leaving their homes in larger numbers than ever before, and the Post Road hamlets continued to fade.

Meanwhile, still newer old men took their seats in the surviving stores of the villages that did not have the steamcars, and talked on. One day, in the new century, they had a new topic: The first horseless carriage came through the village to run down and mangle the first leghorn rooster to be killed thus in all the county.

Never again did it matter much who had the railroad, and who did not. The Iron Horse was no match for the horseless carriage. The branch-line railroads that had served so many Post Road towns started to rust, then to disappear; and in their place came the highway pavements, and the cars. They were no longer the steamcars, but the personal, private vehicles of a nation of tourists.

Never again was it to matter much whether or not a village *had* a railroad station. Of infinitely greater importance, in the new age of tourists, was a well-kept old tavern dating from Colonial times, a graceful church with spire, and a handsome village green complete with elms and a bronze cannon that bore the ordnance markings of George III. . . . Welcome to Tourists.

Chapter 12

Boston West by the Upper Road

T HIS IS PERHAPS a good place for the reader to start ranging the Boston Post Road as it looks today, 280-odd years
after the original postrider completed his first round trip from New
York. Scollay Square will do for a basing point for the three separate routes between Boston and New Haven, where they merge to
become a single route from New Haven to New York.

I propose that we first follow the Upper Road to Springfield, and
south to Hartford; then head back to Boston and take the Middle
Road to Hartford and New Haven; head again to Boston, and
follow the Lower Road. The Lower Road makes its way to New
Haven by three routes. Each will have a chapter by itself. When

The Upper Road

New Haven is reached, all is clear sailing, or rather wheeling, to New York City.

Because, as pointed out earlier, this study makes no pretense to being a guidebook, this tour of the entire Boston Post Road will not pause at every town along the way. It will, however, pause here and there for reasons that will be clear and, I hope, interesting.

One should bear in mind that in terms of age, if not of length, the Boston road is the grandfather of all American post roads. Like all grandparents, it has seen fearful changes in its time. One of the most purposeful of these events was the first concerted movement of Yankees toward the Great West. It was also dramatic. Though the idea and the plan originated in a Boston tavern, the actual movement itself began in what is now the town of Hamilton, some 20 miles east of Boston.

The time was a cool December day in 1787. There were twenty-two men striding beside a great long wagon hauled by four oxen. The wagon was covered its full length with canvas. Painted on each side of the canvas, in a strong bold hand, was a legend: FOR THE OHIO COUNTRY, it said.

Here was evidence that a road worked both ways, east and west. It was a sort of formal early warning of what in time was to be considered New England's greatest export—people. Although the Constitution of the United States was not yet fully ratified, the Yankee exodus had begun in the classic manner. Generations of restless Americans along the Atlantic seaboard were to move west with the sun in covered wagons until that vehicle of pioneers was at last recognized as the incomparable symbol of the American people.

This covered apparition of 1787, with its strange reference to the "Ohio Country," had been fashioned at what then was Ipswich Hamlet, one of the truly lovely names of the Puritan settlers in the northeastern corner of Massachusetts Bay province. The twenty-two men were members of a group that had been organized in the Bunch of Grapes Tavern in Boston's King Street by General Rufus Putnam, Continental Army officer, to receive a grant from Congress of 1½ million acres of land in the new Northwest Territory. These men with the long wagon were the first contingent of the Ohio Company of Associates. At dawn on December 1, they had paraded before the parsonage of Dr. Manasseh Cutler, Congregational minister of Ipswich Hamlet, who gave them Godspeed. The good doctor was to follow later.

The pilgrims moved on to nearby Danvers where they paused to fire a salute, and continued on to Charlestown, across the river from Boston and Cambridge. Here they met and entered upon the Boston Post Road, passing near Harvard College. Proceeding on through Sudbury, Marlboro, and Worcester to Springfield, they paused briefly at Hartford, to greet Colonel Ebenezer Sproat, who was to lead a second contingent due to leave on January 1, 1788.

Some four months later, the forty-eight pioneers started to drive their stakes on the Ohio River. For a while they called the place Adelphia, then thought better of it and named the town Marietta, possibly for the two daughters, Mary and Etta, of General Rufus Putnam. It was the first permanent settlement in all the vast void of the Northwest Territory.

Though the Ohio Company of Associates doubtless made a stir as they passed down the Upper Post Road, and so out of New England history, many a Yankee hamlet was just beginning to feel the heady influence of improved communication and transportation: Levi Pease's stage line, Boston to Hartford, was already five years in business, and due to expand to New York. Ambitious villages were soon setting their sights for great things. One of these, nine miles from Boston, had been carved out of Watertown and named Waltham.

For more than a century, Waltham on the Charles River was known the country over as the Watch City. Before then, and for a lesser period, it was called the Kerosene Capital of New England.

The Upper Road

Even earlier, Francis Cabot Lowell had built in Waltham "the first mill in the world which combined all the operations of converting raw cotton into finished cloth."

When I was last there, in 1960, a new concern was trying to make Waltham into the "Electronics Heartland," and though it seems not to have caught on as a booster phrase or slogan, it at least showed that the old town was trying hard, making a pitch to ride one of the several new waves of the future. The original red brick watch factory still stands beside the river, its elaborate tower typical of New England industrial towns. Two enormous signs still told passers-by that this was the Waltham Watch Company, yet lesser signs indicated the old building housed various other firms.

No watches are made in Waltham now. I learned that one company assembles watches, the parts for which come from Switzerland. Yet somebody remembers the great days; a sign on the Post Road near the factory read, WATCH CITY LIQUORS. The closure of Waltham Watch, which had opened for business as the American Horologue Company, was a tragedy. It was the only local industry of size. Making fine watches was precision work. Many employees never got *any* work again.

Technology has always loomed big in Waltham. When Francis Cabot Lowell's complete cotton mill began making raw cotton into finished cloth, hundreds of hand-weavers were thrown out of work in the region. And candlemakers may well have felt the effect of the Atwood brothers, Luther and William, who had succeeded in producing a fine burning oil from what they called petroleum pitch, and moved to build a kerosene factory in Waltham. The product was a success from the start, but it was soon gobbled up into the United States Chemical Company, which moved the plant to Portland, Maine.

In and around Waltham today are a number of new modern-type plants of the Raytheon Company, which I was told is now the largest employer in the city. It seems likely, however, that Waltham town will be identified with watches until Time itself runs out. Its genius was Aaron Lufkin Dennison, who introduced to American watchmaking the system of interchangeable parts which Eli Whitney, the cotton-gin man, had devised for the making of muskets for the United States Army. The first Waltham watches were ready for market at about the same time railroads were printing their first timetables.

Before the steamcars came, Time, as regulated by clocks and watches, meant comparatively little in the United States. After a number of tragic accidents, however, Time became the god of railroadmen, so many of whom found the Waltham reliable that the company quickly developed into the largest manufacturer of medium-priced watches in America.

It is worth recalling that on the 18th of November, 1883, which was a Sunday, the matter of time on all American railroads was divided into four standard time zones; and although Congress did not see fit to recognize them officially for another thirty-five years, everybody else did. I like to think it somehow or other pleased the watchmakers that when the noon whistle blew in Waltham, they knew for certain it was 11 o'clock in Chicago, 10 o'clock in Denver, and 9 o'clock in San Francisco. Had they not been told often enough, by proud speakers at the Waltham Merchants Exchange, that Waltham Kept Time for the Great West?

On the way out of Watch City to Weston we passed the massive pile of stone called Norumbega Tower, built by E. N. Horsford, a Harvard professor, to mark what he said was the name of a city mentioned in the Norse Saga of Eric the Red. Though Horsford spent a great deal of money to prove Leif Ericson visited Massachusetts, Columbus Day continues to be celebrated in the Commonwealth. What Chemistry Professor Horsford did prove, however, was that phosphoric acid put up in bottles, labeled Acid Phosphates and advertised to the hilt, could make a man a fortune. He himself had done as much.

Unlike Waltham, Weston did not blossom with the coming of the railroad age. Though in Post Road days it could boast more taverns than either neighboring Waltham or Wayland, its incipient industries picked up and moved away about 1840. I learned that the famous old Golden Ball Tavern still stood on the Post Road, as it had since 1751. It is now a private house. In any case, I was anxious to see what the architectural restorers had been able to do for the ruins of the most celebrated tavern in all Massachusetts, that at South Sudbury.

On Sudbury Common stands the First Parish Church. What struck me at once was the brevity and completeness of its history as set down on a sign nearby: "Founded 1640. . . . Unitarian Since 1839. . . . Meeting House Built 1797." There it is in all clarity and honesty. These Sudbury people were Puritans who were gathered, as the ancient phrase had it, into a congregation in 1640 which, for 199 years, adhered as a unit of the Congregational or virtually the then official church of Massachusetts, both Colony and State; and then voted to join the Unitarian, as opposed to the Trinitarian, wing, in 1839, but continued to worship in the same meeting house used since it was built in 1797. Not all, nor even many Protestant churches in Massachusetts, do so well by the stranger to identify its founding, the nature of its current beliefs, and the antiquity of its meeting house.

Sudbury's population reached its climax just before the outbreak of the Revolution, during which some 300 of its citizens served in the army. The town later lost much of its territory to newer towns that were formed around bustling villages. Yet chiefly because of its remarkable family of tavern keepers named Howe, Sudbury has been famous for its public house since early colonial days. It is now and has long since been known as the Wayside Inn.

Long ago I learned it was best, when dealing with famous old houses in New England, so far as dates and even names are concerned, to tread lightly. I'd be the last man to lessen by so much as a year the date claimed for any Yankee antiquity.

For instance, the official booklet given visitors to the Wayside Inn says that the place was "first licensed at the end of the seventeenth century." This is in accord with the replica of the tavern sign on which the oldest date is 1686. This date is doubtless correct. But then, in the official booklet, one reads that this "oldest operating Inn in the country was built in stagecoach days by the Howes of Sudbury." In 1686, and for many a decade more, there were no stagecoaches on the Boston Post Road or on any other road in the American colonies.

In so handsome and otherwise accurate a booklet, issued by The National Trust for Historic Preservation, this effort to get stagecoaches into the act is characteristic of romantic-minded people who wish to believe that transportation in America began with a coach-and-four, and continued until the railroad put the horses in the pasture and the coach into museums. So distinguished a tavern as the Wayside Inn in Sudbury needs no gilding with the stagecoach motif.

When I was in Sudbury some two years ago, it was an afternoon in July. Business with tourists was brisk, and I had to wait to talk with the costumed attendant, who was Mrs. Verna H. Cotter, a woman both gracious and informed, even to a nonpaying visitor. I had been there several times during the years, but not since it was badly damaged by fire in December, 1955, and although my recollections of the place antedated the fire, and were doubtless dimmed by time, the Wayside Inn of 1960 seemed to me as perfect a restoration as could be. This was due less to my knowledge of what had been done, of course, than to mere "feeling," or emotion.

This feeling, I fancy, was due in some part to the work of a poet, Henry Wadsworth Longfellow (1807–1882), one of the greatest and most purposeful publicists in American history. Among many other things, he published a book of verses under the title, *Tales of a Wayside Inn,* which appeared on November 25, 1863. I am convinced that had it not been for this book, all memory of Howe's Red Horse Tavern in Sudbury would have passed with the death in 1860 of Lyman, the last of the Howes, who left no descendants to carry on.

Longfellow probably first visited Howe's tavern in 1826 on his

101

first trip to Europe. This began with a stagecoach journey on the Upper Post Road. Thirty-five years later, when the last Howe was dead and the tavern and contents had been sold at auction, the poet visited the place again in company with James T. Fields, his publisher, to find it "a rambling, tumble-down old building—alas, no longer an inn!" It was, indeed:

> *A kind of old Hobgoblin Hall,*
> *Now somewhat fallen to decay,*
> *With weather-stains upon the wall,*
> *And stairways worn, and crazy doors,*
> *And creaking and uneven floors,*
> *And chimneys huge, and tiled and tall.*

A few days later, Longfellow wrote to Fields to say that "The Sudbury Tales go on famously. I have now five complete, with a great part of the Prelude." These tales were told by a group of characters staying at the inn. All were actually Longfellow's friends: the Landlord (the late Lyman Howe); the Musician, Ole Bull, the celebrated violinist; the Poet, T. W. Parsons, translator of Dante; the Professor, Professor Treadwell of Harvard; the Student, Henry Ware Wales, and so on.

Each character is described in turn, as he takes the floor to tell his story in the parlor of the inn. The host himself is the first to speak, and this, "The Landlord's Tale," is the only one that concerns us here. He begins:

> *Listen, my children, and you shall hear*
> *Of the midnight ride of Paul Revere. . . .*

Soon enough two lights go up in the belfry-tower of the Old North Church, and the Horseman of the American Revolution is riding through Medford and Lexington to Concord, and the fate of a nation is also riding that night.

It was enough. "The Landlord's Tale" alone was sufficient to turn Howe's Red Horse Inn into the Wayside Tavern almost overnight. It does not matter that other men, Dawes and Prescott, rode that same 18th and 19th of April in '75. It was Revere whose ride was touched by the immortalizing agent of genius, and there was room for none other. And though Longfellow had written this and other verses with the idea of publishing them as "Sudbury Tales," a friend of the Poet, Charles Sumner, senator from Massachusetts, thought it a dull title and suggested *Tales of a Wayside Inn.* Sumner, author of a famous speech entitled "The Crime Against Kansas," was no man to be ignored. Both Longfellow and Fields were grateful.

In 1923 Henry Ford, of Detroit, whose interest in the Wayside Inn extended over many years, bought the place to assure its preservation. He enlarged the property, "In order to preserve the natural scenery," then traced its original furnishings which had been scattered in 1861 after auction by the Howe family, and bought all available pieces. Then came the fire of 1955, and subsequent restoration by the National Trust for Historic Preservation. Being a nonprofit enterprise, it is proper to tell prospective visitors that it is "midway between Boston and Worcester, on the old Boston Post Road, now Route 20, 15 minutes north of the Massachusetts Turnpike (Exit 12, Framingham), 15 minutes west of Route 128 (Exit 43). Four hours from New York, and an easy drive to Lexington, Concord, and other landmarks."

Traffic to Sudbury on the Upper Post Road has increased so greatly that in recent years the Massachusetts Highway Board has "twice changed the road so as to leave the old Post Road approach unimpaired and preserve the old oaks which Longfellow repeatedly mentions." I read this item in a "Note to the Visitors' Edition" of the *Tales of a Wayside Inn* which the poet's publishers brought out since 1923, when Henry Ford bought the property.

When I went to a public library, to borrow this latest printing of the *Tales of a Wayside Inn,* the librarian remarked that she didn't know that "anybody read Longfellow any more." Perhaps they don't. Fashions in poetry have a way of coming and going, but no

The Upper Road

American bard other than Longfellow has created and left us legends so durable. Who among us would know of Miles Standish, or Evangeline of Arcadia, without Longfellow? What old native American is so famous as Hiawatha? (Not even Sitting Bull.) As for Paul Revere. . . .

It is no wonder that as the Wayside Inn, Howe's Red Horse Tavern is incomparably the best-known public house on the Old Boston Post Road.

Chapter 13

The Upper Road:
Sudbury to Worcester

BEFORE LEAVING the Wayside, I looked in at the door of the parlor, first room to the left as you enter the inn, to note that "the Sombre Clock" of "The Landlord's Tale" still stood in a corner, "and on the wall no longer bright/ though glimmering with a latent light/ was hung the sword his grandsire wore/ in the rebellious days of yore,/ down there at Concord in the fight,"/ and that the tourists were devouring the scene.

We were heading west for Marlboro where, as I knew, there was nothing to compare with the Wayside Inn as what has entered the language as a "tourist attraction." The aged Williams Tavern in Marlboro, where Washington had slept, and LaFayette, too, had long since been turned into a club. About the only local thing I had heard about and wanted to see was the John Brown Bell. We found it, hanging front and center on the old GAR Building, at the corner of Rawlins Avenue and Main Street, high above the sidewalk. It must be 30 inches in diameter at the flare of the bell, and though it has hung there for more than half a century, it somehow looked unsafe to a stranger. It is now the property of the American Legion, whose hall formerly housed the John A. Rawlins Post, No. 43, Grand Army of the Republic.

It was the Marlboro lads of Company 1, 13th Massachusetts Volunteers, who stole the big bell at Harpers Ferry in 1861, and at last brought it to their home town. Many years later one of them told how it happened in a booklet published in 1910. "On August 23, 1861," he wrote, "we went into camp two miles from the Potomac and about six miles from Harpers Ferry. In vain searching for something to take home with us as a souvenir, we finally decided to take the bell from the Engine House and send it home for the Marlboro Fire Department, because the Hook & Ladder Company had none." (Was there ever, in the long history of looting, a nobler excuse recorded than this effort to improve Marlboro's Hook and Ladder?)

"This was historic ground, and our thoughts naturally turned to the Engine House, for 'twas there that John Brown fought his last fight for liberation of the slaves."

A Lieutenant David L. Brown and fifteen others of Company 1 crossed the Potomac, climbed the engine house roof, disconnected the bell from the belfry, and lowered it. It was then put in a scow and taken across the river. By then, some of the souvenir hunters had second thoughts. "We decided it best to consult authority . . . and permission was received from the War Department." Within a few days, the Marlboro boys were ordered to return to their regiment at Williamsport, Maryland, and "the Bell went along and was landed with us." A long winter awaited them in the little Maryland town, where "A Mrs. Ensminger baked bread for our Company." The bell seemed to grow heavier by the month. On their $11 a month, the boys couldn't figure how they would ever save enough to pay freight to Massachusetts on so weighty a relic. "So, we made a trade with friendly Mrs. Ensminger to care for the Bell until called for."

Years passed. The Marlboro boys left Maryland to serve in various battles in the South, and never returned to Williamsport until twenty-seven years after the war was done. "Then, following the GAR Encampment in 1892, a party of us went to Williamsport." (The narrator doesn't say where the Marlboro boys lodged on this occasion, but it was not at the Williamsport Hotel, whose proprietor was wholly unreconstructed. He refused them as guests.) Mrs. Ensminger, now Mrs. Snyder by remarriage, was delighted to see her old friends of 1861. She said they owed her nothing for hiding the bell, but that over the years she had sent "many boxes of stuff that belonged to the Marlboro soldiers and had been left behind." For this service she accepted $150. The bell came out of hiding and was shipped to Massachusetts.

I had read that the famous bell was exhibited at the World's Fair of 1893 in Chicago. In any case, it arrived at last in Marlboro, and it was still hanging there on the GAR building a year or so ago when the Civil War Centennial got under way.

It had moved me deeply, to see this relic of one of the great moments of our history. Saint or madman, Old Brown himself had rung it when he raided Harpers Ferry in '59. It was like a firebell in the night, people said. It was more. It was a peal heard through the United States, even here in Marlboro, as witness the lads of the 13th Regiment of Massachusetts Volunteers.

"Again, in imagination," wrote one of them, "we could see the old Spartan as he felt the pulse of his dying son with one hand and grasped his rifle with the other." Every little while he pulled the rope again. The bell tolled on.

Fifty years later, in Marlboro, observed a GAR veteran, "the Bell's glad tones floated on the evening breeze as our battle-scarred Comrades marched to the banquet hall on festive occasions." But it was getting terribly late, by 1910, for the boys in blue, and "only too oft has it tolled the knell for some departed comrade."

They are all gone now, the members of John A. Rawlins Post No. 43 of the Grand Army of the Republic, and I wonder if it never occurred to any of them that within the range of sound of their famous bell, there is another bell, this one in Concord, Massachusetts, that was rung on December 2, 1859, the day of Brown's execution?

It was also the day that Henry Thoreau, still an obscurity of Concord, held his own protest meeting and raised one of the first voices in the country in defense of old Brown. It was a courageous thing. The selectmen of Concord refused to have the Town Hall bell in Concord rung for the meeting. Thoreau himself rang it. Meanwhile, "five hundred of his townsmen had damned him for proposing such a meeting." And, that night, John Brown was burned in effigy on Concord Green. (Remember, this was in '59 when there were few abolitionists in Concord.)

But Henry Thoreau spoke his piece, which he called, "A Plea for Captain John Brown." He did not plead to save Brown's life. His address was rather an indictment of the United States for permitting slavery, and it was perhaps as savagely eloquent a charge as anything heard during all the controversy over that subject in Congress.

"Captain Brown," he said, "has sedulously pursued a study of Liberty, for which he had early betrayed a fondness, and having taken many degrees, he finally commenced the public practice of Humanity in Kansas, as you all know. Such were his humanities. . . . He would have left a Greek accent slanting the wrong way, and righted up a fallen man. . . . It would be vain to kill him. He died lately in the time of Cromwell, but he reappeared here. Why should he not? Some of the Puritan stock settled here in New England. They were a class that did something else than celebrate their forefather's day, and eat parched corn in remembrance. . . . They were neither Democrats nor Republicans . . . not thinking much of rulers who did not fear God. . . ."

Sudbury to Worcester

I had been reading Thoreau many years before ever I came to his plea for Old Brown, and it rocked me as did neither Garrison nor Parker nor Sumner. . . .

Bemused in my hotel room in Marlboro, my night thoughts returned again to the John Brown Bell on the GAR Hall, *and* the bell of the Concord Town Hall. Was there not here virtually an invitation to use these historic relics simultaneously to compose a sort of memorial service unique among all the countless memorials we are having during the Centennial years of the Civil War?

How far apart were Concord and Marlboro? My road map indicated not more than 12 miles, as the crow flies or, possibly, as the sound of a big bell would travel. Were there any geographic features, such as hills, to interfere? I could think of none along the Boston Post Road; and anyway back in 1775, did not the people of Spencer, 50-odd miles from Concord, hear the battle? They claimed so.

No, 12 miles would not kill the exchange of the messages; and, in case a head-wind should prevent clarity of one bell or the other, electronics would carry their echoes, and also the voices of Old Brown and his defender Thoreau:

THOREAU   He was an old-fashioned man in his respect for the Declaration of Independence.

BROWN   Does not this, our very foundation, hold that all men are created equal?

THOREAU   It was no Abolition speaker who converted *him*.

BROWN   Steadfast God, I heard Thee, that though all Kansas bleed and burn, it was Thy command.

THOREAU   How did he manage to live in Kansas at all, with the price set upon his head?

BROWN   It was perfectly well understood that I will not be taken.

THOREAU   He did not attribute this foolishly to "his Star," or to any magic. He said it was because his opponents *lacked a cause.*

109

BROWN   I deny everything but what I have all along admitted; of a design on my part to free slaves.

THOREAU   The Engine House at Harpers Ferry, that was the final fort—Old Brown's last stand. Amid the dead and wounded, he heard his young son Oliver calling in his agony, "Oh, kill me, put me out of this suffering."

BROWN   My Son, die like a man!

THOREAU   Toward morning the crying stopped.

BROWN   I guess he's dead. . . .

THOREAU   It was nigh daylight. The Engine House bell did not ring again. . . Then . . .

A VOICE   The hatchet cut the cord. The greased trap fell. And a Virginia colonel called out, "So perish all such enemies of Virginia, all such enemies of the Union, all such foes of the human race."

THOREAU   Captain John Brown has been hanged. He is not Old Brown any longer. He is an angel of light.

A VOICE   Only a little later, all the North, soldiers and civilians, were chanting . . .

MUSIC AND CHORUS   *John Brown's Body.*

(Virtually all of this dialogue is suggested by a rereading of Thoreau's "A Plea for Captain John Brown," and a rearranging of the lines; plus four lines from the late Stephen Vincent Benét's magnificent narrative poem, *John Brown's Body.*)

As we moved out of Marlboro on the Post Road into Northboro and Shrewsbury, the countryside turned woodsy. Here and there, well back from the road, we often saw fine, big old houses beneath healthy elms and maples. In Shrewsbury we stopped to visit the imposing and wonderfully well-cared-for mansion of General Artemas Ward, first Commander in Chief of the Continental Army. It is now the property of Harvard College. It presents two front entrances, two main chimneys, and two hitching posts. It is open, free of charge, to the public and there was a most courteous caretaker on the grounds. For her attentions, I was doubly grateful. No other largely forgotten hero of the Revolution deserves them more than General Ward. Why this is so is an odd story:

His health broken by hardships as an officer in the French and Indian War, the old soldier (he was forty-eight in 1775) was lying ill at his home when the news of Lexington and Concord was brought to him. Next morning he called for his sword and his horse, and mounted and rode to Cambridge where he assumed command of the Patriot forces, as had been ordered by the second Provincial Congress. During following weeks he directed the siege of Boston and began conversion of the undisciplined militia bands into an army. When the Continental Congress made Washington supreme commander, it also named Ward as second-in-command; and Ward performed heroically until forced by illness to resign.

At war's end the public memory of General Ward was doubtless a little hazy; but later his name was to undergo complete confusion when a writer, Charles F. Browne (1834–1867), became the best-known humorist in the United States, and also lectured the country, and England, as "Artemus Ward." And as Artemus Ward his fame was such that President Lincoln interrupted meetings in wartime to read Ward to his Cabinet.

It seems unlikely that large numbers of tourists on the Boston Post Road are stopped by a sign that says, THE HOME OF GENERAL ARTEMAS WARD. General Ward? Who *was* he? Even the literate may be confused as between Artemus and Artemas, and the military title overlooked.

Quite the opposite is true of a tavern character named Richard Grimes who, on occasion, used to ride his horse into the taproom of the Baldwin Inn here in Shrewsbury. Posthumous fame came to him as "Old Grimes" in doggerel credited to an Albert G. Green:

> *Old Grimes is dead, that good old man,*
> *We ne'er shall see him more;*
> *He used to wear a long blue coat*
> *All buttoned down before.*

111

The Upper Road

All I know about Old Grimes is that he was not a fictitious charac-
ter, but a "rather disreputable one," according to Mary Caroline
Crawford, who in one of her books printed all of the doggerel by
Mr. Green.

In Shrewsbury I hoped to see a historical marker about Farrar's
Tavern, which I knew Levi Pease, the Stagecoach King, had bought
when he retired from business; but failed to find it among the many
older buildings. I also missed a historical plaque, said to have been
set near the tavern, marking the spot where Mary Goodenow, victim
of an Indian attack, was buried.

Westboro was strikingly different from Shrewsbury. This was
probably due in some part to the building of the highly successful
Boston–Worcester Turnpike, which missed Shrewsbury by a good
mile or more, but ran right through the middle of Westboro, and
was closely followed by what became the Boston & Albany Railroad.
In those times, being on the railroad meant a great deal, and Westboro grew rapidly from manufacture of boots and shoes, straw hats,
tools, and, in former times, sleighs. On Main Street is the site of the
birthplace of one of the town's most illustrious citizens, Eli Whitney.
Half a mile out of town is a pond called Chauncy, to remind one that
Westboro was once named Chauncy, for the second president of
Harvard College.

As the Boston Post Road is entering Worcester, it crosses an arm,
or bay, of Lake Quincigamond which, I learned, caused that city
to become "prominent for years as the home of many oarsmen" and
which at least once was the scene of the celebrated Harvard–Yale
boat race.

Chapter 14

The Upper Road: Worcester

NO OTHER TOWN between New York and Boston had so much influence on the Post Road connecting them as Worcester. Though neither man was a native, both Levi Pease and Ginery Twichell became rightly identified with Worcester, and justly celebrated variously, as already indicated, as postriders, stage drivers, promoters of turnpikes, innovators, and even as Stagecoach Kings.

Worcester has a personality and a social climate all its own. Both its industry boosters and its cultural leaders have been valued equally in the community, with the happy result that the town has a fine balance between its commercial and intellectual aspects. Let the visitor go to see the city's Art Museum, listen to its musical affairs, visit its many educational institutions. And do not overlook its unique and incomparable American Antiquarian Society.

Meanwhile, the visitor cannot but be impressed with the extent *and* variety of Worcester's industries.

But there is no point to *telling* readers what the Worcester of today has to offer visitors. Let me attempt rather to indicate how the town came by its unusual personality. To do so, I'd prefer to play Worcester strictly by ear, and to choose things from its long history that are either unique, or at least striking examples of Worcester-in-the-making. But a warning: let the reader with no interest in the past skip the next several pages. They will bore him, I fear, even to learn about my favorite inventor of all time, who was Joshua Stoddard, a Worcester bee keeper when he improbably gave to the world what he called the American Steam Piano, and we know as the steam calliope.

No other sound, unless it be the magic voice of the locomotive, has had so powerful an effect on migration as this great, sweet, lusty voice of the outdoors. It has removed from the farms uncounted young men, and put them on the road to wander to the far corners of the United States. Its urgent and promising notes have also sent ribbon clerks and grocer boys to the Wild West to fight Indians, dig gold, and lasso longhorn steers in Texas.

Stoddard himself was a farm boy, born in Vermont, where he married, then moved to Worcester and continued to keep bees and devote his spare time, in typical Yankee style, to tinkering. He wanted to improve the common horse-drawn hayrake. But being something of a poet and mystic and bemused by the new locomotives, his mind wandered from the starkly utilitarian hayrake and set him to work on the "useless," by all good Yankee standards, steam piano. This was in the early forties.

For his new invention, Stoddard made fifteen steam whistles of graduated sizes and attached them to the top of a steam chest. There was no keyboard to his first model. He adapted the basic idea of the music box by providing a long cylinder with pins so placed that when revolved, the pins pressed the valve stems and thus blew whistles to play a tune. He had no difficulty getting a patent; and on the Fourth of July (1855) he gave a demonstration on Worcester Common, with his daughter Jennie turning the cylinder.

Although it had to compete with a battery of artillery firing salutes to Liberty, the American Steam Piano was a complete success. Later that year the instrument was placed on board a flatcar of a railroad excursion to Fitchburg. Its great voice gave forth with music the like of which had never been heard before, and created a sensation for miles on each side of the track. With others, Stoddard incorporated the American Steam Music Company and began manufacture, "for use on steamboats and railroad trains."

Oddly enough, in view of its subsequent history, the steam piano's first thumping success was on steamboats running between New York and Albany. Then John Van Ambergh bought one to use with his circus, and it was away and running fast in a cloud of steam, smoke, and music. Somebody called it "Calliope." Pronunciation was never a thing of agreement. Both cally-ope and cal-eye-o-pee were used, and a bard made use of both styles in *Reedy's Mirror,* in verses beginning:

> *Proud folk stare after me,*
> *Call me Calliope*
> *Tooting joy, tooting hope,*
> *I am the Calliope.*

Stoddard's invention, now with a keyboard, went on to classic success in circus street parades. Its position in the procession was at the very end of the line. As for the inventor, he was naturally pushed out of the manufacturing company, with nothing for his pains. He resumed labors on his improved hayrake, receiving patents, and the rake was manufactured and sold under his name. He went on to invent a fire escape, and a fruit-paring machine. Nothing much came from either. But his beloved bees were faithful to the end, and the end came as Stoddard reached his eighty-eighth year in April, 1902, just when a score or so of circuses were taking to the road all over America. In every parade was one of his patent steam pianos—sizzling, smoking, rocking, vibrating, blowing the living daylights out of *Over the Waves,* telling the villages and the cities that the big show was about to begin, charming alike the city folk and the rustics as Calliope of old, mother of Orpheus and chief of the Muses, had charmed in her time, calling from the farms the plowboys, the milkers, the pitchers of hay as the Sirens had called mariners—sometimes, to be sure, to their doom, but always to their instruction. There has never been any other sound quite like it, this bewitching voice of the old bee keeper of Pawlet and Worcester.

For many years a Worcester man, Ichabod Washburn, had something to do with conventional, or nonsteam, pianos. Back in the 1830s he entered the wire business, which until then had been using crude machines capable of drawing no more than fifty pounds a day. Washburn devised the wire drawblock, increasing his production more than tenfold, and built up an enormous business supplying machinery for carding and spinning wool. One day soon came Jonas Chickering of Boston, pioneer of American piano manufacture, to suggest the type of steel wire he wanted. Washburn was ready, and his product was so good that Chickering did away with imported wire.

Taking his twin brother, Charles, in partnership, and soon adding a son-in-law, Philip L. Moen, the firm of Washburn and Moen went ahead to introduce the first galvanized telegraph wire, in time to greet the demand created by Samuel F. B. Morse's new invention; and also to acquire practically the whole of the hoop-skirt business which, when the girls really got going, called for 1,500 tons of tempered steel wire annually.

Then, in about 1876, Washburn and Moen paid $60,000 to an Illinois farmer named Joseph Farwell Glidden for manufacturing rights to what he called barbed wire. This, of course, was the product the great plains of the West had needed desperately since the first homestead was settled.

Joe Glidden was born in New Hampshire, in 1813, and had

116

worked on his father's farm and taught school until 1843, when he decided to go West. No Erie Canal for him. He bought two second-hand threshing machines, hitched on a couple of rugged teams, and started *threshing* his way west, pausing here and there in season, to thresh for farmers in Ohio, Indiana, Michigan, and Illinois, where he settled near De Kalb. He was a man who liked to keep up with things, to be "well posted," as he said, and he never missed a county fair. At one of these events, he saw an exhibit of barbed wire. It had been a failure; it wouldn't work. Joe saw what was wrong; the barbs would not stay in place.

Glidden began to experiment at home, using two strands instead of one. It was typical of his kind—a man who migrated west *in* a threshing machine—that he rigged up an old coffee mill so that by turning the crank, the wires were twisted to hold the barbs firmly in place. He thought he had something pretty good. He got a patent, turned out enough of the product to fence his own acres, found that it worked, then started manufacture for sale in a small way. He was soon broke and in debt. But in 1876 he showed the invention to Washburn and Moen of Worcester.

Although he had to fight infringement suits and to stage several of his own, Glidden's barbed wire was here to stay. In 1876 a mere 600,000 pounds was made and sold. A year later the figure passed 1 million pounds. By 1901, it ran to 300 million pounds.

For all its hospitality to new inventions, Worcester was also to achieve in the nineteenth century a reputation for intellectual or cultural progress second to no other city. In Worcester was built the first hospital in the United States for treating and caring for the mentally unbalanced. It was in Worcester, too, where John B. Gough first spoke in public against Rum and went on to be the most effective enemy of potable alcohol ever heard in the country. Worcester was also the place chosen by the badgered friends of Women's Rights to stage their first national convention.

Though that historic meeting, in 1850, had no direct connection with an event of sixty-eight years before, I like to think it was due to Worcester's general climate that the first authentic female soldier

117

enlisted here to fight the enemy England; and, moreover, did fight, with regulation issue musket and bayonet. It is perhaps the strangest story to come out of the Revolutionary War and it began in Worcester where, in 1782, Miss Deborah Sampson was accepted for Army service by a possibly myopic recruiting sergeant.

Miss Sampson meant business. She had walked into town from Middleboro Four Corners, a matter of seventy-five miles, dressed in male clothing, her hair short, to enlist as Private "Robert Shurtleff" in Captain George Webb's company of the 4th Massachusetts Regiment of foot which, in early June 1782, started the long march to West Point Camp on the Hudson River.

One wonders what Captain Webb would have thought of a twenty-two-year-old woman in his company. And what of Captain Webb's men? It is a subject that soldiers of all times and all nations have discussed, this possibility of a female soldier. But there seems to have been no suspicion, then or later, until an improbable accident brought about a denouement.

What was she like, this Amazon who lived with and fought with soldiers? It was agreed, much later, that she was some five feet eight inches tall, quick, erect, strong, and "as fleet as a Gazell, bounding through swamps often many rods ahead of her companions." She had given serious thought to her general outline for, after the war, she said she had bound a bandage tightly around her breast which "had compressed the bosom whilst the waist had every natural convenience for augmentation." One may guess that when Deborah was encased in her bandages and the shapeless homespun male clothing of the period, she had the shape, or lack of shape, of her comrades.

In any event, she was In The Army Now, and soon saw action in a sharp skirmish near Tappan Bay during which she suffered a wound from an enemy saber. A bit later she was hit in the side by a musketball, at East Chester on the Boston Post Road. She told the surgeon it was only a scratch, then hid herself in the woods for a few days, living alone. (She feared "discovery more than she feared bleeding to death.") The musketball was never removed from her body.

Private "Robert Shurtleff" was sent to Fort Ticonderoga with a detachment, then into western New York. Deborah must have conducted herself well, for she was made an orderly on the staff of General Patterson in Philadelphia. Fever was epidemic in this city. Deborah was stricken, and put into the "hopeless" ward of an Army infirmary. As she lay unconscious on a pallet, a Doctor Binney came through on his rounds and stopped to put his ear to the patient's chest to learn if the heart was still beating. It was, and good Doc Binney's heart may have well skipped a beat. He went to tell the head nurse of his discovery. Private Deborah Sampson was moved elsewhere.

When General Patterson learned of the kind of orderly he had on his staff, he delivered himself of an observation worth recording. "Why," he cried, "this is truly theatrical!" When Deborah had recovered, General Patterson sent her to West Point, and there she was permitted to don female garb and to parade down the ranks of her comrades-in-arms, not one of whom recognized the tall young woman as the recent Private Shurtleff.

In November 1783, Deborah Sampson was honorably discharged at Worcester and returned, briefly, to Middleboro Four Corners. But that town could no longer contain her. She married Benjamin Gannett of Sharon, Massachusetts, and became the mother of three children. It is pleasant to know that in 1792, the Massachusetts General Court, taking cognizance of the state's unique veteran, granted the sum of £34 to Mrs. Gannett. In 1805, the Federal pension office granted her $4 a month, later increased to $8, for life. She died April 29, 1827, aged about sixty-seven years. A street in Sharon was named for her. In 1944, I was delighted to read that a Liberty Ship, just launched from the Bethlehem yards, honored her name.

Were the Navy not so hidebound in the matter of naming its fighting ships, it could do worse than to have a cruiser *Deborah Gannett,* or at least a destroyer. It is, however, particularly pleasing to reflect that Deborah's descendants are alone of the status that, if they cared to, they might join the Daughters of the American Revolution solely on the strength of a female ancestor.

There were no formal battles of the Revolution fought in or near Worcester, but that city was in the very storm center of the serious aftermath in 1786–87 known as Shays' Rebellion. There are historic markers in many towns throughout western Massachusetts, no few of them along the Upper Post Road, or near it, that refer to the rebellion. It was a most purposeful revolt. From it came the convention that drew up and put into force the great Constitution of the United States of America.

The fighting war was over by 1783, but the Revolution, in a manner of speaking, continued. Since 1777 the thirteen jealous colonies had been loosely joined by the Articles of Confederation and Perpetual Union. This was at best a leaky vessel. Its great weakness was that it rested wholly on the good will of what at war's end were the sovereign states. Congress could not tax. It could not lay customs duties. It had no money. Times were hard and getting worse. Anarchy seemed to many to be just around the corner, and so it was. Nearly all the returned soldiers were farmers, and farmers everywhere found themselves heavily in debt to the merchant and trading class. Courts were bogged down with suits for debts against farmers.

Conditions of the farmers in the rocky hills around Worcester and in the Berkshires were especially tough. The ex-soldiers had been waiting a good while for a Man on Horseback. Suddenly he appeared in the spring of 1786 in the hill country. He was Captain Daniel Shays, a gigantic man who had been cited for exceptional bravery during the war. He was persuaded to act as spokesman for the discontented.

Shays was both brave and completely honest. He attended meetings which passed resolutions demanding reforms of the General

Court. They were ignored. In September, a party of eighty men, who described themselves as Captain Shays' partisans, suddenly appeared in Worcester, took possession of the court house, and said they had come to prevent the sitting of the fall term of court. When the judges showed up, they were denied entry. Next day, the insurgents numbered 400. They marched down Main Street, some with muskets, others with clubs. There was as yet no open violence. The judges, beleaguered in the United States Arms Tavern, voted to adjourn all cases to the next term.

A little later, Captain Shays himself appeared in nearby Shrewsbury with several hundred armed followers. Governor Bowdoin called out the militia. They failed to respond, and for several days Worcester was in control of Shays and his by now nearly 800 armed insurgents. Shays withdrew, then moved halfway across the state to attack the United States Arsenal at Springfield. Here he ran head-on into the waiting militia, who attacked and dispersed the rebels.

Shays retreated to Amherst, where he was joined by his lieutenant, Luke Day, and other forces. General Benjamin Lincoln of Massachusetts demanded surrender. Shays stalled, then asked for an armistice until petitions could be presented to the General Court. Lincoln, however, was without authority to delay operations. And on the night of February 2, 1787, he led his militia troops through a heavy snow storm and fell on Shays' army in the big woods around Petersham, routing them by gunfire, then tracking them down one by one in the deep snow. Shays' Rebellion was over. (Note that it neither began nor ended in Worcester, but the rebels massed there—doubtless because they needed publicity and thought Worcester was less likely to shoot them down than other towns.)

The effects of the uprising were tremendous. It had put the fear of anarchy into the hearts of all conservatives, and many others. Shays had done something else too: he had shown that a government, itself founded on rebellion, could also deal with a rebellion. From the emotional surge of fear and despair that swept through the bickering states, as mentioned before, came demand for the Constitutional Convention.

The Upper Road

Though Daniel Shays was specifically excepted in a general pardon of the rebels, and condemned to die by a court, he was later pardoned. He moved to New York State, to settle and farm at Sparta, and died in 1825.

It has been mentioned that Worcester was not to be favored with a battle of the Revolution, and thus share the glory that has since attended all such fortunate places. Yet, because the city had the courage to welcome a refugee printer named Isaiah Thomas, it can and does take pride as the place where the *Massachusetts Spy* was published. No more famous newspaper was published in all the American colonies. It began its seditious editorials as early as 1770, when Thomas established it in Boston, and at once came into conflict with Crown authorities. They were looking for him by April 1775 when, on the sixteenth, he managed to get his press and type through the British lines, and hidden temporarily while he, two nights later, joined Revere and Dawes in spreading the alarm, and then, with musket in hand, took part in the fighting at Lexington and Concord. On April 20, Thomas arrived in Worcester to reestablish the *Spy*. From that day to the end of the war, the *Massachusetts Spy* was one of the most fearless and potent voices in the colonies; and from New Hampshire to Carolina, Isaiah Thomas was known as the Patriot Printer.

Thomas remained in Worcester, where the *Spy* was published, and where the Patriot Printer became a leading citizen, and is remembered also for the founding, in 1812, of the American Antiquarian Society, for "the preservation and study of the materials of American history." One after the other, in order to house its staggering collections of Americana properly, it has outgrown its buildings until recently a new wing was erected. There is nothing else in New England remotely like it. It is visited by scholars and others from all over the world, yet it cannot, I fear, be called with accuracy "a Tourist Attraction," for which some of us tourists are devoutly thankful.

Chapter 15

The Upper Road: Worcester to Springfield

WEST OF WORCESTER, the villages on the Upper Post Road have memories of Shays' Rebellion all the way to Springfield, where several of Shays' partisans were shot and killed during the attack upon the United States Armory. Later, one of the eighteen others who were convicted of treason, Henry Gale of Spencer, got as far as Worcester with a rope around his neck, when all were pardoned.

Another indication of the Worcester orbit was Pliny Earle, of Leicester, who invented or improved cards used in cotton and wool spinning. He also experimented with the local cultivation of mulberry trees when the silkworm craze promised, ever so briefly, to add a new line to New England textiles. There were many Earles here on the Upper Road, among them Ralph and James, both painters. It was Ralph who hastened to Lexington and Concord before the smoke had hardly settled, to depict the battles from the accounts of participants. (As works of art, said a critic, they deserve "faint praise, but they are justly famous as being among the first historical paintings done in this country.")

Originally a part of Leicester, the adjacent town of Spencer got a slow start after its incorporation and did not obtain full town rights until after the Revolution. Possibly it displayed too much independence for a democracy. As early as 1725 Spencer was cited by a Court of Quarter Sessions for not having bridged the Seven Mile River. It was cited again years later before the town fathers, grudgingly and in no great hurry, at last took action. Even then, the town called for censure, and in 1800 the attorney general of Massachusetts was complaining of "the badness of the Great Post Road there, and the State made an attempt to convert it into a turnpike." But a local historian wrote that "the people of Spencer successfully resisted the scheme."

Even so, Spencer was noted on the Post Road for its three taverns and "it was no unusual thing to see fifteen coaches here at the noon hour." All of these public houses have gone. On the site of the most famous of them is the "new or 1912" Massasoit House, which today advertises a cocktail lounge but has no place to eat. In searching for a restaurant in Spencer, I also attempted to find an ancient milestone reading "59 Mi to Boston," said to stand at Maple and Mechanic Streets, but failed. Local history has it that workmen were busy at this spot, setting out sapling trees, on June 17, 1775, and "could hear noise of the Battles of Lexington and Concord." (This noise, of course, included the "Shot Heard Round the World.")

In front of Spencer's Town Hall was a monument to tell the stranger that here in this town were born three famous inventors, William, Tyler, and Elias Howe, all born in the same house, locally known as the Old Howe Homestead. Perhaps because all three names were familiar to me, I wanted to see the single source from which had stemmed the wooden truss bridge, William; the Patent Spring Bed, Tyler; and the first lock-stitch sewing machine, Elias. Finding the site of the Old Howe Homestead, however, was something else.

It began when a courteous and substantial-looking employee of the Town of Spencer, whom we accosted in his office in the Town Hall, waved an arm to indicate the general direction we should take, and told us the Howe Homestead was "eight minutes" distant on *that* road. After a good eight minutes, we paused at a farm house where the housewife, who was just as courteous as the Town Hall man had been, said she had never heard of such a place. "No neighbors name of Howe on *this* road," she said. I explained that the Howes I was looking for had been dead for many years; they were famous historic characters. She gave it thought for a moment. "I don't believe nobody name of Howe never lived around here," she said, adding, "leastways, if they did, I never heard of them."

We were now well into the country, and we drove on, passing hills, dales, fields, woods, streams, and ponds, stopping now and again to ask about the Howe Homestead. All wanted to be helpful, but were of no help at all until, by my watch, we had driven forty-odd minutes from the Spencer Town Hall, and we stopped to ask some children. A boy, possibly ten years old, said that there was a Howe *Pond,* "quite a piece back where you come from." We turned around, and headed for Spencer again. In about twenty minutes we came to a small roadside sign: Howe Memorial State Park. A simple turn left led us through handsome woods to an open place and *there* was a marker about the three Howes—Elias was nephew to William and Tyler—and behind it the outlines of a foundation of stone. The Old Howe Homestead.

I'm sure everyone has had a similar experience somewhere or other. It is likely we misunderstood the Town Hall man, our first "guide." If we did, then I am still shocked that we met no one else in Spencer who appeared to have heard of at least the inventor of the sewing machine. I am given pause, however, when I recall that in 1928, or thereabout, when in Baltimore, not only could I not find a drugstore or newsstand that had on sale a postcard of Henry L. Mencken's home, but no one seemed to have ever heard of H. L. Mencken.

The Upper Road

But it is largely chance that determines what sort, if any, information a stranger gets from a native or resident of a given town. This was brought home to me in what used to be the very next township beyond Spencer—namely Brookfield, an enormous expanse of land, which was later cut up to make towns named Brookfield, East Brookfield, West Brookfield, and Western. The name of the latter was changed to Warren, for patriot Doctor Joseph Warren who fell at the Battle of Bunker Hill.

My especial interest in Warren was an organization of which I had long heard of but of which I knew nothing: The Warren Thief Detecting Society. We drove first to the public square, or the green, in Warren, and parked. Knowing no one in this village, I tried the door of the slick modern bank. It was after three; closed for the day. Nearby was a stretch of small business shops fronting this side of the square. Entering the hardware store, I waited until the proprietor finished with customers, then approached him. He was Robert A. Buck, a young man in his forties, carrying on the business his father had founded.

As briefly as possible, I said I was a stranger, a sort of tourist, who wanted to learn something about the Warren Thief Detecting Society. Could he tell me whom I should see? He said the society's current president was a Mr. William G. Wood, and that likely he would be glad, etc., etc., then started to tell me where I might find him. Having just experienced the complications of finding the site of the Old Howe Homestead in Spencer, to say nothing of other searches into the New England past, I asked Mr. Buck if there happened to be any members of the society right here on the square. Well, yes, he had been a member for six years, and had recently been appointed to the Pursuing Committee.

I replied that if there was anyone I wanted to see in all Warren town, it was a member of the society's Pursuing Committee. We talked a few minutes, and then came the astonisher. "I live upstairs," he said, "and business isn't rushing. Let's go up to my living quarters, and sit down where we can talk. I'll lock the store for a while." And he did. If you don't think this was a stunner, then it's because you

126

don't know too much about Yankee storekeepers or, for that matter, about Yankees.

In the Bucks' attractive and comfortable home—Mrs. Buck was out—the genial member of the Pursuing Committee gave me high-lights in the long history of the Thief Detecting Society of Warren, Massachusetts. "Our early records," he said, "were unfortunately lost, probably in a fire, sometime before January 5, 1847, which is the date of the first entry in our present record book. This book bears a label, 'Constitution of the Society for the Detection of Horse Thieves, etc.,' and is printed in gold, yet the minutes of that 1847 meeting, and all subsequent events, refer to 'The Warren Thief Detecting Society.'

"The constitution states that the purpose was to unite the members of a society of mutual aid in detecting thieves and perpetrators of malicious mischief in Warren, and to recover property stolen from any of its members."

Though the society has never been disbanded, it gradually ceased to function for its original purpose, and became a social group of forty members, elected for life, as are those chosen to fill vacancies due to death. It meets once a year to dine and elect new officers. Mr. Buck supplied me with a woodcut, still used on its annual programs, and otherwise, as a sort of trademark or symbol of the society. It is a lively and authentic woodcut depicting four members of the Pursuing Committee, riding hell-for-leather after a thief, also mounted. The leading detector, in tall beaver hat, and armed with a wicked club, is obviously making the classic hue-and-cry with which "felons were anciently pursued." From his mouth is issuing STOP THIEF in letters so large and black that one does not miss the conventional exclamation mark.

That this woodcut must antedate by many years the sole surviving record book of the Society (1847) is indicated by the thief himself, whose beaver hat has been blown from his head revealing his *hair streaming back in a pigtail.*

It would seem likely that the Warren vigilantes were organized during the "disturbed period" after the Revolution when "the people had not yet readjusted themselves to the new social and political conditions." There were many breaches of the peace "with pilferings and robberies, while horse and cattle stealing flourished." Shays' Rebellion in Massachusetts comes to mind.

Mr. Buck said that a surviving tradition of the group is that at the very first meeting, when the society was organized, cold weather was in the air and on the ground and, when the proceedings were under way in some farmhouse, thieves stole the very blankets off the backs of the tethered horses in the barn and sheds, and made clean away with the loot.

"Our constitution provides that members of the Pursuing Committee," Mr. Buck said, "were required to hold themselves in readiness at all times to assign members to the chase and apprehension of the thief or thieves whenever a robbery was reported, and to give directions in which each was to travel. For this, they were paid a reasonable compensation for their services and expenses."

A historian of Warren wrote long ago that the example of the Thief Detectors was "followed in other places with similar success." * In any event Warren has done well in perpetuating the memory of those who in earlier days "stood ready to perform a needed duty." All glory to Warren, and to "Western" as it was known when it was first removed from ancient Brookfield, which was organized and incorporated in 1673, almost ready to greet the first eastbound rider on the Boston Post Road in January of that year.

The Post Road east out of Springfield soon enters into the Quaboag River valley, which it follows from near Palmer to pass through the Warrens and the Brookfields. This was real Indian country, and though John Eliot, the missionary, had visited and preached among these Quaboags and they and the few settlers had lived in amity for

---

* There was and probably still is a Society for the Detection of Horse Thieves and Robbers in Enfield, Connecticut, described (1938) as having a roster of 300 members and keeping $500 in its treasury.

almost a decade, when King Philip's war broke out, the local tribe joined Philip and the warlike Nipmucks in the attack and destruction of the twenty dwelling houses that constituted Brookfield. "The town lay in ashes for several years," wrote a historian, "and the inhabitants were dispersed."

Resettlement began in 1686, many of the newcomers being from Marlboro, Suffield, and Hadley. But the troubles were not done. A raid in 1688 prompted the building of Gilbert's Fort, which managed to fend off or defeat several more attempts; and the General Court felt need to forbid abandonment of frontier towns, of which Brookfield was surely one, without permission. In 1710, again in 1713, savage bands struck Brookfield and killed at least five settlers. Not until the latter raid were the inhabitants of this sorely tried town to be free of the hostilities which had lasted forty years.

The town survived the Revolution, and at its end was "the third town in age and the first in wealth and population in the County of Worcester." It could not have held such a high position for long. When the industrial revolution got under way, both Springfield to the west on the Post Road, and Worcester to the east, grew rapidly, while Brookfield remained little more than an important tavern and relay depot for stagecoach lines on the Upper Post Road.

Yet, somehow or other West Brookfield has stuck in my mind as an intellectually superior town. Possibly this is because Isaiah Thomas, founder-editor of the *Massachusetts Spy* and New England's great publisher of fine books, once edited the first newspaper in Brookfield, and sold it to Ebenezer Merriam and Company. Out of this concern in due time came the famous publishing house of G. and C. Merriam, of Springfield, whose dictionaries by Noah Webster (born on the Middle Post Road at West Hartford, Connecticut) it has published since the revised edition of 1840.

And possibly the great beauty of West Brookfield Common had some influence on the town's reputation. We came to it with the sun at our backs, the great green oval, longer than Lexington Green, curving gracefully past magnificent maples and a few elms, past fine old houses, both brick and white pine, of both Georgian ("colonial") and Federal vintage, past the Congregational Meeting House, no Wren, perhaps, but superb in line and essence.

Weeks later, I went back to look again at West Brookfield Common. In the meantime I had seen, between Greenwich, Connecticut, and Amesbury, Massachusetts, on the New Hampshire border, perhaps a hundred, certainly eighty village commons or greens in three New England states. All of them were handsome, a few like Lexington, which I had known for years, moved me deeply. But none obliterated my delight in West Brookfield as the perfect scene for a generic picture, either photograph or painting, to be entitled, "The Village Green, New England." Just that and no more tells everything.

Like almost every other town between Worcester and Springfield, West Brookfield was shaken by Shays' Rebellion. Among Daniel Shays' shakers and lieutenants who had led a large group of West Brookfield's discontented on the march to Worcester was the great-grandfather of Lucy Stone, born here in 1818. Lucy herself was so discontented with cooking, weaving, spinning, milking cows, and making butter that when sixteen years old she asked her mother: "Is there nothing to put an end to me?" But there wasn't, and little Miss Stone went away from West Brookfield to shine, and often to glitter as the very morning star in the dreary night of an all-male world. In short, Lucy Stone became one of the first and greatest leaders in the Rights of Women Movement; and in the home of her parents here, hard by the handsome village green, she was wed to Henry Brown Blackwell in the most widely known marriage of 1855.

As soon as the ceremony was done, bride and groom read the soon-to-be-notorious Protest, which the Reverend Thomas Wentworth Higginson thought so just and rational that he sent it to the *Worcester Spy* for publication. Summed up, this document was a protest against the whole system by which "the legal existence of the wife is suspended in marriage." Miss Lucy Stone did not become

Mrs. Henry B. Blackwell. She was *Mrs.* Lucy Stone. And a new phrase had been added to American speech: "a Lucy-Stoner."

Having already seen the Brookfields and the Warrens, only two more places, Palmer and Wilbraham, remained on the Upper Road to Springfield. Yet, because Brimfield was an adjacent town to Warren, and on the way to Palmer Old Center anyhow, we drove out of Warren on the Brimfield road, to pass the spot where in 1759 Lord Jeffrey Amherst and ten thousand troops camped on their way to Ticonderoga and Crown Point, during the French-and-Indian War. In Brimfield, I found few markers, but should the residents of this pretty hamlet care to honor their native men of importance, they could cite Samuel Guthrie, born in 1782, a doctor of medicine who experimented with chemicals and in 1831 produced what he called "chloric ether," which turned out to be what we know as chloroform, antedating discoveries of the same compound in France and Germany; and Brimfield could also mention the Fairbanks Brothers, Erastus and Thaddeus, who in 1815 moved into the wilds of northern Vermont and there started to build weighing scales so good that they were to be found in every country of the world.

It is doubtful, however, if Brimfield would care to recall a visit there, in about 1835, of two extremely forward thinkers, who called themselves Brother John Humphrey Noyes and Brother Simon Lovett, and lectured on a new sort of religion they called Perfectionism. The audience that evening included "a coterie of handsome and emotionally exuberant young women of Brimfield, two of whom late that night made their way to the bedroom of the forward-thinking lecturers." The news got around in the village, then out of the village, and became known as the Brimfield Scandal. Things like that may not have the proper tourist appeal, yet they do add a certain flavor to a place. (Brother Noyes was of course the founder of Oneida Community in York State, soon to be vilified or praised for its marital or domestic arrangements.)

The Upper Road

Early in the nineteenth century both Wilbraham and Palmer attracted many industries to the banks of the Chicopee River, among them flax, paper, and jute mills. They were hard hit in the early 1920s when wage differentials began to affect all Yankee manufacturing, and textile and other plants took off for the South. But Yankee educational plants not only survived but often grew, both in stature and size. This happened to Wilbraham Academy, moved here in 1817 from Newmarket, New Hampshire, to become a college preparatory school for boys. The buildings stand on the site of Wilbraham's first settlement.

My interest in neighboring Palmer Town had to do neither with education nor industry; it was plain curiosity to see the place where Hall Jackson Kelley spent much of his long and seemingly futile, frustrated life. Kelley was the strange and consecrated character who considered himself God's own messenger in respect to what in his day was called, vaguely enough, The Oregon Country. By consecrated I mean that although he had never been nearer to Oregon than the junction of the Connecticut and Chicopee rivers, in 1831, Kelley felt urged to incorporate, under Massachusetts laws, the American Society for Encouraging Settlement of the Oregon Country.

What might be called Kelley's Oregon Booster Club was a dismal failure; yet, from it stemmed a succession of emigrants and events which were to have an incalculable effect in founding and shaping the states of Oregon and Washington, to say nothing of making the whole Pacific Northwest, south of 49°, American rather than British territory. Since I first heard of Kelley, some twenty-five years ago, he has been one of my favorite "Lost Men of American History."

Being pretty sure that nobody in present-day Palmer had ever heard of him, I wanted to visit the town where he had lost a modest fortune in the Three Rivers Manufacturing Company of Palmer Old Center, Massachusetts, in 1829, and spent the next forty-five years trying to get his "American Society for, etc.," off the ground. This is no place to go further into Kelley's great dream (which I have long since discussed in two previous books), other than to re-

132

mark that though he was a most cantankerous crank, impossible to live with, he was a truly impressive fanatic. If there is a Chamber of Commerce in Palmer Old Center today, its manager might well consider Hall Jackson Kelley as fit for a modest historical marker somewhere in the village. After all, George Washington never slept in this town. His diary (1789) says of Palmer merely that he had breakfast "at the House of one Scott."

Chapter 16

The Upper Road: Springfield

The Bunch
of Grapes

AT SPRINGFIELD FERRY, as it was often called, traffic west on the Upper Post Road crossed to the west bank of the Connecticut River, then turned south to pass through Agawam, and so into Connecticut at Suffield and Windsor to reach Hartford, where it merged with the Middle Post Road from Boston.

Agawam was the original name of William Pynchon's "plantation" which in time spread to both sides of the river. At the town meeting of April 16, 1640, it was voted to become Springfield, honoring the native town, in Essex, England, of Pynchon, who had purchased land here on New England's longest river from the Agawam tribe. It can be doubted that few towns in this region were more bedeviled by assorted troubles than was Agawam-Springfield.

Springfield

To begin with, Founder Pynchon had bought the site in the belief it was a part of the Connecticut Patents. It wasn't. After action in the courts, Agawam was declared to be well within the bounds of Massachusetts Bay Colony. Disputes like this were naturally discouraging to prospective settlers, and possibly had that effect on Agawam-Springfield. In any event, there was no rush to the new town.

Pynchon was elected magistrate, and the records of his court, kept in his own hand, indicated that he aimed to do justice rather than to follow the rules. Separated by a hundred miles of wilderness from Boston, Magistrate Pynchon ruled the community with a cabinet consisting of his son John, his two sons-in-law, Elizur Holyoke and Henry Smith, and the minister George Moxon. Despite the nepotism, Pynchon seems to have been fair enough. And when the first case of witchcraft in western Massachusetts erupted in Springfield, he did not lose his head, as had other judges and court officers closer to Boston and the General Court.

In 1651, Hugh Parsons of Springfield was accused by his wife and neighbors of being in league with Satan. Poor Hugh was a dyspeptic. His wife was subject to fits, probably epileptic. She soon accused herself, whereupon she was convicted, but died before further action could be taken. As for Hugh, Magistrate Pynchon had the great good sense to send him to Boston, where the legislative assembly "refused to confirm the verdict of guilty and he was set free."

But Springfield had little more than recovered from the Parsons' witchcraft affair than all hell broke out in both Boston and Ipswich, Massachusetts Bay Colony. Just before the witch-hunt, Magistrate Pynchon had had published in London a little tract entitled "The Meritorious Price of Our Redemption." In it he attacked the current ultraorthodox view of the Atonement. When the first copy of it reached Massachusetts, a committee of clergy, headed by the Reverend John Norton, denounced both book and author as heretical.

One need know little or nothing of the abstractions of theology to appreciate the seriousness of this charge. It is enough to know that the Reverend John Norton of Ipswich was, even in that time, notoriously bigoted, narrow-minded, and tyrannical, and staunch for the application of the death penalty in matters of heresy. (The Quakers were soon to feel his heavy hand.) Pynchon's tract was publicly burned by the hangman. Pynchon was ordered to appear before the court to retract his heresies. Instead, he deeded his Springfield property to his son John, and his son-in-law Holyoke, and sailed for England. It is worth marking that with him went the Reverend George Moxon, who apparently shared his heretical views.

Young John Pynchon, according to repute, was "able and astute, honest and just in his dealings." Under his direction Springfield grew steadily. One of his earliest projects was to build the first brick house in the Connecticut Valley. This was no status symbol. When King Philip's massed savages attacked the town, Pynchon's new house, virtually a fort, became a safe refuge for the townspeople. All the raiders could do was to set afire all the other homes and the barns. Had it not been for the brick fort, the loss of life doubtless would have numbered more than 200. Pynchon himself was in Hadley when the attack on Springfield came; and in a forced march at the head of militia he relieved the siege with the loss of but three men.

Though the village was in ashes, save for the fort, it was rebuilt quickly and well under Pynchon's able leadership. Thus, after all its early troubles, Springfield was to justify the two Pynchons. For 300 years it has battened and flourished by its strategic position, first on the Boston Post Road *and* the mail route to Albany, and later on the railroads, in the traffic with New York City and the West.

Like almost every other New England city of mature age, Springfield has accumulated no few monuments to its great or prominent men, and many markers to remind a forgetful public of its historically notable events. Among my favorites are the Miles Morgan Statue, in Court Square, and the Boston Road Marker at Federal and State Streets. Who was Miles Morgan, and why did the Boston Road need identification other than the usual milestone?

Miles Morgan was a settler in this town before its name became

Springfield

Springfield by action of the town meeting in 1640. He came from Bristol, England, and on the passage over he met a Miss Gilbert, who settled with her family at Beverly, not far from Boston, while Morgan walked halfway across Massachusetts Bay Colony to set up as farmer and butcher in Pynchon's new settlement. He had been much taken by Miss Gilbert, and according to the local account, "Miles Morgan wooed her by proxy and, in 1643, accompanied by two neighbors and an Indian, he made the journey back to Beverly and was married to her." Miss Gilbert must have been a stout character, worthy of the best tradition of Bay Colony pioneers, for "It is told that the bridal party walked all the way back to Springfield, the bride riding the only horse the party had."

The happy couple set up housekeeping here by the banks of the Connecticut River. Morgan seemingly did well in his occupations of farmer and butcher; though he could not write—this was no unusual condition in the 1640s—Morgan's fellow-townsmen elected him to "many important positions." One might wonder if these modest contributions were such as to warrant the noble statue of Miles Morgan. In any event, one of his descendants was John Pierpont Morgan, which may have helped; and the likeness of Miles "was erected by one of the fifth generation in the line of descent."

The story of the Boston Road Marker is much simpler. There was no interposition of proud descendants. It was erected by one Joseph Wait, Esq., described only as a "Merchant of Brookfield" (Massachusetts) who, on some unfortunate day prior to 1763, lost his way in a blinding snow storm and wandered out of the well-traveled path of the Boston Post Road. It must have been a nerve-shattering experience, for Esquire Wait promptly ordered the elaborately chiseled marker—quaintly embellished with Masonic symbols, a Sun, a Moon, and a Star, against a background of what appears to be a front door and steps (welcome enough without a mat saying as much)—to be erected, to quote the guide stone's simple legend, FOR THE BENEFIT OF TRAVELLERS.

The stone stood directly opposite the Rockingham House, a brick hotel and tavern where the postriders stopped and later the stagecoaches paused for refreshment of man and beast. If any rider or driver or foot traveler wandered from the Upper Post Road after 1763, it was not for lack of warning by Joseph Wait, merchant of Brookfield, some 20 miles eastward on the way to Boston.

Mr. Wait's guide stone happened also to be near what for many years was "the Principal Building in Springfield." This was of course the United States Armory and Arsenal. For almost two centuries this establishment has been Springfield's pride and, occasionally, one of its trials. The site, near the top of the hill on State Street, which was the Boston Post Road, is said to have been selected in 1776, by General George Washington and his close friend, David Mason, also of Virginia. The Continental Congress then leased the grounds. Contrary to popular fancy, no firearms were manufactured here for the Revolution. The first Springfield muskets were made in 1795, when 245 were turned out during the year. But the arsenal was ready for the War of 1812, and all American wars since.

Washington stopped in Springfield, to "inspect the Government stores," as he wrote in his diary, while making his inaugural tour of New England in 1789. But Daniel Shays and his rebels had already been there two years before, and were put to rout by General Sheppard and troops, and several killed.

It was the Civil War that really boomed production. Some 3,000 workmen flocked to Springfield to turn out 1,000 muskets or rifles a day. "Springfield" became a noun meaning rifle, and continues so, despite the almost continuously changing mechanism of the chief weapon of the United States infantry.

In 1864, an unsuccessful attempt was made by enemy agents to blow up the arsenal, and Springfield people learned that making guns is not always a comfortable industry to live with. (Back in 1824, the armory was partially destroyed by fire, which had nothing to do with war.)

Longfellow, New England's peripatetic bard, visited the arsenal while on his wedding trip in 1843 and, to please his bride, who remarked that the tiers of arms reminded her of an organ, followed up the simile:

Springfield

This is the Arsenal. From floor to ceiling,
Like a huge organ, rise the burnished arms;
But from their silent pipes no anthem pealing
Startles the villagers with strange alarms.

Nevertheless, the United States, for all of our pious disclaimer of warlike attitudes, has managed a fairly respectable record of major and minor wars since Springfield went into the arms business. The sporadic demands for "armorers," followed by almost as sudden layoffs when the shooting stopped, created municipal problems for Springfield, and also for the shipbuilding ports, that were unknown to other towns until World War I brought total, or rather universal, war. Since then, it has been a poor town indeed that was not engaged in supplying some product or other used by the armed forces.

Incidentally, it was in Springfield where John Brown, later of Kansas and Harpers Ferry, Virginia, operated the last of his civilian enterprises before he started to raise and arm an army of his own. In Springfield he opened a warehouse for Brown and Perkins, wool merchants, in 1847. Like all of his other business ventures, this one soon ended in bankruptcy. He was already organizing his new League of Gileadites among the increasing number of Negroes in Springfield. Visions of an insurrection far greater than that of Daniel Shays had taken his cloudy mind. Frederick Douglass, the remarkable "Escaped Slave" of New Bedford, visited him. A year later Brown left Springfield for the West. He was to return to Massachusetts later to get a wagon load, said one of his biographers, "of rifles and ammunition." By then the time was 1857. The goal was Kansas.

Whether or not the rifles had been made in Springfield, the driver of this traveling arsenal, his blue-gray eyes aglitter, the Voice in his ear, knew where he was going. There was a plenty of the grapes of wrath stored in Kansas. Old Brown would trample them.

By the end of the stagecoach era, there were six lines serving Springfield, yet the town was still little more than a cluster of business houses, including many taverns, along the main street, which was the Upper Post Road. With the advent of the steamcars, however, the town grew so mightily that the *Republican,* founded by Samuel Bowles in 1824, was hard put to express the wonder of "modern transportation." New industries sprang up in such variety that Springfield seems never to have been known as a cotton town, a woolen town, or even a textile town. It was no more noted for shoes than for dictionaries. "In Springfield," said an official of the Merchants Exchange, "we manufacture everything."

Doubtless, Springfield did manufacture everything. But because young people are often, if not always, impervious to all else save what currently seems important, my boyhood opinions of Springfield's greatness was based on three items: It was where you changed cars—no matter where you were going—in a railroad station that seemed second in size only to Grand Central in New York City; and even better because in Springfield you could buy small switchman's lanterns filled with brightly colored hard candies. It was in Springfield also where a God-given outfit named Milton Bradley made Parcheesi boards and games called Pit and Flinch. And, Springfield was the home of the Guy Brothers Minstrels.

These varied things, as I say, were what, early in this century, set Springfield apart from all other and lesser cities, at least to me and many of my generation of farm and village boys in New England.

One reason the Springfield Union Depot was impressive is that to get from the train shed to the waiting room you had to go underground through a long echoing tunnel. As for Milton and Bradley, in addition to the games they made, they turned out a line of wax crayons fairly blinding with colors. As for Guy Brothers Minstrels, they were, like Barnum and Bailey in a larger field, a New England institution, not only in the cities and Post Road towns of Massachusetts and Rhode Island (though not Connecticut), but in the remotest parts of Maine, New Hampshire, and Vermont.

Just when the Guy Brothers started trouping I do not know. My mother recalled seeing them during her Tilden Female Seminary days of the late Eighties at West Lebanon, New Hampshire. I know that they were a full-blown and famous attraction as early as 1882, when they posed to have their picture taken standing in front of (old) Dartmouth Hall. I was to see them later, in both Vermont and New Hampshire. Among them were the six sons and one daughter of the founder, George Guy, Sr., and the wives of three of the sons. All were musical; all could sing or dance, and also double in brass for the parade and concert. With from ten to twenty other performers, Guy Brothers Minstrels could muster a respectable company for the town hall and opera house trade in the days before movies. They were good enough for the clientele, too; and in time they became a sort of standard fixed holiday, like the Fourth of July and Memorial Day.

Founder George Guy, a distinguished-looking white-haired gentleman of the old-school type, wore his silk topper set straight upon his head, and there were no diamonds, real or otherwise, on his fingers or in the studs of his boiled white shirt. He never failed to pay a call on the local Congregational minister, and on the Sabbath several of the veritable members of the family, and often non-family members in the company, attended services in a body. It was almost as if the Guys were citizens of the town or village.

I must have attended shows by Guy Brothers Minstrels half-a-dozen times between 1904 and, say, 1916. Though the gags of Mister Bones and Mister Interlocutor were insufferable, as were those of the big-time minstrels of Lew Dockstader, the soft-shoe or "Essence" dancing of the Guys was superb. Indeed, Eddie Guy occasionally did a song and dance act over the B. F. Keith Circuit as a single.

But it was when four of the Guys, including Eddie, simultaneously came forward to front and center, and took stance for their ballad by quartette, that we incipient barbershop harmonizers sat up in our seats in the gallery:

"Ladies and gentlemen," announced the Interlocutor, "by special request, our sweet singing four will render that old favorite, 'She May Have Seen Better Days.'" Then, high and clear came the tender voice of the top tenor, who may have been Arthur Guy, telling the sad old story of the country girl gone wrong in the city. As the verse ended, the house lights went down, ever so little, the four singers took a deep breath, and then softly came the refrain of purest melody, in lyrics already ten years old but still fit for the fashion of the times:

> *She may have seen better days,*
> *When she was in her prime;*
> *She may have seen better days,*
> *Once upon a time . . .*

At this point the lead tenor took solo, thus:

> *Though by the wayside she fell . . .*

Then all four cut loose with great power:

> *She may yet mend her ways . . .*

to hold "her ways" into a swelling climactic chord, while the bass repeated the line, grunting it down, down the scale to a marvelous cellar note.

Then the full quartette went sweetly *diminuendo:*

> *Some poor old mother*
> *Is waiting for her . . .*

and took breath for the final line, *forte:*

> *Who has seen . . . better . . . days.*

"There was not a dry eye in the opera house," observed the Newport (Vermont) *Express,* adding that "The Guy Brothers seem to improve each season." And so, too, observed the *Coos County Democrat,* Lancaster, New Hampshire; the *Daily Commercial,* Bangor, Maine; the *Standard-Times,* New Bedford, Massachusetts, and possibly even the *Journal* of Providence, Rhode Island.

In New York City, the *Clipper* might have noted something to the effect that "The Guy Bros., minstrels, after summering in their home town of Springfield, Mass., have taken to the road for their thirty-second annual tour of Northern New England."

The Guys were not the last minstrel show to tour New England, but they must surely have been one of the last family troupes to do so—the sort whose members would visit public schools, had personal friends among leading merchants, bought tickets for the Firemen's Annual Ball, and attended church services on the Sabbath. Their era started to fade with the first nickelodeon, the first Woolworth, and the first Stanley Steamer.

Chapter 17

The Upper Road: Springfield to Windsor

IN THE DAY of postriders, the Upper Road ferried westbound traffic by Springfield Ferry to the west side of the Connecticut into Agawam, the original settlement. Because the west side had much the better soil, with rich natural meadows, it was lawful for many years for the east siders to move their horses and cattle into Agawam for grazing purposes from spring until November. The district became known, as it is to the present day, as the Feeding Hills.

Although Agawam village does not appear to have been a regular stop, when stagecoaches took over the mails, it is clear however that they passed through Agawam township on the way south, to enter Connecticut at Suffield, where they stopped, as they did also at

Springfield to Windsor

Windsor Locks and Windsor, all three being on the west side of the river. On the east side, in this stretch of Connecticut, are the towns of Thompsonville and Enfield, which were doubtless served by alternate stages. In any event I shall consider them all as Post towns on the Upper Road between Springfield and Hartford.

Suffield village has been described as "a sedate little town," its main street and long narrow green bordered by many substantial old homes, a few dating from late eighteenth century. Historically it is important for its leadership in the making of cigars from Connecticut-grown tobacco. The tobacco industry has changed. American cigars are now made elsewhere, yet the Connecticut River valley produces much of the shade-grown broadleaf that is used to wrap, or roll the better grade of domestic cigars.

On the way from Springfield, we passed mile upon mile of tobacco fields, staked to support the netting that filters the sunlight and thus —said a tobacco man—makes the wrapper leaf "thinner in body and lighter in color." It is said to be the most expensive tobacco grown in the United States. I learned that by 1921, its peak year, Connecticut shade-grown was a crop of 45 million pounds. Since then, due to the popularity of the cigarette and the slow steady decline of the cigar, Connecticut leaf has followed the prevailing trend; yet, the casual visitor would never guess it.

It seems that native tobacco has been a leading product around here since colonial times. It was used in large part for pipe-smoking until the cigar was introduced by far-ranging Yankees whose ships had touched at Spanish ports in Cuba and Mexico. It was amusing to learn that at least here in Connecticut the great hero of the cigar was none other than Israel Putnam. This almost native son of Pomfret returned to Connecticut in 1762, from an expedition against Havana, so wildly enthusiastic about cigars that with him he brought "three donkey-loads of Havana seegars."

I was already so familiar with Connecticut's all-around folk hero that if the story had concerned only one donkey-load, I should have dismissed it as myth; but three donkey-loads was quite in the Putnam tradition, and Old Put thereupon became and has remained of heroic tradition as one of America's three most potent boosters of tobacco in the form of cigars. General U. S. Grant was the most widely known; but it was John Quincy Adams who was revered in the Yankee tobacco trade because it was he who "made the seegar proper for Bostonians."

As for Israel Putnam his celebrated return to Connecticut inspired a Suffield tobacco grower, Simeon Viets, to import a professional from Cuba to teach the women of Suffield how to roll cigars properly, and presently Viets expanded his business to neighboring Windsor, and his factories began turning out thousands of cheroots daily. These became known as Windsor Particulars: the Long Nines were pencil-thin; the Short Sixes merely not so long; the Supers were finished with a twist. The Short Sixes were the favorites in taverns, and were called "Twofers," meaning not two-for-five-cents, but two-for-one-penny.

The sudden rise and continued popularity of the cigar indicated that Connecticut's legislators, who for a century had been wrestling with laws to regulate use of the vile weed, had failed miserably, as had been the case elsewhere. In view of this continual struggle, it is singularly ironic that right in Suffield was born and reared Sylvester Graham, unquestionably America's greatest enemy of tobacco in all its forms. Once known the world over as the founder of Grahamism, a dietary reform based on bread made of the whole of the wheat, unbolted and coarsely ground, his system also prohibited tobacco and rum.

Grahamism swept the country. There were Grahamite hotels and boarding houses. Millers began barreling Graham flour. In Boston a mob of bakers and butchers (Grahamites were forbidden meat) attacked Graham in person. Still, up and down the country he went, lecturing on "the Science of Human Life," lambasting The Enemy, including Suffield's "Genuine Spanish Seegars," to die, aged almost fifty-seven years.

Suffield seems not to have honored its famous reformer. I could find no monument or marker. Still Webster remembers him with an entry: "Graham flour." (After Sylvester Graham, 1794–1851.)

Springfield to Windsor

In the south part of Suffield we could see the upper or headlock of the Windsor Locks canal, built about 1826 to by-pass the wicked Enfield Falls. The canal is 6 miles long. Until it was built, Warehouse Point at Windsor was virtually the head of navigation on the Connecticut River. Though shallow-draft flatboats were developed that could be poled up the rapids, it was slow going. The canal and locks speeded the haul up-river for only eighteen years, when the new railroads began to take away much of the river transportation. One might wonder why the canal set-up was still in use in the 1960s. But it provides water to the several mills left along the old towpath in Windsor Mills. The old canal company is ready to operate the locks free of toll charges for the many pleasure boats that run up and down the river from spring to freeze-up. The company also permits visitors to walk the old towpath, which has changed not at all since it was laid 135 years ago.

The Locks did not turn Windsor into the mighty port that enthusiasts envisioned. What the Locks did was to bring all river traffic to a halt, briefly, and provide taverns on both sides of the river to cater to the captains and crews of boats, to the passengers, and drovers, and the army of river drivers accompanying the rafts and booms of logs that were cut far up the river in Vermont and New Hampshire. Though most of this timber was sawed into lumber in the mills around Mount Tom, in Massachusetts, there were other plants between Hartford and Saybrook awaiting logs.

Then, there were the powdermen, moving ton upon ton of the explosive made in Hazardville near Enfield, by employees of the Hazard Powder Company, named for its chief owner, Augustus G. Hazard, of the able and prolific Hazards of Rhode Island. The powder came in kegs of 25 pounds each, and 13,000 kegs might be stacked on a single barge. For obvious reasons, crews moving the product were often hard to recruit. Legend has it that these powdermen were not only well paid but good spenders; and when both powder and logs were going through the Locks, the taverns at Windsor Hill, at Point Rocks, and at the Locks, were so noisy the festivities could be heard in Hartford, 12 miles distant.

The Upper Road

Legend has it that there was little that a man wanted that could not be found at Windsor Locks.

Antedating both the Locks, and the powder factory (bought by DuPont in 1876), were the Shakers who came to found an Enfield colony in 1790. Officially, Shakers were the United Society of Believers, followers of "Mother" Ann Lee, a group of gentle, devout, and energetically independent people whose metaphysics did not permit marriage or even sexual intercourse. Adult members were converts, but an infinitely larger number came from orphan asylums.

That a factory for the manufacture of powder, the first necessity of war, should have come to settle next to the Shaker village of peace lovers was ironic, but no more so than that a cluster of distilleries, which needed 300 bushels of grain daily, had grown up at Warehouse Point.

Despite which, the sect survived by tending closely to its own business, which was mainly the growing of garden and flower seeds of so superior a quality that the Shakers here, as in their other villages in New York State, Massachusetts, New Hampshire, Maine, Ohio, and Kentucky, never lacked for customers. It was the changing times, and the increasing difficulty of getting new members which, at last, in 1917, caused the closing of the village at Enfield, Connecticut. These dedicated people had lived here by the rapids for 127 years. When they went away, during World War I, there was still, across the river at Windsor Locks, a business firm that had been there before even the Shakers came. This was and is the venerable C. H. Dexter and Sons, Inc., makers of paper for the past 194 years. In terms of events, the House of Dexter was founded in 1767, the same year John Quincy Adams and Andrew Jackson were born, the former in Braintree, Massachusetts, the latter in Waxhaw, South Carolina; and six years before the Boston Tea Party. (Item: In less than another four years, Dexter can and probably will observe its bicentennial.)

Because I had known something of this concern before coming

to Windsor Locks, the youth of President David L. Coffin in no manner astonished me. When at thirty-one he became head of the firm he was the third oldest of the three Dexters and four Coffins who have served it as president. He remarked that his company has been characterized by two factors: young leadership, and strong emphasis and dependence on research.

When I wanted to know what the specialty products were that had kept Dexter and Sons away down front in the paper business, Mr. Coffin prefaced his reply by saying that, "The most fruitful development in our business took place during my father's and grandfather's period of management." (There had been a Great-grandfather Coffin, too.) "This, in fact, represents the technical foundation of our present operation to a very large degree." Then he got down to cases.

"Among many things," he said, "Dexter and Sons introduced the first packaged sheet of toilet paper. With it was a wire loop so that it could be hung on a convenient hook. . . . But don't seek this product at your local supermarket. It was abandoned in the early 1930s, the last customer being S. S. Pierce of Boston." (Mr. Coffin recalled that there had been a large number of illuminating anecdotes concerning this specific product and many of the old families of Boston's Back Bay.)

"For years," he continued, "we made a special paper for the camera and Kodak industry, which permitted the autographic feature of films, and was very popular. Then, in 1922, Grandfather Coffin engaged Fay Osborne, a young graduate of the Massachusetts Institute of Technology. He is now our vice-president and technical director. His great contribution was the development that permitted the use of long fibers on a papermaking machine, and it brought about Dexter's leadership in several product fields. For instance, the porous teabag paper which we introduced in the 1930s. The same technology also permitted development of fibrous meat casing, stencil base tissue, and a general line of absorbent and filter papers."

At my request, Mr. Coffin gave me a copy of an address he was preparing about his company's history for the Newcomen Society. In it I found an item characteristic of inventive Yankees since time began: Back in earlier days, Founder C. H. Dexter experimented with manila rope and successfully made wrapping paper of such quality that "it took a man with a strong pull to tear it." Meanwhile, he was perhaps the first papermaker to use lime in cooking stock, and the first to make "jute manila." For this product he used the old saltpeter bags he obtained from the Hazard powder mills across the river. Mr. Coffin believes that these and other empirical experiments brought in little or no profit, but they served to answer questions posed by technology.

Today, with a total payroll of only 300 employees, it is obvious that Dexter and Sons has chosen goals other than mere size. That one of these goals concerns new products is clear enough from a remarkable record that reaches back into colonial times when master papermakers wore pig-tails.

In addition to the paper products of C. H. Dexter and Sons, the gunpowder from Hazardville, and the gin and whiskey made at Warehouse Point, there was still another commodity of this overall community that was shipped down the river: the seemingly endless rolls of floor covering produced by the Thompsonville Carpet Manufacturing Company. Thompsonville was a town that became noted as the place of the most important strike in Connecticut history. In 1833, employees quit work to enforce a demand for higher wages; the company countered with a suit against the strike leaders, charging them with conspiracy to ruin the business. After three years and numerous trials, a verdict was rendered in 1836 that was to bedevil industrial struggles for another hundred years: the court found it was legal to combine in order to raise wages but unlawful to ruin an employer's business. It is a fine point indeed.

Some astute, if ribald, member of the Windsor bar remarked of this decision that it was comparable to the attitude and practice of the Enfield Shakers: It was perfectly all right to combine to raise seeds in vast quantity for the support of their members, but "improper, impious, and illegal" to manufacture children.

Age, good luck, and a respect for the past have combined to leave today's Windsor with an unusual number of old houses of varied architecture. These include the seventeenth-century home of Joseph Loomis, which is now in the grounds of Loomis School (founded 1874, opened in 1914, an independent boarding and day school for boys); the 1822 home of James Loomis, father of the founders of Loomis School; the Hezekiah Chaffee House, perhaps the oldest (1757) brick house in Connecticut, now used by the Chaffee School (the girls' division [day students only] of the Loomis Institute, which includes both the Loomis and the Chaffee schools).

Now owned by the Windsor Historical Society is the Walter Fyler House (1640), said to be the oldest frame building in the state. The privately owned Captain Thomas Allyn Homestead dates from 1670. Elmwood, the home of Oliver Ellsworth, noted jurist and statesman, probably the town's most eminent native son, is now the property of the local chapter of the Daughters of the American Revolution.

Chapter 18

The Middle Road: Boston to Hartford

H AVING REACHED the north environs of Hartford and the
end of the Upper Road, we headed back to Boston by the
Massachusetts Turnpike, then to resume the post route by the Middle
Road.

At the site of the Parting Stone in Roxbury, the Upper Road turns
right for Cambridge, and the Middle turns left for Dedham. Here
at Dedham, the route separates again, when the Middle proceeds
right toward Medfield and the other, by taking off left for Norwood
and Walpole, has become the Lower Road.

The three routes out of Boston will meet in New Haven, to form
a single Post Road to New York.

Boston to Hartford

Ancient Dedham is no town to be by-passed by mere reference to the famous remark of a Boston woman who when visiting friends on the Pacific Coast was asked by which route she had come to the Far West. She replied, briskly enough, it was "by way of Dedham."

Although back in 1635, when Dedham settlers made their pitch, they voted to name their town "Contentment," the place failed to live up to its rather smug name. It was Dedham where the most discontented "Suffolk Resolves" were passed in the Woodward Tavern; and these protests "lighted the match that kindled the mighty conflagration of the American Revolution." Or, so says a tablet in the Norfolk County Registry Building.

Much later, during the anti-Masonic excitement of the 1830s, when Dedham Masons were stoned in the streets, Dr. Elisha Thayer put a polished Square and Compass on the front door of his house where it remained for generations and, for all I know, is still there. But Dedham's greatest excitement of all came in the 1920s with the trials of Sacco and Vanzetti, on murder charges, before Judge Webster Thayer. These occupied much of six years, and resulted in executions of both defendants. The news echoed around the world.

Adjacent Westwood, originally a part of Dedham, was not incorporated as a town until 1897. In early times, Indians roamed this neighborhood, and are said to have used a local rock formation as a sort of community bake oven; but Westwood escaped the fury visited upon neighboring Medfield, more than half of which was burned when King Philip's War began. Just beyond Medfield, the Post Road skirts, between Millis and Medway, the Black Swamps, a once-sinister place said to be a favorite hideout for Philip's braves.

Back in 1845, when post roads began to feel the first effects of steam, Milford was the lucky town in this region: the Boston & Albany Railroad built a Milford branch, and the village boomed with boot and shoe factories, and with a quarry producing pink granite. Things began to taper off after 1900. Milford's boosters started to look around for things to brag about. Had no great or famous men been born here? It was discovered that nearby Bellingham was the native home of William T. Adams, who under the name of "Oliver Optic" had written 126 books for boys. Well, everybody couldn't have a Hawthorne, and Oliver Optic went into the guidebooks because he had discovered a genius.

Between writing his own books, Bellingham's Adams edited a goody-goody magazine called *Student and Schoolmate;* and one day there came to him, from an unknown writer, a story entitled "Ragged Dick." It was signed by Horatio Alger, Jr. It is clear that Editor Adams knew good rich tripe when he saw it. He took one look at Alger's first story and rushed it to the printer. The rest is history—135 different versions of "Ragged Dick," and 250 million copies of Alger's books.

Not long before "lucky Milford Got the Railroad" and started to teem with industries, a Utopian group headed by Adin Ballou, Universalist preacher and reformer, bought some 500 acres of farm land in the Mendon district, to test his radical theory of "practical Christianity." The new village was named Hopedale Community, owned and operated by a joint stock company organized by thirty-two members and capitalized at $4,000.

Adin Ballou had become one of the better-known reformers in New England; and Hopedale attracted many who were discontented with conventional churches. As usual with Utopian experiments, Hopedale's disciples included a sizable number of free-riders, but also a sufficient leaven of dedicated souls who were willing to work. Fifteen years later, Hopedale had 110 members, busy with farming and various small industries. It was supporting a good school and a good library. The community stock property was valued at $40,-000. Yet, discovery that liabilities exceeded resources caused two of the heaviest stockholders, George and Ebenezer Draper, to withdraw from the enterprise.

The community lingered on as a sort of moral association until 1868, when it was merged with the Hopedale (Unitarian) Parish, of which Adin Ballou was pastor.

It may be said for Hopedale that it was probably the only

Utopian community—save Oneida, in New York State—that wound up paying all its bills. As for old Mendon, from which 500 acres were sold to Hopedale, it not only did not "Get the Railroad," it was the second town burned by King Philip's raiders. Industry passed it by, and so did population. Even in the 1960s Hopedale has twice the population of Mendon, which has remained chiefly agricultural. Perhaps it has been more fortunate than its citizens have realized. Of the two other villages which withdrew from Mendon, both Blackstone and Millville attracted several industries, including two or three really big plants. But all of them have gone. Several left in the 1920s, others a decade or so later.

Beyond Mendon we came to Uxbridge, the first of the several "bridge-named" towns, which include Northbridge, Southbridge, Sturbridge, and Old Sturbridge Village. Uxbridge alone is fair on the Post Road; and Uxbridge still characterizes, for me, this general portion of the Middle Road: It is the mellow flavor of a largely rural region, with here and there a small spot of industry.

In Uxbridge we passed a lone worsted mill in the midst of mile upon mile of meadows, hayfields. In July, when we were there, they were the most fragrant hayfields I could recall. It was not just a whiff here and there in passing, but a continuous fragrance from what we commonly call sweetgrass, and which Webster says is one or more species of genus *Glyceria*. (Says Gray's *New Manual of Botany: Anthoxanthum odoratum.*)

Here at Uxbridge we left the Middle Post Road to pay a call at Old Sturbridge Village which I had visited periodically ever since it was first opened in 1946 as a "Living Museum," which seeks "to preserve and present the story of New England farm and village life of yesterday."

Like many other good things, Old Sturbridge Village is a by-product of Yankee industry. It grew from the hobby of two brothers, Albert B. Wells and J. Cheney Wells, of the American Optical Company, whose immense plant at Southbridge employs several thousand people and is the most important business in the town.

The Middle Road

Early in the 1920s, the brothers were smitten with the collecting urge, and went at it with much the same energy and attention they devoted to the family business. First, it was chairs, tables, mirrors, chests, and clocks; then came woodenware, tinware, pottery, glass, china; and pewter, copper and brass; by the time they had got to hardware, like latches, hinges, saws, axes, windvanes, andirons and early stoves, they began to see what was happening; and in South-bridge, near the American Optical plant, they built the Wells Museum to house their collection.

One thing led to another and at last to Old Sturbridge Village. This is not a restoration of an actual historical place, but the re-crea-tion of an imaginary representative New England community of the period 1790 to 1840. The Commonwealth granted a charter establishing the village as an independent nonprofit educational in-stitution. To this organization the two Wells brothers gave their collections, the buildings, and the site. It should be said here that the village receives no public funds. All revenues are used for its support.

On the way from Uxbridge to Sturbridge, we passed through Southbridge, with its humming American Optical plant. We also came to something I had never seen before and did not know existed. In the center of Southbridge village was a churchlike structure of little distinction which we passed before I saw that it was indeed a church. We not only stopped, but backed up, to learn if my eyes had played me wrong. But no, three separate signs on the church indicated that three denominations were meeting there. This in it-self was not so strange. But the fact that Seventh-day Adventists used the same premises as the Universalists and the Assembly of God was odd enough. I knew that Adventists were more than chary of worship in a structure used by others; and have since learned that only a temporary emergency condones it.

But by now we had come to Old Sturbridge Village, where the two church buildings are properly called meeting houses, as they were known when and where they were built, the tall and stately Baptist Meeting House in 1832, in Sturbridge itself, and the Friends Meeting House in 1796, at Bolton, north of Marlboro on the Upper Road.

Sturbridge Village stands on 200 acres of farmland just off the Massachusetts Turnpike. It is truly a living museum. Several hundred thousand people visit it each year, and what they get is a tour in time and history. Centering on the village green, with the meeting houses, stocks, pillory, the little brick powder house, and a general store, along with half-a-dozen old homes ranging from simplicity to magnificence, the outlying fields and pasture are spotted here and there with a sawmill, a gristmill, blacksmith shop, boot shop, gun shop, printing office, and a covered bridge.

There is no gimcrack to Sturbridge. Virtually all of the thirty-odd buildings are the identical structures that were moved here from their original sites in neighboring towns. So, too, were their furnishings. Here is the New England village of, say, 1800–1830, in the days of the Post Road, before the railroad came. It was a self-sufficient community. I know of nothing else like Old Sturbridge. The illusion of time past becomes so powerful that, after a good long look, many a visitor has to shake himself for assurance that he has not somehow slipped into the fourth dimension.

Returning to strike the Middle Road again at Thompson, Connecticut, we were in the corner where that state touches both Massachusetts and Rhode Island, and thus approached the orbit of Thomas Dorr, instigator of Dorr's Rebellion in 1841. When he fled Rhode Island with $5,000 on his head, Dorr came here to Thompson to hide in Stiles Tavern where, so goes the story, he evaded the agents sent to arrest him, by "using the complicated series of stairways in the old Tavern."

Neighboring Putnam, named for the Revolutionary hero, Got the Railroad and became the industrial center, depopulating nearby villages to supply operatives for the Belding mill, said to be one of the largest silk thread factories in the country. We drove through Putnam's mill districts, where the company houses seemed to display great use of outside wallboard, much of it as imitation-brick siding. In some community around here, a sign called attention to a plant of Colt's *Plastic* Division. The italics are mine, for I did not know of this astonishing diversification of the traditional products of the old firm.

Pomfret, too, Got the Railroad, but too late, I heard, to revive the village after 1837, when widespread panic ruined the numerous small water-power mills that promised to make Pomfret an important city. This panic came at just about the right time to flatten many a budding textile baron. The home looms had been disappearing since the early 1830s, and the weaving previously done in the kitchen became a community venture under a new and tough capitalist. If Pomfret was never to become a Fall River or a Lowell, nature, Israel Putnam, and mythology combined to give Pomfret one of the finest "tourist attractions" possible. The sign directing traffic to it, in the crossroads hamlet of Abington, in Pomfret Town, says "Israel Putnam's Wolf Den."

I'd like to know what sort of a tourist would look at an authentic textile baron, complete with mill, if he could see instead an alleged wolf den into which, once upon a time, Connecticut's hero was allegedly lowered by a rope, to grab the vicious beast by the ears, and be hauled with wolf to the surface. If strangers do not already know it, they should be told that Putnam, like Ethan Allen and Davy Crockett, was the sort of character on whom contemporaries like to pile legends. Indeed, years later when fame touched Putnam, and sketches of his life began to appear in books and pamphlets, one of the favorite illustrations had to do with his work in the she-wolf's den in Pomfret. "In the fissured granite walls," says a guidebook, "the Daughters of the American Revolution have erected a tablet in honor of the exploit." (Because old Put will appear again in this book, let us move on through the several Mansfields—the Center, the Four Corners, the Depot—which with nearby South Manchester,

"The Silk City," comprise Connecticut's present-day silk industry.)

Silk culture in, of all places, New England is quite a story, and all but forgotten. Now and then, on the Yankee horizon, appeared an idea that seemed to hold salvation for the decaying towns, the communities which had been by-passed by the railroads. One of these notions was the raising of silkworms and the manufacture of raw silk. Here at South Manchester, Ward Cheney and three brothers had been experimenting with a tree, *Morus multicaulis,* a variety of mulberry.

The first bushes had long been familiar in Connecticut. To encourage their culture, the legislature had distributed a sample package of seeds to every town in the state, and in Mansfield a silk mill had successfully reeled raw silk from native cocoons by water power.

What the Cheneys did was to put silkworms into mass production in two immense nurseries. Newspaper editors did the rest. Here was the first good news about home industry and agriculture since the grow-ginseng-and-get-rich bust of forty years before. Wild stories of sensational profits made by the Cheneys filled the New England press. They were evidence that the Lord had at last pointed the way to His own people in these times of their great woe. Did not God make the mulberry bush and the worm? Plant now, and produce fine silk in the sight of the Lord.

Almost at once, in 1834, a mania took hold in Connecticut and spread, within weeks, to four other Yankee states. (Only Maine seemed immune.) Up in far and cold New Hampshire, at Candia, for example, more than one hundred miles north of Manchester, Connecticut, the silkworm virus struck like the plague. Wrote the village historian: "In 1835, Dr. Isaiah Lane and Captain Abraham Fitts, together with a group of fellow citizens, bought a large stock of mulberry shoots and a colony of cocoons and planted the trees with utmost assurance. It cost a lot of money, but almost everybody wanted a few dollars in it. A young school mistress invested all of her savings. . . ." Farmers, teamsters, cobblers, mechanics, preachers, merchants—one and all, they demanded admission to the ranks of stockholders. Then, in autumn, came the "harvest." It did not take long: ". . . Hannah Lane and two or three other women managed to reel silk enough to make a few small skeins for sewing."

"It was found," the historian remembered, "that the climate was rather cold for the silkworms." (One doesn't doubt it.) The host of mulberry bushes in Candia were permitted to "go wild," as the expression was, and thus join the uncounted other tree farms for silkworms in New Hampshire, Vermont, Massachusetts, Rhode Island, and, of course, Connecticut. By 1841, even the Cheney brothers had quit the nursery business. Yet, they were in the silk business for good, or at least for the next 120 years.

In 1838, while the silkworm craze was still booming, Ward Cheney, with brothers Ralph, Rush, and Fred, together with Edward Arnold, had organized the Mount Nebo Silk Manufacturing Company at South Manchester, Connecticut, capitalized at $50,000. Both the plant, and the several fine residences of the Cheney family still stand in South Manchester, and the very name Cheney has come to mean silk in the American textile industry. Among artists and engravers, however, the names of two other brothers of Ward Cheney, John and Seth, are remembered for their outstanding skill with a sheet of copper and a burin.

It seemed best to include *the* silk city of South Manchester with the traditionally silken Mansfields. To do so it was necessary to skip the communities of Coventry, Andover, and Bolton. But if only because Nathan Hale was born in what used to be South Coventry, but has now dropped the adjective, we had to see the native town of the famous martyr spy of the Revolution. Unlike several other noted men who were born, or had lived or died, within sight or sound of the Boston Post Road, and whose markers or plaques seemed to have been hidden from the public with unusual cunning, the very geography of Coventry was as if dedicated to making memory of the town's incomparable patriot easily available to the stranger.

Boston to Hartford

Up a short steep hill, yet almost within the village, is the Nathan Hale Cemetery, with an imposing granite obelisk 45 feet in height. Within the yard is the Hale family plot, and the grave of Asher Wright, described as Hale's orderly. Near the village green on Monument Hill is the Huntington House (1763) where Nathan Hale was prepared for Yale College by the Reverend Joseph Huntington; and within 3 miles of Coventry Village is Nathan Hale's birthplace, built by his father. Just east of the house is a replica of the Bela Pratt statue of Hale at Yale University.

The Hale tour was both scenic and effortless, but I could find neither memorial nor even memory of Daniel Halladay in Coventry. This was not astonishing. He was not a hero. I doubt if he was known outside what must be the comparatively narrow field of windmills and pumps. Yet he is credited in the American West with invention of the third of the three products that made possible the settlement of the Great Plains, also known in former days, and designated as such on the map, as the Great American Desert. The products were: the Colt's revolver, invented and manufactured by Samuel Colt of Hartford; the barbed wire perfected and patented by Joseph Farwell Glidden, and manufactured in Worcester; and the Halladay windmill, perfected and patented by young Daniel Halladay, of South Coventry, Connecticut.

The value of the Colts in border country is obvious. Not until barbed wire was perfected could the 160-acre homestead be protected against the open range—and not even then in the arid regions. These wastes awaited a fence no more than they awaited a dependable supply of water.

What Halladay did was to devise a windmill "which governed itself by centrifugal force, being held to the wind by the governing weight and so arranged that when it revolved too fast this weight would slowly rise and thereby reduce the area of sail presented to the wind." Out of this invention grew the Halladay Windmill Company of South Coventry, Connecticut, which in turn became, in 1857, the United States Wind Engine and Pump Company of Batavia, Illinois. Halladay continued to improve the device. The Union

The Middle Road

Pacific gave it a fine boost when it ordered seventy windmills to supply water to its locomotives while making grade and laying rails across the dry plains. During the seventies and eighties the manufacture and sale of windmills increased in about the same proportion as that of barbed wire. The two final necessities for homesteading the Great American Desert had arrived.

Well, towns on the Boston Post Road had supplied those necessities. I had visited the Colt factory in Hartford, and the barbed-wire mills in Worcester. I could not claim Batavia, Illinois, as on my beat; but had hoped against hope to dig up some forgotten information about Halladay's long-ago windmill concern in South Coventry.

In such case, the first thing a sane researcher always does is to consult a library, or a librarian, or both. We were in Coventry, Connecticut, on July 20, 1960, a Wednesday. The Booth and Dimock Memorial Library was closed, and thoroughly locked. Next door was the big old general store owned and operated by Miss Annie Wellwood and her brother. Behind the counter was a tall, gray-haired woman whose alert face and quick stance belied all sign of age.

I made my pitch, saying I was a reporter working on a book about the Boston Post Road and, wanting to learn more about a famous businessman of long-ago Coventry, had just tried to visit the public library next door. Miss Annie Wellwood eyed me for a brief moment and then spoke:

"The library's shut tight four days a week, and this is one of them." It sounded final, but Miss Annie wasn't done. Reaching up to a shelf behind her, she came back with a ring of keys. "Come on," she said, "I can let you in if you can find the books you want." And away she went out the door with us in her wake. Two minutes later we were within the Booth and Dimock Memorial Library where, to the glory of Coventry, all books were catalogued in professional style, and I had no difficulty in locating volumes dealing with Connecticut and with Tolland County.

But inventor Daniel Halladay had escaped notice of those state and local historians represented on the shelves. Despite which, I applied the almost automatic rule used (by writers) to grade Coventry's Public Library; and ranked it better than good. (It had no less than four of my own books.) Back in the Wellwood store again, I mentioned Halladay's name and his windmill. Neither was known to the several customers. Much later, in the Midwest, I was given a handsome advertising brochure entitled "When the Mill Goes Round," done in four colors, copyrighted in 1895 by United States Wind Engine and Pump Company, Batavia, Illinois, which indicated the manufacturers of "Halladay Standard Wind Mill, U.S. Solid Wheel, and Gem Steel Wind Engine" were still going strong.

As we prepared to leave, Miss Annie invited us into the old house of her family that stood between the store and the public library. It is a splendid period piece, authentic with low ceilings and narrow stairs, and especially fit for a native of Connecticut. In the parlor and kitchen were more than a dozen handsome clocks. I noticed that all of them were in working order.

But my companion also wanted to visit the store again. Hanging high from a shelf there, a set of sleighbells was what had caught his eye. They were for sale. I thought the asking price was high, but he said it was "reasonable" because of the quality of the bells. Now he bought them, cash on the drumhead, and we left Coventry, Connecticut, on a hot July afternoon to the music one associates with December and a one-horse open sleigh.

We had already visited Storrs, with its fine buildings comprising the University of Connecticut established in 1881, and were reminded of the many big dairy farms in the rolling hills of Pomfret, where Holsteins appeared to be favorites. (In a college restaurant, the waitresses were conversing in German. On the way

into Storrs, we passed, near Ashford, a prosperous-looking structure labeled Hungarian Social Club.)

We had no calls to make in Andover and Bolton, so drove on
through Manchester to Hartford, musing on the bright colors of
the newspaper mailboxes in this region: Red for the *Courant,* Green
for the *Times,* both of Hartford, and a startling Yellow for the
Willimantic *Chronicle.*

Chapter 19

The Middle Road: Hartford to New Haven

AT HARTFORD, the capital of Connecticut, the Middle Road we had been following is joined by the Upper Road coming down from Springfield and the combined single Post Road proceeds south to New Haven.

Hartford has been a key city in relation to the Post Road since its beginning in 1673, when it was selected as "the first stage [stop] designed for the postrider to change his horse and where he should constantly have a fresh one lye." More than a century later, it was the original goal set by Levi Pease, of Boston, the stagecoach operator, for his "Western terminal" before his ambition shifted to New York City itself.

Before the railroads came, Hartford was an important seaport to which many industries in northwestern Connecticut toted their products for shipment by vessel to the Far West, and to far countries. Among these were the products of two factories located *off* the Post Road but which became so noted for excellence that they deserve mention in any account of Yankee industry, namely Hitchcock chairs, and the edged tools of the Collins Company.

We drove west on US 44 some 10 miles to Canton (town) and so into the village of Collinsville in the Farmington River valley. Before we reached the office of Collins Company, on the east bank of the river, we were well aware of industry by the insistent pounding of the forge, and soon had a panoramic view of the complex of buildings stretching along the river banks. The buildings indicated the various decades of their construction, and, why not? The company made its first ax in 1826 in what was reputedly the "first ax factory in the United States."

I found Clair M. Elston, who has headed the old firm for many years, to be as proud of the company as he was cognizant of its history, which is not always the case with the high brass. But Elston just happens to be "a fourth generation Collins man." He said that his company was founded by brothers Samuel W. and David C. Collins, nephews of David Watkinson, a noted iron merchant of Hartford, who did well in his business and was inspired to give the reference library that bore his name in the Wadsworth Atheneum in Hartford and since 1952 has been a part of the Trinity College Library Collections.

Doubtless encouraged by their iron-dealing uncle, the Collins boys, together with a cousin, William Wells, took over an old grist mill in the town of South Canton, Connecticut, and started to make axes. In that time, 130 years ago, when you wanted an ax you made it yourself, said Mr. Elston, or got a blacksmith to do the job. The Collins boys quickly discovered a vigorous demand for their product. And in 1831, they received a single order from New York for 1,500 dozen axes.

So vast an order startled the Collins brothers. It called for prompt and radical action. One of the boys took off at once to seek blacksmiths and other workers in metal throughout New England. The other two partners started to build forty-odd houses for workmen near the factory. Among these early employees was a mechanic, Elisha K. Root, who was to become factory superintendent, then chief advisor to the Collinses, before he returned to Hartford to head Colt's Patent Fire Arms Manufacturing Company.

The Collins management must have kept up with the times. Within four years after founding, they quit cutting trees for charcoal and introduced Lehigh coal to Yankee industry. As early as 1829, ". . . we altered our bell hour from twelve to ten hours." They subsidized a four-horse stage from the Albany turnpike to run regularly through what was already named Collinsville, to Hartford; and won a post office which, for the next quarter of a century, used a cancellation in the outline form of a Collins Company Ax. (Not bad for a "naive" period.)

Then early in the 1850s, machetes were added to the Collins line, and soon were pushing axes for first place, as they are more than a century later when, as Mr. Elston said, "in a score of countries, plantation workers ask for 'a Collins' when they want a machete." It was from Collinsville, too, that in 1859 John Brown obtained pikes for use at Harpers Ferry. Only a couple of years later, the Collins Company began delivering thousands of bayonets to the makers of the Springfield, Sharps, and Colt muskets and rifles.

The Hitchcock chair story begins in 1818, when Lambert Hitchcock, a Yankee cabinet-maker set up shop in the hamlet of Barkhamstead, Connecticut, some 12 miles north of Collinsville, and started making chairs. Even in that day of superb handcraftsmen, his product was so good that within three years he was employing fifty men. By 1826 he had more than a hundred workmen in a new brick factory, three stories high, topped with a cupola, and the new post office took the name of Hitchcocksville. For another forty years the chairs went forth in increasing numbers to Hartford, then by ship, post road, and railroad to the world.

The Middle Road

The Hitchcock products had a distinctive design. You could have them with rush or cane or wooden seats, and their patterns of decoration, using black and red and gilt stencils, were called Turtle, Crown, Pillow, and Federal Eagle. These were applied with unusual care. And so, one imagines, was the stencil of warranty by L. Hitchcock, Hitchcocksville, Connecticut.

When Lambert Hitchcock died in 1852, his brother-in-law partner, Arba Alford, took charge of the business for twelve years, then sold the factory to a firm engaged in making carpenters' rulers. At about this time began the confusion of mail with Hotchkissville, and the name of the village at the Hitchcock factory was changed to Riverton. It also began to fade as first one concern, then another failed to find the right product to take the place of Hitchcock chairs.

By 1946, Riverton was long since a ghostly village, the Hitchcock factory a melancholy relic. Not a chair had come out its doors in eighty-two years, when it caught the eye of young John T. Kenney, a native of Northampton, Massachusetts, who had become a successful Hartford merchant. Though his retail stores dealt in quality shoes for men and women, Kenney was familiar with Hitchcock chairs. Since before he could remember, they had been sought by antique dealers and collectors. He took over the echoing factory at Riverton, spent two years restoring it and in locating furniture craftsmen, and by Thanksgiving 1948, the first chairs since 1864 came from the original old plant of Lambert Hitchcock.

So, I went to Riverton to see what the imaginative John Kenney had been doing there with his Hitchcock Chair Company. The three-story main plant of painted brick, with ell and nostalgic cupola, faces the road just before you cross the Farmington River to the excellent Riverton Inn, formerly the Ives Tavern of staging days. The factory stands handsomely white against the green of lawn and trees. Inside were 150 employees engaged in making Hitchcock chairs and cabinet furniture, no few of them, men and women, handweaving the rush seats that are still popular. The company maintains market showrooms in Chicago and other Western cities.

When I was at Riverton, President Kenney had just returned

from Texas, where he had installed a showroom in wildly-growing Dallas. Six-feet-five, dynamic and personable, he even looks like the kind of man who would and could and did take over an abandoned and boarded-up plant that was sinking back into the scenery, and revive the honored name of "L. HITCHCOCK. HITCHCOCKS-VILLE. CONN. WARRANTED," that is stamped on each of the thousands of quality chairs and other furniture that have been going out from old Hitchcocksville every year for the past decade and a half. As we returned to Hartford and the Post Road, I reflected that the Hitchcock story is one of the most heart-warming I had met with; while that of Collinsville, with a record of continuous production for 135 years, is as remarkable as anything in New England industry.

Leaving Hartford to resume the Middle Road to New Haven, we came first to Wethersfield, which one guidebook calls a "suburb of Hartford on a plain along the west bank of the Connecticut River." I can think of Wethersfield only as a distinctive entity, a rather serene village with a main street of fine old houses, several of which are particularly distinguished by their associations with history. The town was settled in 1634, a year ahead of Hartford, by a group of adventurous men from Massachusetts.

That we came into old Wethersfield by the Silas Deane Highway indicated that the damaged reputation of the town's longtime leading citizen and member of the Continental Congress, who had died in disgrace and in exile, had been "cleared unto honor." I had the good fortune to find the Silas Deane House, 202 Main Street, under repair, and during the lunch hour, walked in to admire the handsomely proportioned rooms and hallway, and the truly elegant staircase.

Right next door was the Webb House, called Hospitality Hall and now maintained by the Society of Colonial Dames. Though on his first visit to Wethersfield, in 1775, Washington had slept in the Deane home, on his next call, in May 1781, he, together with Rochambeau, held council for four days in the Webbs' north parlor, making final plans for the joint action resulting in the Battle of Yorktown and war's end. Across Main Street is the splendid "First

The Middle Road

Church of Christ in Wethersfield, Congregational, Est. 1634, Rev. Keith M. Jones." It is of eighteenth-century brick, has an open belfry and a particularly graceful spire.

These old structures are merely a start on the town's architectural and historic treasures. By actual count, there are twelve more old homes or buildings in Wethersfield that warrant descriptive plaques, including the present home of the warden of the Connecticut State Prison, built in 1774 for one of the prominent Welles family. Nearby is the site of the home of Governor Thomas Welles.

Wethersfield was settled early enough to suffer a massacre (nine dead) by the Pequot Indians, and to suffer from the witchcraft hysteria (three hanged). It took the lead as an inland port when, in 1649, the first Connecticut-built ship, *The Tryall,* was launched here. Exports included furs, bricks, leghorn-type hats, brooms, plows, tobacco, and for one period, "more than one million bunches of onions annually."

In the town's new public library we soon discovered, through the efforts of Mrs. Ellis Backman, reference librarian, that "Ancient Wethersfield" had a typically Yankee background of industrial ingenuity. "It was a Wethersfield man, Levi Dickinson, who made the first broom from broom corn, in 1797," wrote town historian Henry R. Stiles. "He began at the same time to cultivate the corn, native in the East Indies, and it soon became an important industry here and in other Connecticut Valley towns. In 1845, three local factories manufactured 5,500 brooms. Large crops of broom corn were grown here as late as 1880." Then, there was the charming Miss Sophia Woodhouse of Wethersfield and her leghorn hats. (In several Post-road villages I had come across references to leghorn bonnets.)

"Miss Woodhouse, who married Gurdon Welles in 1819," chattily begins Historian George S. Roberts, "should not be passed by. Miss Woodhouse made the bonnets of red-top and spear-grass which grew in Wethersfield (her shop was in the present Titus Buck Place, 583 Main Street), using the upper portion of the stalks. In 1821, the Society of Arts, in London, England, awarded her a prize of twenty guineas for a bonnet she had made of those grasses. In the same year, she was granted a patent by the United States. The color and fineness of her hats was said to be superior to the best leghorn."

All in all, ancient Wethersfield turned out to be one of the most friendly and interesting stops we made on the Boston Post Road. The town even shared in one of the greatest mysteries of eighteenth-century England. It concerned a London housemaid, Elizabeth Canning, who in 1753 disappeared, only to return home four weeks later, with the story that she had been kidnapped. It is much too long to go into here, other than to say that after a sensational trial which made her known the world over—even to Henry Fielding and Voltaire, who wrote pamphlets about her—Elizabeth was convicted of "perjury wilful and corrupt, and sentenced in 1753 to be transported to His Majesty's Colonies in America."

Wethersfield was the scene of her exile. For several years she lived in and was later married from one of those great old houses on elm-shaded Broad Street. (Probably 249, said Mrs. Backman.) London did not hear of her again until in 1773 the *Connecticut Courant,* for June 22 to 29, arrived from His Majesty's Colonies in America. Said an item in that issue of the periodical:

> *Hartford, June 22. Last week died very suddenly, at Wethersfield, Mrs. Elizabeth Treat, wife of Mr. Treat, formerly the famous Elizabeth Canning.*

We drove through Rocky Hill, in former days the chief port of Wethersfield, on the way to Berlin. A tourist guidebook called attention to the fact that Berlin was the birthplace of Emma Hart Willard and Almira Hart Lincoln Phelps, "Educators and Authors." We found two houses in the village with signs, one "About 1790, Jesse Hart," the other a positive "1786, Jesse Hart"; but getting a line on the Hart women was something else. We had to hunt, and had all but given up when we stopped to ask men engaged in haying the roadside. As if they had been merely waiting for someone to inquire, a man with a scythe stepped across the road, and with several strokes into the tall grass uncovered a boulder telling of Emma who, among other things, founded the Troy Female Seminary. She also wrote a poem, "Rocked in the Cradle of the Deep," which, when set to music, became a favorite solo number for generations of bass singers. I thanked the alert man with the scythe, and here thank the Berlin Chapter of the DAR, for the plaque (1910) on the boulder. Years ago, I had written about Emma Willard, to say she had undergone enough ridicule and persecution to have broken most women.

I had wanted to visit Berlin (and Rocky Hill, too) for another reason. The persuasive Storrs Lee, the historian, had convinced me that of all the numerous claims to the contrary, Berlin, Connecticut, was the original depot of the Yankee Peddler, America's eighteenth-century merchant on foot, whose heirs, and peers, were the Jews and Armenians who carried on into the first decade of the twentieth century.

It is true that peddlers with packs had been making the rounds of the Post Road villages long before 1740, but this was the date when "Berlin introduced a new economic order and a new psychology of salesmanship." In that year, tinsmiths William and Edward Pattison arrived from Ireland with a large quantity of tinned sheet iron, and started cutting, shaping and soldering a handsome line of tin dinner plates, tin cups and saucers.

Nothing remotely like these dishes had been seen in Connecticut, or in America. Their flashing brilliance was stunning. The beholder was quite helpless to do anything but buy, or barter, for these irresistible new wares, and the Pattisons could scarcely keep up with the demand. In neighboring Rocky Hill, Thomas Danforth, pewterer and village storekeeper, "remaindered" his line of pewter Yankee notions and stocked up with new tinware until his shelves and counters were blinding. Now he began to advertise that his store was "Headquarters of Peddlers," and went on to open stores in Philadelphia and other cities.

Back in Berlin, the Pattison brothers were hard put to get sufficient tinned sheet iron to fill orders. They soon had scores of young apprentices hammering away at long workbenches—pans, pots, pails, candlesticks and sconces, teapots, lanterns. Even serious young Emma Hart was impressed. She composed a free advertisement in rhyme for one of the Pattison's tin platters, that began, "Oh, what's that lordly dish so rare/ that glitters forth in splendorous glare?" The fad for tinware became a mania.

The ingenious Pattisons showed the peddlers how to load their trunks and shoulder-packs: Into shining coffeepots were crammed spools of thread, papers of pins, cards of buttons, cakes of shaving soap; bolts of ribbon could be stuffed into pepper boxes and tea caddies; other pieces of tinware hid calico, handkerchiefs, scarves. When a Yankee Peddler left Berlin or Rocky Hill, he was *loaded*.

They had gimmicks, too. During the Revolution, soldiers tired of fighting, or even of discipline, went AWOL, being careful to wear a cockade in their headgear (it served as a pass or furlough) and took to the post roads with an outsize knapsack of notions. They called themselves Yankee Peddlers.

Timothy Dwight, president of Yale College at New Haven, enjoyed dining off the tin plates in private homes and public houses, but he noted a steady moral decay of the peddlers. Many young men entered this business with modesty and principle, he observed. Soon enough, "Their sobriety is exchanged for cunning; their honesty for imposition . . . no course of life tends more rapidly to eradicate every moral feeling."

Steadily the great horde of Yankee Peddlers increased their cunning until their kind was ridiculed and burlesqued in a literary character, *Sam Slick of Slickville* (1835), a Yankee of Yankees, peddler of Connecticut clocks, who vied with lightning-rod salesmen in disrepute. Storekeepers complained to legislatures; and in Connecticut and Massachusetts the itinerants were all but taxed out of existence. The Yankees were soon outnumbered by first-generation Jewish peddlers and, later, Armenians. But not before much of the United States had come to believe the legend of the Yankee Peddler whose line of goods included wooden nutmegs that were never identified otherwise than as a product of *Connecticut* manufacture.

It is possible that neighboring Middletown made some of the

The Middle Road

Yankee notions that went into the packs of peddlers along with the overwhelming tinware of Berlin. Yet Middletown's traditions appear to be more in the academic line, and in other parts of the country it is known chiefly for Wesleyan University, founded as a nonsectarian institution in 1831 by the Methodist Conference. Due to chance, this institution opened its doors with a plant already built for something named "the American Literary, Scientific, and Military Academy," organized by Captain Alden Partridge, former West Point superintendent. Middletown citizens provided funds to rear two stone structures in 1825, but nothing more happened, and Captain Partridge, with his plans and charter, took off for Norwich, Vermont, where Norwich Military Academy arose on the west bank of the Connecticut River opposite Hanover, New Hampshire. In 1866, fire razed the Academy building, and a year later the school, now Norwich University, moved again, to Northfield, Vermont, where it has flourished.

The two brownstone buildings in Middletown, still vacant in 1831, together with the grounds, were a bargain at $33,000 for the organizers of Wesleyan University, a going concern from the day it opened. The stone for these buildings came from the quarries of Portland, across the river from Middletown; and so did a great deal more of the same stuff that gave its name to an era—The Brown Decades, or simply Brownstone. For a whole generation no new millionaire in New York was content until he and his family were residing behind a facade of the massive elegance that came in large part from Connecticut and much of that from Portland. In a continuous procession down the river went barges loaded with brownstone, bound for cities along the Eastern seaboard until Manhattan's Fifth Avenue from the one end to the other was veneered with what Webster came to describe, singly, as a "brownstone front—a house with front of brownstone, a mark of wealth in the middle of the 19th century."

We did not visit Portland on the Post Road tour, but a friend told me most of the Portland quarries are "now as dead as the dinosaurs whose tracks the quarry men keep turning up in their blasting." They did not die, however, until they had put their mark on Eastern

United States, and in lesser degree on cities as distant as Seattle, Portland, and San Francisco. Nor has it yet been wholly obliterated, despite the great swinging iron ball of the wreckers, enemy of traditionalists, which most up-and-coming Americans seem to consider the very pendulum of Progress.

As we swung south into Durham, and at a sharp turn up a hill, we came suddenly upon a factory of the Lyman Gun Sight Corporation, of which until then I had never heard. On the hilltop was a great handsome mansion, which a sign said was the old John Lyman place, upholding a tradition of early New England industry, namely, that the boss of a mill or factory ought to live where he had the plant constantly under his eye. Later, from friends in Meriden, I learned that the Lyman Gun Sight outfit attracts wealthy riflemen from all over the world who come here to have their special rifles equipped with ivory and gold bead sights.

What I wanted to see in Durham, however, were two things. One was the birthplace of Moses Austin, whose plan led directly to the settlement of Texas by his son, Stephen Austin, for whom the capital city was named. The modest house, dating from 1743, was on the main highway. A sign said "Tourists Taken." Then, I wanted to find Allyn's Brook, and did. It crossed the highway not far from the Austin place.

In an old account of this section of Connecticut, I had read that one of the worst disasters on the Boston Post Road had occurred on February 21, 1822, at the bridge over Allyn's Brook. The stream was in flood. The coach driver was cautioned about the bridge, whose abutments appeared to be seriously in danger. There was one type of stage driver who did not welcome any advice from ordinary people, which was to say, passengers. This particular driver "answered the caution with bravado." He started to cross, the bridge gave way, and "a number of passengers were drowned."

This is neither good nor complete reporting; I had hoped that in Durham, despite the passage of 138 years, there might be some local historian who could fill me in with details. But there was none. We went to the spot. Running west, Allyn's Brook comes out of the woods, forms a deep pond, then passes under a big cement culvert which supports the highway. I stood a while to ponder the scene as it may have been in 1822, and calculated that the coach could well have fallen 20 feet from the Post Road into the flooding stream. Noting a woman in the yard of an attractive house near the disaster spot, I went to explain my reason for loitering, and asked if she had ever heard of the accident. She hadn't heard, and was obviously shaken that anybody should have asked about anything that happened in 1822. As I left, she repeated her astonishment and made it sound like an indictment: "In eighteen twenty-two!" she said.

On to Meriden, where we called on Blanch and Wayne Smith, old friends and publishers of the *Daily Record*, asking to be put in touch with somebody in Wallingford who could guide us to any relics of that outpost of Oneida Community. They arranged matters. Then we drove on for a fine dinner in the Yankee Silversmith Inn, considerably richer, I am sure, than was the Perfectionist diet in old Wallingford, and a night in a motel at least near, if not on, what used to be the Boston Post Road.

A guidebook identified Wallingford with Choate School, "an exclusive preparatory school for boys"; and also as one of the foremost centers for manufacture of silverware and Britannia ware (an alloy of tin, antimony, and copper). Robert Wallace is mentioned here in connection with plated ware, but there is nothing to indicate Wallingford as the place where the "Christian Communists" of Prophet John Humphrey Noyes got into the silverware business, which was why I wanted to visit Wallingford.

Back in the 1840s, Noyes, a refugee from Vermont, had founded Oneida Community in upstate New York, generally considered a group of eccentrics given to free love, birth control, and other deplorable practices. Despite this, they flourished and grew prosperous by their manufacture of the finest steel traps in the world. (The Hudson's Bay Company of Canada was their largest customer.) In about 1851, Henry Allen, a farmer of Wallingford, had become so convinced that the Perfectionist doctrines expounded by

Hartford to New Haven

Prophet Noyes were both right and rational, that he adopted them for his own family, and invited others to join in founding a Perfectionist colony.

Some forty persons, including a few from Oneida, did join, and Allen donated his farm and buildings for the experiment. More land was bought. Several buildings for communal living were erected. So was a factory. Prophet Noyes himself visited the new colony, and moved Oneida's publishing business to Wallingford. By the early 1870s, the Wallingford group started to manufacture large quantities of plated spoons for the Meriden Britannia Company. Knives and forks were soon added to the line, and Oneida Community, Ltd., built a factory at Niagara Falls, New York, to manufacture what became a sensationally successful line under style of Community Silver.

Wallingford meanwhile had another use. This was as a sort of "disciplinary barracks," to help in breaking up the "special" or "idolatrous" attachments between members at the main colony at Oneida. One or the other partner of the romance was sent to the Connecticut branch to cool off. This may explain the unusual number of young Oneidans who were graduated from Yale Medical School, in nearby New Haven.

On our visit to Wallingford, jovial Dr. Craig gave us a hearty welcome, and proceeded to guide us past Community Pond, where the Perfectionists got their water-power to run their newspaper press, and to make their spoons. High on a hill above the pond still stood the four-story structure that had been Perfectionist headquarters for the Wallingford community. Dr. Craig also took us to meet Mrs. Clara Newell, who lives in the Masonic Home. She was working on a manuscript dealing with Wallingford and the Perfectionists, many of whose descendants still live there.

Apparently, the name of Community Pond is the sole reminder in Wallingford of the Perfectionists. There is no plaque on their former headquarters here, which, in any case, is merely a boxlike house four stories high. Yet, there remains in Wallingford one structure I should like to buy and move to some safer place as an incomparable relic of a period that seems more remote than anything else I saw that day. This is the Wallingford station of the New York, New Haven, & Hartford Railroad, a wondrous depot complete with mansard, gingerbread, and curlicue.

Is there no individual or group in the neighborhood to preserve this perfect piece of a railroad period when Grant was President, locomotives came in three colors, and architects dreamed of openwork patterns in jigsaw?

There was one more place I wanted to see before we reached New Haven. This was the crossroads hamlet of Clintonville. Here for many years was the tremendously busy factory of the Kickapoo Indian Medicine Company which employed some 300 people who manufactured Kickapoo Sagwa, Kickapoo Oil, and a complete line of remedies good for man or beast. Although I knew the factory had been torn down several years ago, I wanted to see the place, and did. The site is still vacant, on Connecticut 22, not far from the Pond Hill Road in North Haven, and near the grass-grown tracks of the old Airline Railway, New Haven to Willimantic, over which in the great days of therapy, came the hogsheads of rum and of molasses that constituted the formula for Kickapoo Indian Cough Syrup.

Because champions in any line of endeavor deserve better of history than New Haven and Connecticut have accorded the Kickapoo Indian Medicine Company, I trust that some seeker of a Ph.D. at Yale will consider the now misty firm of Healy and Bigelow, of Clintonville, who organized this giant of the medicine-show business, and retired with fortunes.

We finished the Middle Post Road tour at the edge of New Haven, then headed back to Boston, to start on the Lower Road.

Chapter 20

The Lower Road:
Boston to New Haven
(By 1st Route)

"Attleborough, Providence, Scituate,
Norwich & New London"

WE COME NOW to the third and last of the post roads between Boston and New Haven. We are facing south toward
Rhode Island, which is not only the smallest state; there is perhaps none other so broken into segments by the Atlantic Ocean.
This may account for the several stage routes that were needed to

pick up the mails and care for the passengers before leaving Rhode Island at Westerly, then to follow the Connecticut shore almost to the Hudson River and New York City.

Gaine's Almanac of the 1770s refers to the Lower Road as the *Old* Boston Post Road, and lists the stage as leaving Boston by way of Dedham, Wrentham, then Providence. Yet this was by no means the only route taken by Lower Road stages for New York. And let me be wary *now* of writers-of-letters who delight in "correcting" the spelling of names of towns that may well have been changed twice in the past two hundred years, or the moving of a road that has already been moved half-a-dozen times and is now not even in its original township. Above all, let no pseudo-purist tell me just where the Boston Post Road made its way through Rhode Island or, for that matter, elsewhere. Far too much has happened to towns and roads since 1700, or thereabout.

In 1826, the *Farmer's Almanac,* Boston, compiled by Robert B. Thomas, listed three important routes all on the Lower Post Road through Rhode Island. One was by Dedham, Attleboro, Providence, Scituate, and Coventry, to Norwich and New London, Connecticut. Another left Boston by Dedham and Walpole, then quaintly, "over Seekonk, through Rehoboth," and into Rhode Island to Warren, Bristol, and "Ferry House to Newport." The third route went by Dorchester, Milton (Baker's Chocolate and Bent's Water Crackers), through Canton and other Massachusetts towns including "Swansey" (now Swansea), to enter Rhode Island at Warren and Bristol, then "over the bridge to Newport." There was nothing beyond Newport but water. There you had to ferry to Jamestown, on Conanicut Island, in Narragansett Bay, and so to the mainland again at Kingston.

So, if the order in which towns appear, in the Lower Post Road tour of this book, seems occasionally out of sequence, let the reader bear up as best he can. I found no few of them among the most rewarding stops imaginable. One should keep in mind that the goal, so to speak, of the Lower Post Road, is New Haven, where it is joined by the Upper and Middle Roads that have come down the Connecticut River from Springfield and Hartford. The shortest of the three Lower Roads to New Haven is that by way of Dedham to Providence, then west through Scituate and Coventry, Rhode Island, on to Norwich, Connecticut, and to New London on the Connecticut shore.

Having again passed through Dedham, where the Parting Stone used to stand, we took the lefthand road into Norwood, about which I knew little, save that it, together with neighboring Walpole and nearby Wrentham and Attleboro, had been much harassed when King Philip's painted braves came through here in 1675. In Norwood, however, a later war is recalled by the legend cut in a boulder on a lawn:

> *Near this spot*
> *Captain Aaron Guild*
> *On April 19, 1775*
> *Left plow in furrow, oxen standing*
> *And departing for Lexington*
> *Arrived in time to fire upon*
> *The retreating British*

Though this is an eminent libel upon the British, who were *not* retreating at Lexington, but advancing to Concord, I was delighted to learn that Israel Putnam was not the only patriot whose urgency for battle was such as to leave his plow in a furrow. Since early schooldays my vision of Old Put had him, musket on shoulder, waving good-by to the plow and unfinished furrow on his Connecticut farm, heading for Boston. It was good now to share the legend with brave Captain Guild of Norwood, Massachusetts.

Along this Lower Road, there seemed to be striking contrasts of concentrated industry and the open spaces of undeveloped country. Here and there, between factories along the Neponset River, were spots of wild marshes of reeds, and cattails, swarming with red-winged blackbirds. It was easy to forget that in this neighborhood is a sizable share of the specialty jewelry manufacture in the United States, and also an immense plant making roofing materials.

In Attleboro, I learned about but did not see a slate monument erected about 1640, in Plainfield Center, to mark the line between Plymouth Colony and Massachusetts Bay Colony, and was told that originally this marker carried a warning, thus: "Beyond this Line Roger Williams may not go." Which was also notice we were not far from Providence Plantations.

The best known of the thirteen members of the Proprietors Company for Providence Plantations, Roger Williams, had already tried both Massachusetts Bay and Plymouth before he fled Salem, in 1636, under banishment for preaching seditious doctrines, to settle in what is now East Providence on the east side of the Seekonk River. Within a year or so came other exiles, Anne Hutchinson among them, to settle on what the Indians called Aquidneck, an island in Narragansett Bay, and was renamed the Isle of Rhodes, or Rhode Island. The settlement itself was called Portsmouth. By 1647, the new colony got under legislative way with four towns voting— Providence, Warwick, Portsmouth, and Newport.

All of these pioneer settlers were dissenters from the Puritan church of Massachusetts Bay. And though a small group had founded the first Baptist Society in America, in 1639, Williams soon left it to become a Seeker; accepting no organized religion during his lifetime. He also sought to keep the new colony free from the doctrinal troubles that had long since beset the rest of New England. For the Rhode Island Charter he declared to "hold forth a lively experiment that a most flourishing civil state may stand and best be maintained with full liberty in religious concernments."

Little wonder if both Plymouth and Massachusetts Bay wanted

Boston to New Haven (By 1st Route)

Roger Williams to stay south of that deadline marker near Attleboro.

Twenty-odd years ago I spent some days in Providence, as a reporter, getting material for an article in a national magazine about New England industry. I liked the town, but was confused until I discovered it was much like Boston, which I knew fairly well, in one respect: It was largely an agglomeration of towns and villages which long ago developed around a local industry, or even a single factory; a few of these old villages have maintained a personality that still sets them apart from the adjoining community. On older maps many of these villages appeared as separate entities along the post roads. On today's motor maps they are clustered solidly as Greater Providence—Cranston, Crompton, Coventry, Anthony, Rumford, Greenwich, the Warwicks, Fiskville, Arctic, Arkright, Lippit, and others. In them for many years were made lace, velvet, cottons, woolens, and much else, including jewelry, and Rumford baking powder, known from Alaska to Patagonia.

Let us not forget Perry Davis who, at 74 High Street, in the center of Providence, manufactured after 1840 the Painkiller that bore his name. No captain who made port at Providence failed to call at 74 High Street, to pass the time of day with Mr. Davis and leave a generous order for this balm; and thus it "conquered its way around the world before the end of the century." (It is still made, in New York, but now is called Perry Davis Liniment (Painkiller Brand), yet on each bottle, as of yore, is the likeness of Mr. Davis, a man of distinguished mien, who peers forth from the antique steel engraving with a serene if somewhat austere countenance. Beneath the portrait is the legend: Alcohol 51%.)

The folklore of Providence has it that among the thousands of French-Canadians attracted to the textile and other mills in the city's orbit, all or nearly all of the town's pioneer industrialists, merchants, shipping men, and even educators were named Brown. Though "Brown" approaches "Smith" in the category of Anglo-Saxon families, there does seem to have been an unusually large number of prominent Browns in Providence history, including Nicholas (1769–1841) for whom the former Rhode Island Col-

183

lege was renamed Brown University. (In the *Dictionary of American Biography* there are seventy-four prominent Americans named Brown, a good many of them identified with either Providence or Rhode Island, or both. In the Rhode Island volume of the American Guide Series are twenty-two Browns connected with Providence. The folklore of the mill workers is understandable.)

Getting back to the Boston Post Road: The list of towns on the Lower Road in 1826 naturally included Providence, and the name of the recommended innkeeper was Rice. This was Henry Rice whose Golden Ball Inn stood at 159 Benefit Street, opened in 1783. Four stories high, it had a "commanding position" on a hill, and became immediately popular with townspeople as a social meeting place. It was Washington's headquarters in 1790, when as President he made his first visit to Rhode Island. (He had been in Newport, during the war, to confer with Rochambeau.) On his inauguration tour of New England (1789), he purposely did not visit Rhode Island, which did not ratify the Constitution until May 1790. But in August of that year, he thought best to "make a short tour" of the recalcitrant state, which he did, landing first in Newport, August 17, where the official salute was fired at the fort. He was escorted to his lodgings by the usual "principal inhabitants," and later was given a very elegant dinner at the town hall. Next morning at nine o'clock "the President and his company embarked for Providence." This was the occasion when Landlord Rice entertained at his imposing Golden Ball Inn.

I do not know what route the stage for New Haven and New York took on its way west and south from the Golden Ball. Several old maps I dug up indicate it could have been by way of Scituate or Coventry, both of which we visited and are now virtually suburbs of Providence. Yet the maps stirred memories of the Rhode Island I learned about many years ago in grade school: What set it apart was that both Providence and Newport were marked with the as-

Boston to New Haven (By 1st Route)

terisk used to designate capitals of states. In my *Morse's Geography* (1849) a brief question-and-answer section has this to say:

> Q. Name the capitals of Rhode Island.
> A. Providence and Newport.

Apparently, the two cities took turns at the job for many years, until 1901, after which the new State House in Providence became the state's only capitol. (Something similar occurred in Connecticut, with New Haven and Hartford, but I do not recall maps which indicated two capitals.)

On resuming the Lower Road tour, we struck out for Norwich, Connecticut, detouring a bit through Plainfield, to see the town where C. L. Tiffany, the great Yankee jeweler, got such formal education as he had, at Plainfield Academy. Somehow or other, there were two highly successful Yankee businessmen whose occupations have always struck me as out of character. One was the native Vermonter, Louis Sherry, who became one of New York City's most elegant and famous restaurateurs; and Charles Lewis Tiffany, born in Killingly, Connecticut, and founder of the most famous jewel shop on Fifth Avenue. Neither was born on the Boston Post Road, but Tiffany got his schooling here in Plainfield, on the Lower Road, a few miles from his birthplace, hence "belongs" in any account of its outstanding Yankees. The old Academy (founded about 1778) still stands on its original site in Plainfield.

We moved on to Norwich, about which I had done sufficient reading to reflect that if visitors to Providence might come to believe Rhode Island's chief city was largely the work of pioneers named Brown, the same might be said in regard to pioneers named Huntington and the city of Norwich, Connecticut. In the Connecticut Index of Historic Houses are no less than half a dozen relics identified with Norwich Huntingtons named Jabez, Jedediah, Joshua, Samuel, and Simon. Among them and their close kinsmen were merchants, bishops, a university president, a physician, a novelist, a painter, a governor of Connecticut, a governor of Ohio, and a signer of the Declaration.

Although Norwich seems not to have been originally a regular stop on the Boston Post Road, it was one of the earliest railroad towns in Connecticut. It flourished mightily as a terminal city of the Norwich & Worcester, with the added impetus of a steamboat line from New York to Allyn's Point, 8 miles down-river from Norwich, reached when the Thames was frozen, by the special stagecoach line of the incomparable Ginery Twichell.

Before the railroad came, Norwich was served by a sort of alternate route of the Lower Post Road from Providence. That is the way we came to the now busy industrial city and shopping center of eastern Connecticut. Because I had read a few rich lines about her native town by Lydia Howard Huntley Sigourney (1791–1865), I was prepared to see Norwich "like a citadel, guarded by parapets of rock, and embosomed in an amphitheatre of hills whose summits mark the horizon with a waving line of forest green." Although I missed that waving line of forest green, Norwich's northwest hillside section is proof of both age and wealth. From Georgian through Greek Revival and to purest Mansard and General Grant, the mansions indicate that citizens of this old town made a good deal of money and were not averse to keeping up with generations of Joneses.

As for Mrs. Lydia Sigourney, by 1830 she was pouring a steady stream of prose and verse into twenty magazines. Ten years later she was widely known both here and abroad, and was possibly the most prosperous female author in the United States. Much of this magazine tonnage was later processed into books, which, in time, numbered sixty-seven. Among her many verses dealing with disasters on land and sea—a favorite subject—one had to do with the tragedy of a local steamship, the *Atlantic,* lost in Long Island Sound, November 25, 1846. Entitled "The Bell of the Wreck," this poem called for a program note: "The bell of the *Atlantic,* being supported by portions of the wreck and a contiguous rock, continued to

toll, swept by wind and surge, the requiem of the dead." Then came
the pitiless stanzas:

> *Toll, toll, toll*
> *Thou bell by billows swung,*
> *And night and day thy warning words*
> *Repeat with mournful tongue!*
>
> *Toll for the queenly boat*
> *Wreck'd on yon rocky shore;*
> *Sea-wind is in her palace-halls,*
> *She rides the surge no more.*

Not bad by any standard of the period. But the theme of most
of her writing was death; and the inevitable regularity with which
her poetic tribute followed the demise of any prominent person
caused a wisecracking critic to declare that "Mrs. Sigourney has
added a new terror to death."

There was no Mrs. Sigourney to bid us welcome to New London,
at the mouth of the Thames, and its sister town across the river,
Groton. We were back on the original Lower Post Road, and we
were also back again in the American Revolution orbit. Here on
September 6, 1781, New London was attacked by British troops,
led by Benedict Arnold (a native of the town up the river we had
just left), whose loyalty had only recently been purchased by Sir
Henry Clinton. The redcoats set the town afire, then attacked Fort
Griswold in Groton. Arnold is said to have watched as the British
Regulars slaughtered many of the patriot militiamen after they surrendered. It is perhaps with more justification than usual in such
affairs, that the marker at the site of Fort Griswold declares the
engagement to have been a *massacre*. In any case, I am quite content to leave it that way, so far as the British commander is concerned.

Before, during, and after the Revolution, men of New London

and Groton were notable mariners, and shipbuilders. The lower river was lined with their yards and warehouses. They were early in the West Indian trade, and among the first whalers. The two towns claim that their number of whaleships exceeded that of Nantucket, and was only one less than the New Bedford fleet.

There are two museums in Groton. One is at Fort Griswold State Park, which has a whaling collection and also relics of the Revolution. The other is sponsored by the Electric Boat Company and is devoted to submarine craft. Nearby Mystic is noted for "Mystic Seaport," a reconstructed village with a whaling museum, sail lofts, and rope walks, and is a major tourist attraction.

Both Groton and New London seemed swarming with sailors of the United States Coast Guard Academy, the "Annapolis" of this Federal branch which, in earlier days, was called the Revenue Cutter Service.

Groton and New London brought to mind a district in the old Western Reserve in Ohio called the Firelands, sometimes known as the Sufferers' Lands. This half a million acres was set aside by Connecticut in 1792 for the benefit of citizens of Connecticut shore towns who suffered immense property losses in destruction by British troops. Beside the two towns we were visiting, they included the several Havens: Norwalk, Danbury, Greenwich, and Ridgefield. It was in Ohio, not Connecticut, where I learned that though the latter state had done a generous and logical thing, in the Firelands matter, it was thirty years before they were properly surveyed and open for settlement. And the Firelands settled very slowly indeed. Forty-year-old men who lost their homes in the war were now in their seventies, rather old to migrate. But their descendants at last moved into the new country; and one of the Firelands settlements was named Norwalk, for the martyred village back home.

Chapter 21

The Lower Road:
Boston to New Haven
(By 2nd Route)

"Over Seekonk, through Rehoboth, &
The Ferry to Newport"

AT NEW LONDON ended the first of the three stage routes
used on the Lower Post Road to New York. Now, back in
Boston, begins the second Lower route. Like the first it starts by
way of Dedham, Walpole, and Attleboro, as if its goal were Providence, but then it veers east at Pawtucket, Rhode Island, to cross

the Seekonk River into Massachusetts again, and after a stop at Rehoboth, returns to Rhode Island.

In a stage guide for 1826—corrected to 1825, it says—the listing for the Lower Post Road describes this route with what, due in part to the felicity of place names, is virtually a poetic invocation to travel. What tourist of the 1960s would fail to find an appeal in a route that promised in so many words to take him, "Over Seekonk, Through Rehoboth, and to The Ferry House for Newport"?

The route appealed to me, even if the meaning of "Over Seekonk" was not at all clear until I studied a map of Greater Providence to find the Seekonk River on the city's east side, indicating that, as of 1826, the stage did not touch Providence at all, but had turned east, perhaps at what is now Pawtucket, and was heading, surely, as if to go "Through Rehoboth."

I had to go back to Old Bradford's *Of Plimouth Plantation* to learn that the original settlement at Rehoboth was also once called Seekonk, and that Captain John Smith himself had once rallied soldiers there to defend Plymouth Colony against Indians. Bradford gives no reason for the change from Seekonk to Rehoboth. It being a biblical name, perhaps the settlers thought best to remove the obviously pagan flavor of Seekonk. (My Concordance translates Rehoboth merely as "breadth, room." But Rehoboam was one of King Solomon's sons.)

On the 1826 stage route, Rehoboth was the only stop mentioned between Attleboro and Warren which, with Bristol, comprise most of the population on Mt. Hope Peninsula. Warren was first settled, in 1632, from Plymouth, as a trading post. This was the region where the great Massasoit had one of his several homes. He was the all-powerful Sachem of the Wampanoags, King of the Country, who visited Plymouth in 1621, and until his death was a faithful friend to the English settlers. One of his sons, however, became the much-feared King Philip, who began his war by wiping out the Swansee settlement.

At the close of Philip's war, which seems to have made almost as much history in New England as did the War of the Revolution, Plymouth claimed all the lands around Mt. Hope, and the town of Bristol was founded in 1681. In these colonial times, Warren took the lead. It had organized in 1764 a Baptist Society, and with it the College of Rhode Island which was later moved to Providence, and its name changed, as said, to Brown University.

Men of both Warren and Bristol had a part in the *Gaspee* Affair, which was Rhode Island's counterpart of the Boston Massacre and the Boston Tea Party. The *Gaspee* was the Crown's revenue cutter stationed in Narragansett Bay to hamper Rhode Island's chief industry of the period, which was smuggling. In June 1772 she ran aground, near Warwick, and a fast-ebbing tide left her high.

John Brown, the Providence merchant, acted with commendable speed. Mustering sixty-four men, he put them into longboats, boarded the beached cutter, took off her crew, and set her afire. Presently she blew up, and sank. It created an "incident" that Rhode Islanders still like to claim as the "first battle of the Revolution." The Crown offered a large reward, and John Brown was arrested. But no witnesses could be found. During the war both Warren and Bristol suffered depredations by English and Hessian troops, and there was shooting, burning and pillage.

With the return of peace, the people of Mt. Hope Peninsula resumed their maritime occupations, which already included shipbuilding and slaving. And now began the richest period for New England seaports. It was to last from 1785 to the election of Andrew Jackson in 1828.

During this nearly half a century, the fortunes of Boston and Providence were largely made in the China trade, those of Salem in the East Indies, and those of New Bedford, Nantucket, and New London in whaling. "As for Bristol," declared a member of one of that old port's first families, "almost alone among the seaports, it owed its wealth to the slave trade and privateering, which is only a politer name for piracy, and soon became poor again when the two professions were at last outlawed."

The Lower Road

The deWolf clan of Bristol and environs was as numerous as were the Browns in Providence. Mark Anthony deWolf was their chief. He married into the numerous Potter clan. Then came the Howes, Dimans, Bradfords. These were Yankees who had to wage a perpetual battle between conscience and cupidity. They were generous and skinflint. They were irreverent and pious. They were "antlike for work, catlike for fighting." (Famous among their later generations was DeWolf Hopper, noted actor, and Mark Anthony deWolf Howe, Boston author.)

These God-fearing and God-damning Bristolites were to pass through several golden ages in the first 300 years in Rhode Island. They became fat on the slave trade, then on privateering, and on outright piracy. Then, after decades of doldrums, they sought tardily to enter the "new" Age of Steam by the manufacture of textiles, firearms, and rubber goods. The profits, especially of Bristol slavers, had been enormous, and mansions rose to line Bristol streets.

But the risks, too, were staggering. Nearly all of the great mansions became boarding houses, or saloons with contingent barbershops and poolhalls. And when the last slaver made her last voyage, Bristol and Warren were left swarming with master mariners, able seamen, ships carpenters, and messboys—all of them spoiled for such tame business as the China trade. They didn't like whaling, either.

As privateers in 1861–65, the Mt. Hope mariners had just what they liked. It did not last, and the waterfronts again turned ghostly, until shipowners began registering their vessels in Bolivia, and Bristol boys were happy to sign on as members of crews of the Bolivian Navy. This navy flew the Jolly Roger. But piracy did not endure, and Bristol, loathing every moment of it, was at last forced to work in and live with factories.

When we visited Bristol, to drive down the long street through the center of town, it was lined with fine healthy elms. We noticed that what in the north end were rather modest homes, gradually grew more imposing, then changed into what looked like estates, before we came, not as the old stage schedule had it, to "The Ferry House," but to the bridge across Mt. Hope Bay to the Island of Rhode Island, and the towns of Portsmouth, Middletown, and Newport.

It may be recalled that when the Colony of Rhode Island got under legislative way in 1647, one of its four voting towns was Portsmouth. But this early promise failed to match the growth of Providence, Newport, or even Warwick. It is possible that many of the original settlers, who were known to have pulled up their stakes and moved out of Portsmouth, did so because among the newcomers was the remarkable Anne Hutchinson, the very rebel of rebels.

Anne had been, like Roger Williams, a controversial if not a downright dangerous character from the first. One imagines she was probably hard to get along with, and she is thought to have tried to take over political control of the new settlement, then known as Pocasset. Whatever happened, Anne herself still was not content and soon moved on, this time to Long Island Sound where, at Pelham Bay, she and several of her children were massacred by Indians.

But Newport itself was not without its troubles; and long before the Revolution, a division took place when a sufficient number of its citizens voted to remove a portion of the settlement from Newport Town and incorporate what is still Middletown.

The Revolution went hard with all of this section of the province, that is, the Island of Rhode Island. The British occupied Newport for three years. Battles large and small were fought on the Island, and much property destroyed. One account estimates that about one-fourth of the Island's inhabitants left for other parts. Only Newport recovered and flourished.

We drove into Newport from the north to stop at an information booth to get our bearings. A Mrs. Robbins there was gracious and helpful with a map of Newport and Middletown, which carefully indicates the famous resort's antiquities: Whitehall (1729), the "Old Houses at The Point" (1750), Touro Synagogue (founded 1648, the building dedicated 1765), the town's "Vast Naval Establishments," and at last what Newport actually means to most people who have heard of the place—the estates, invariably known as "cottages," of America's Gilded Age.

Though I had written a sizable book about many of the moguls who had built their incredible cottages at Newport, I knew considerably more about how they made their fortunes than how they spent the money; and I turned to Mr. Cleveland Amory's amusing study, *The Last Resorts,* to learn what they did for and to Newport.

Without a mention of the late Thorstein Veblen, Mr. Amory documented almost every observation of that authority on *The Theory of the Leisure Class,* including the remark that "the canon of reputability must adapt itself to . . . the degree of spiritual maturity of the particular class whose scheme of life it is to regulate." This seemed reasonable enough, and we prepared to set out to see what the canon of reputability was like on Bellevue Avenue.

Before we left the information booth, my eye was taken by what looked like a set of medieval-like ruins, stark against the sky toward the west. I was told only that they were the remains of a recent fire at "the Budlong Mansion." Then, we started our unguided tour of Newport, stopping first near the vast gate of The Breakers, a Vanderbilt property, recently leased by its owner to the Newport Preservation Society for the sum of one dollar, and now open to the public, at $1.50 a throw, for those who want to visit a cottage that may be termed of vintage quality. The place was doing a brisk business the day we were there.

Mr. Amory remarked in his book that The Breakers had cost 5 million dollars to build, and could not now "be duplicated for 20 million dollars." Because of my inability to conceive of a house costing 5 million dollars, I was less impressed with the figure than I was when Mr. Amory went on to say that the ornamental wrought-iron gate and fence of this property "currently costs over five thousand dollars a year just to keep painted." I realized then that we were, indeed, looking at what had impressed the late President Calvin Coolidge. "It's quite a place," he said.

We went on, to range slowly past the other surviving monsters of the era, partly hidden by walls and hedges, here and there one a bit shabby, but mostly well kept—Swanhurst, Edghill, the Marble Palace, then into the older part of the town.

Here were the narrow, crooked, and cobblestoned streets of historic Newport. The Newport Historical Society was closed; but next door Touro Synagogue was open, and busy with visitors, of which I was an interested one. We donned the small round ritual cap supplied by the attendant and purchased a set of well-printed postcards telling, among other things, that in 1790 George Washington wrote to Jeshuat Israel Congregation to say, "Happily the Government of the United States . . . gives to Bigotry no Sanction, to Persecution no Assistance."

Since 1947, this synagogue has been a National Historic Site, along with The Wayside Inn at Sudbury, and several more Yankee-dedicated spots in New England.

As for the rest of fascinating Newport, I was content to leave it in the hands of a host of historical and descriptive writers, save for one item: I wanted to see those House-of-Usher ruins I had caught sight of on the far west side of Newport. I recalled being told they were remnants of a fire at "the Budlong estate." I happened to know the younger generations of two families of that name, and got to wondering.

After driving two or three miles along the western shore of the town, we rounded a wide curve and there they were, almost in front of us: half-a-dozen or more naked chimneys rearing up here and there around a tall stucco tower. Below was a porte-cochere of rugged stone and stucco, a rounded wide porch, and broken, blackened, and blank windows. Up and around this shambles on every side had grown the stunted trees and weeds characteristic of the Rhode Island shore. No sign of yard or lawn was left. In another year or so, the encroaching ground cover would start to attack the house itself, to crush what remained.

This house had never been, by Newport standards, more than a minor mansion, or cottage. Of its owner, I learned only that his name was Budlong and he was dead. It had burned "about five or six years ago" and had been left as I saw it, the charred remains scattered around in the brush. This was because "the only surviving member of the Budlong family" was in some rest home, or other institution, hence "it had been impossible to close or probate the estate." And there the matter rested.

The late Mr. Budlong was surely no major millionaire, yet I have never seen more romantically satisfying ruins than those on this west shore of Newport. I looked at them a long time before I set out on foot to see them close. The jungle was such that I needed half an hour to push my way a few yards through the growth to the porte-cochere.

The place obviously had been popular with vandals. In the past few years they must have lugged away tons of debris. It was stripped now, and, crawling over its naked sides and timbers and stone and stucco, as if to cover the shame, were the urgent vines, with now and then a full-grown berry bush coming up through cracks in floors. One-half of one sash was still in one window. The rest were staring. A single shutter swung from an upper story.

The lighting, on that July day, was perfect for ruins—bright sun part of the time, then chased by clouds that were as night, and sinister. (Perhaps I had read too much of Mrs. Sigourney and her "Toll, toll, toll.") Yet the shadows cast by moving clouds did things to this devastated relic. As I said, it was not in the imposing class of Jay Gould's old town house at Fifth Avenue and Forty-Seventh Street in Manhattan which, before it was razed by wreckers, had become a gigantic antique shop; nor was it an eighteenth-century farmhouse, still graceful though deserted while it went down, ever so slowly, before the termites and the weather had made of it a victim of the Yankee exodus.

Still, about this pitiable remnant of a place and an era that had been called Gilded, was all the melancholy of a deserted village and the foreboding of the House of Usher. I made my way back to the road, and when we drove away, I looked back once to see if the Budlong place had started actually to crumble.

Chapter 22

The Lower Road: Boston to New Haven (By 3rd Route)

"Canton, Taunton, Bristol, & Over The Bridge to Newport"

LATE IN HIS LONG LIFE Paul Revere dabbled occasionally in verse, and in one of his efforts sought to identify himself with the village just out of Boston where he founded industries that added to his fame as horseman and craftsman in silver:

Boston to New Haven (By 3rd Route)

Not distant far from Taunton Road
In Canton Dale is my abode....

At Canton in those days began the third stage route of the Lower Post Road to New Haven. By 1808 the already weathered old village was beginning to get its second wind. The new Boston and Taunton Turnpike had made it a station. Businessman Revere had only recently moved his copper rolling mill and bell foundry to Canton from Boston's North End. Among other notable jobs, he had supplied copper sheets valued at $4,232 for the new Massachusetts State House for which, incidentally, he had laid the cornerstone. He had also coppered the frigate *Constitution* (Old Ironsides) when she came into Boston Harbor for repairs.

A part of Revere's plant at Canton had originally been the Continental Government powder mill in which, during the first three years of the war, Revere manufactured much of the gunpowder used by the Provincial Army. He must have felt right at home when he returned to Canton after the war. It was here he recast the bronze and silver bell of King's Chapel, made in England, which had cracked in 1814, and also manufactured many more bells. These are still cherished by congregations throughout New England, including one in the belfry of Canton's First Parish Church.

One day in Canton, while walking the streets Revere knew so well, I was passing this church when the sun flashed on an object set high above the front entrance. It turned out to be a "Golden Pineapple" and it had been there, as a "symbol of hospitality and welcome," I was told, for some 130 years. It was like nothing I had seen on a church before. For all I know, it is unique, though a member of the Canton church said the pineapple symbol was familiar as a motif in early American furniture and on the doorsteps of old Salem, Massachusetts. Maybe so. In any event, the brilliant glint of this small object high on the front of the plain white structure sent me to learn more about the pineapple and the craftsman who made it.

He was, like Revere, of French descent, James Bazin, a cabinet-

The Lower Road

maker and all-around master craftsman of Stoughton, who carved the symbol in about 1825, and gilded it. He also made several miniature pineapples. These were affixed to pews indicating, in a time when it was customary for members to purchase pews, that these seats welcomed strangers. One could not imagine a more graceful manner of extending courtesies.

In nearby Sharon, during Revere's years in Canton, lived Deborah Sampson Gannett, the famous Female Soldier mentioned before. Revere's biographer, Miss Esther Forbes, says that Deborah was seeking a pension and asked Revere's aid. The old hero not only wrote Congress a letter that did the trick, but he was also glad to give her what she was pleased to call "a loan of ten dollars for a short time." Even before Longfellow's poem, the antique figure of Paul Revere, who never discarded the small clothes of the eighteenth century, was a familiar sight in Boston and Canton. He seems to have enjoyed stopping his horse at Mrs. Gannett's to chat "with this conversable woman." At his death in 1818, he left sons to carry on the Revere Copper Company of Canton which, through mergers, became what is now a division of Revere Copper and Brass, Inc. (Canton's first industry today is the Draper Brothers Company, manufacturers of paper-mill felts for the past 101 years.)

One cannot know how much effect the Boston and Taunton Turnpike had on Canton, but on Taunton it must have been remarkable. The record indicates that "more than 200 industries there had come into being before 1850." Among these was the Taunton Locomotive Works which made some of the most beautiful and efficient steam engines in the country. Later came stoves, silverware, a copper rolling syndicate that was to merge with Revere Copper, and much else. (Item: In 1892 Taunton suddenly became nationally prominent when the Lizzie Borden trial was held there; and so was nearby Swansea, simply because the Borden family of Fall River owned two farms in that town which sisters Emma and Lizzie used often to visit.)

Dighton, Somerset, and Swansey (old spelling) were not on the turnpike but were listed as regular stops on this route of the Lower

200

Boston to New Haven (By 3rd Route)

Post Road, before it led into Rhode Island at Warren and Bristol. Then, as the Boston Stage Office had it: ". . . over the Bridge to Newport." At Newport we could resume our tour of the main Lower Road at the Jamestown Ferry.

And it was here, either in Wickford, or maybe North Kingstown, or perhaps even Hamilton, that things, or at least geography, began to go to pieces. I have since got them sorted out, I think—but on that July evening two years ago, we stayed at a motel in what my 1954 map said was Wickford and my 1960 map said was North Kingstown. Yet, before we had settled down, we seemed to be in a place named Hamilton and noticed a road marker pointing toward Kingston and a West Kingston. (Note no "W.")

I had planned to visit the birthplace of Gilbert Stuart, the noted portraitist, said to stand in one of these towns, but failed to make it among signs pointing variously to "Boston Post Road," to simply "Post Road," and once merely to "Turnpike." So, when we saw a "US Alt. 1," we were glad enough to follow it; and, soon enough it brought us, if all unwittingly, to one of the most appealing hamlets in New England. On the window of the post office was the legend: Peace Dale, R.I.

We came upon Peace Dale suddenly at about seven in the morning. It was almost as if the curtain of a theater had rolled up as we watched, to reveal the stage set for a ghost town. Not the conventional ghost town of the West, with its false fronts, saloons, and hitching rack, nor yet the conventional deserted and shabby industrial section of a New England village. I can only call it unique.

We were obviously in the center of Peace Dale, the village square. On the left was the post office. Opposite was the Hazard Memorial Library, on which a plaque mentioned Rowland Gibson Hazard, born in South Kingston October 9, 1801, died in Peace Dale, June 24, 1888. Straight ahead, facing us, and occupying the entire side of the square was an immense stone factory. It was obviously long deserted by its original industry, and a few of its hundreds of windows were broken. A new sign indicated that its sole occupant was a print-maker and dealer in antiques. The library-giver was not the only local worthy memorialized. On the well-kept green in the square was a monument to the Department Members of Narragansett Steam Fire Engine Company No. 1.

We parked on the square, and I got out to sit on the library steps and contemplate the scene. Peace Dale was magnificent in the seven o'clock hush which I knew was not to be broken by factory whistle this morning, or any other morning. Peace Dale had reached its era when the number of spindles and the number of looms no longer counted. All but hermetically sealed in that immense factory was an account of the rise, the flowering, and the decline of a segment of Yankee industry.

What the first Rowland Hazard had done was to found (1800) a new village in South Kingston, name it Peace Dale, to honor the family of his wife, Mary Peace, and establish the Peace Dale Manufacturing Company. It was in an effort to match him that Francis C. Lowell later erected the first modern cotton factory at Waltham.

Hazard was the first to apply power to the spinning of wool, then to introduce the first power loom to weave broad woolen goods in the same factory. Generations of Hazards carried on the business. Some Hazards, meanwhile, attained stature in other ways. Rowland G. of the library became a philosopher and attracted the attention of John Stuart Mill; Augustus G. founded the great Hazard Powder Works in Connecticut; Thomas R. became a social reformer of note; Miss Caroline was long the president of Wellesley College; the first Thomas had been one of the founders of Newport; the second Thomas was the reputed political dictator of Rhode Island. Most of these "Narragansett Hazards" were Friends (Quakers), and among these had been still another Thomas who, as early as 1774, was an ardent abolitionist, rare in those days.

We drove south some four miles out of Peace Dale to the village of Narragansett. In that brief stretch of road we covered Time at the rate of approximately twenty-five years a mile, coming forward from, say, 1860 to the present. Mellow Peace Dale, built for the centuries, had already lived out its first, and the vast stone factory was ready for a second; but somehow its time schedule went awry. Its clock had stopped.

And here at Narragansett, ten miles distant, was contrast to blur the eye. To a visitor, it gave the impression of a collection, or perhaps "display" is the better word, of one big bathing club after another —sundeck, clubhouse, sundeck, clubhouse. Everything was "modern" to the very moment, or possibly running a little ahead of the moment. Architecturally one cliché stood back to back with another. The builders knew exactly what was wanted: a slickness of surface and line, yet of material that lent itself readily to removal within a short time, to be replaced with a newer cliché, which I fancy may be called *Beachhouse Centennial 1970.*

There was nothing of nostalgia about *this* Old Swimming Hole of Narragansett. The last curlicue of gingerbread had been plowed under along with the last two-piece bathing suit. All was slick. And all looked as prosperous as it doubtless was. It is possible that here and there was a vacationist who wondered if he or she could afford another week at a tony bathing club; but this would be unthinkable behind the long thick hedgerows of the estates which take over where commercial Narragansett leaves off. I was told that the resort was "booked up for all summer."

Half an hour later we were passing through Wakefield, next village to Peace Dale, where we saw the Oliver Hazard Perry House, old home of the naval hero of Lake Erie. (Did his middle name come from one of the many Hazards in this area?) The house is also identified with his younger brother, Matthew Calbraith Perry, he who "opened the ports of Japan." Five miles beyond Wakefield we passed the hamlet of Perryville.

At Westerly we reached the western limits of Rhode Island, and crossed the Pawcatuck into Stonington, Connecticut, which likes to claim it has been "The Nursery of Seamen," citing its many distinguished mariners, including noted whaling captains, whose efforts had made it a port of entry complete with customhouse. Although one guidebook says Stonington was "off the Boston Post Road," an old post-office route map shows it as a regular stop from the earliest times. Quiet now, and still stony, it is pretty much one long narrow street down a peninsula, at the very point of which we came to a marker commemorating what was doubtless the old town's greatest day in American history:

This is to Remember
Here the Brave Men of Stonington Defeated
a Landing Force from HMS Ramillies, Bent
on Burning the Town and Its Shipping
Aug. 10, 1814

This was the climax of a four-day bombardment by a British fleet in command of Captain Thomas Masterman Hardy, one of Lord Nelson's officers at Trafalgar. Here at Stonington, Hardy's fleet, mounting a total of 140 guns, suffered ninety-four casualties and was "successfully repulsed by Connecticut militia with two cannon." It must have been an off-day for Hardy's gunners: "British cannon balls fell harmlessly so thick in Stonington fields and woods that they have been among the town's most valued relics."

Having previously visited New London and Norwich, when running the *first* alternate route of the Lower Road, we drove on to Old Saybrook where the Connecticut River enters Long Island Sound. Near New London we had entered the Connecticut Turnpike; and from there westward we would remain virtually turnpike-bound all the way to Manhattan. That is, such would have been the case if we had merely driven to New York by the shortest route.

But the Connecticut Turnpike, which I came to think of as the *Groove*, and the Boston Post Road have little in common except general direction. From here at Old Saybrook in Connecticut to, say, Pelham Manor, New York, it will be best to attempt no specific identification with the Boston Post Road. It is a matter of on again, off again. Much of the way the actual centers of the old towns are not on the turnpike, and can be reached only by leaving it at this or that exit (called "gates" on the oldtime pikes) and driving anywhere from a mile or so to 10 miles over highways that may once have been portions of US 1, or even of the Boston Post Road. On my 1960 road maps (Copyright, Rand McNally) is the legend: Connecticut Turnpike: Total Distance 120 miles. *There are 90 Interchanges.*

Saybrook friends, being on the side of angels, and thus preferring the back roads to throughways, took us up the big river to Ely's Ferry Road, near the village of Hamburg in the town of Lyme. For many years Ely's was the best run and most popular ferry in this stretch of the Connecticut. Still standing near the landing was the old home of ferryman Ely himself, which had been built over into a sizable mansion. In the dense brush near the water we saw the stone foundations of a former inn and store that served stage passengers and the many drovers who came this way.

From the landing, we drove several miles on a veritable wilderness road, barely passable by car, and ended near a farm that is still operated chiefly with oxen. Yet at this same spot, we were less than "three crow miles" from the Connecticut Turnpike. It seemed almost incredible. On the way back into Old Lyme, we stopped while our host took us beside the old highway to show us what was probably "the sole remaining marker" of the King's Highway or Post Road in Old Lyme. It was of sandstone. On its face was chiseled: "14 M. to N.L.," which referred to New London.

Saybrook, across the Connecticut River's mouth, dates from 1635 and because of its strategic location at the mouth of the Connecticut was an important place from its first settlement. During much of its first 200 years it was guarded by forts erected variously against Indians, Dutch, Massachusetts settlers, British, and "to discourage attacks by the Confederate Navy." I had known that Saybrook was also the original (1701) site of Yale University when it was called The Collegiate School; but until our Saybrook host told me, I had no idea that the town had a rough time to prevent its removal to New Haven in about 1716. The Post Road was treated to the most ungenteel sight of Saybrookers attacking the New Havenites' cavalcade en route, to free their horses and damage the wagons filled with books; and later removing the planks from the larger bridges and demolishing the culverts.

The Lower Road

In their three centuries, both Saybrook and Lyme have given many distinguished men to the United States. Among them all, the two I should be most interested to meet are David Bushnell, a native of Saybrook, and Sergeant Ezra Lee of Old Lyme. Bushnell, Yale 1775, devised or invented in that same year a sea-going craft he named the *American Turtle*. It was a primitive submarine, built of oak, 6 feet high, with a water-tight compartment and pumps for submerging and rising. Motive power came from two sets of paddles, operated by a hand crank. On its back the *Turtle* carried an explosive bomb. Bushnell's idea: The sub would approach a warship under water, its operator would attach the bomb to the vessel's keel, set a clock mechanism to working, then go away from there.

By the summer of 1776, a suitable target in the British fleet lay in New York Harbor near Whitehall Stairs, on the Post Road near the Battery. All inventor Bushnell needed was a suitable operator, so, into this floating coffin crawled Sergeant Ezra Lee, of Old Lyme and the Connecticut Militia, to be fairly bolted into position, and away he churned into the night to attach the *Turtle* to the hull of the *Eagle,* sixty-four guns, Lord Howe's mighty flagship. Lee was foiled by the new copper sheathing of the battleship. Well, dawn was breaking. But Sergeant Ezra Lee was no man to take a torpedo to sea and bring it back; and when a barge of British marines started to pursue the *Turtle,* Lee pulled the pin of his charge and cut it loose. The marines zigzagged out of danger. Lee's torpedo went up in one mighty blast, tossing columns of water and hunks of wood and iron high in the air. The force of the explosion, "a report like thunder," was noted all over the tip of Manhattan.

General Rufus Putnam of Connecticut witnessed Lee's cold-courage effort, and welcomed him when the *Turtle* made shore. General Washington congratulated the Navy's first submarine commander and promoted him to some sort of special duty on the General Staff. After Yorktown, veteran Ezra Lee returned to his native home in Old Lyme where he died in 1821, aged seventy-two, full of honors as an outstanding if "minor" hero of the Revolution.

Boston to New Haven (*By 3rd Route*)

Had a Longfellow but fastened upon him, he would be as famous today as a Paul Revere.

At Old Saybrook we stayed the night with friends in the Fenwick borough, named for Mr. George Fenwick, "the only Puritan aristocrat to settle here." It faces the ocean and has a large number of big turn-of-the-century homes. In the morning, we were reminded that the Connecticut shore is in the hurricane country. When we drove back to the Post Road, the long causeway was covered with more than a foot of water that had been rolling in ahead of the breakers. Radio warnings were being broadcast as we passed through Clinton whose chief industry, despite the town's maritime tradition, was once said to be the manufacture of Pond's Extract, made "from native witch hazel," *Hamamelis virginiana.* Clinton also has a hero, General Horatio G. Wright who was born here in 1820, at 95 East Main Street, and was to repel Jubal Early's raid in 1864 at the very edge of Washington, and had a brilliant record throughout the war. Indeed, says one of his biographers, Wright's "very excellencies have minimized his reputation." Perhaps his misfortune was to have commanded the Army at Cedar Creek when General Philip Sheridan arrived from Winchester, and a poet, Thomas Buchanan Read, wrote *Sheridan's Ride,* indicating that Little Phil's appearance had "saved the day." It is committing no injustice to say that Sheridan did nothing of the kind, but *that* is not the manner in which popular verse is written.

Because Clinton was once a part of Killingworth before its incorporation as a separate town, we drove north into those wooded slopes to see if the Killingworth hill-dwellers were still busy, as alleged, in the distilling of witch-hazel extract for "the town's leading industry." We saw no stills, though there was hazel brush to spare. It was an astonishing trip. For 25 miles we ranged the hill roads and did not once see a house or a person. At what I suppose was Killingworth Hamlet was one small store, one farm house, and a building to house the fire department, doubtless needed to control forest fires.

But something new had been added. We learned as much from small posters tacked to trees along the road. This was advertised as "Cowboy Valley," a sort of Western corral and dude-ranch attraction. Pretty soon we saw people in the road ahead. They were half a dozen ballyhoo characters, in Stetsons and chaps, two guns in belts, and they tried to flag us down. We did not stop, but could see their corral in an opening, stocked with a few ponies, and a small group of adolescents, waving hats and shooting cap-pistols. It was an incongruous sight and a most potent commentary on the influence of television.

What impressed us most of all about Killingworth was that in teeming Connecticut there could be so much vacant land in a township as here. It was obvious that customers of Cowboy Valley would have to come from elsewhere.

We drove back to the shore at Madison, a small village with a wealth of old houses with plaques attesting their historical significance. I was sorry, however, to find no mention that Madison was the birthplace of Professor C. F. Dowd, who conceived of and urged adoption of what we know as the Standard Time Belts, or zones, which went into effect on October 11, 1883. Though seldom if ever mentioned in our history books, standard time deserves notice as one of the great events of late nineteenth century.

We continued on through Guilford to Branford, said to be the place where the founding of Yale College was first proposed. It seemed to be a good spot in which to base the Post Road expedition for a few days, not only because of the provenance of Yale, but also because we had just passed a grade crossing which, a sign said clearly enough, was the property of the Branford *Steam* Railroad Company. (The italics are mine.) In these days one might well have secret doubt about this virtual bragging of "steam," but such skepticism is not admitted by dedicated proponents of the motive power of trains in the golden age of the rails.

Branford was formerly a region called Totoket, a grant to Samuel

Boston to New Haven (By 3rd Route)

Eaton, one of two brothers associated with John Davenport in the founding of New Haven Colony. The other brother, Theophilus, was to govern the colony nineteen years "in a course marked by wisdom, justice, firmness, and prudence." Branford settlement must have flourished from the first, for there remain a number of fine old houses, one surviving from 1685, though only a marker commemorates the site of the Samuel Russell House where, in 1701, ten ministers of Colony churches met to discuss the founding of the Collegiate School and to donate books for it.

In cruising the Branford country, we discovered that the Branford Steam Railroad was allied with the New Haven Traprock Company, whose quarry was not far from the village. We also visited Traprock's loading dock near Stony Creek, a delightful hamlet; and came to believe that the Steam Railroad must be the busiest freight line in all New England. During two days we saw more long trains in Branford town than one would readily have believed. But the "Steam" had of course turned to Diesel. One more hope went glimmering.

Both Branford and Stony Creek had once been stations on the Connecticut Company System, whose slogan was "Travel by Trolley" and whose lines comprised no less than 803 miles "of well maintained track over which is operated modern equipment at frequent and regular intervals." The trolleys have long since disappeared, though we saw remnants of overhead tracks in several towns along the Connecticut shore; and a friend presented us with a facsimile of the Company's (undated) map of operations, with a plea to "Ship by Trolley Express." The brochure also made a strong pitch about "Rapidity in transit, promptness in delivery and reasonableness in Rates." It all had the sound of antiquity as remote almost as a reference to "Fast Stages" in schedules on the Boston Post Road. Indeed about 1½ miles of old trolley line, with the original cars (not to mention some forty other examples of this art form collected all over the country), are still operating in the town, at the Branford Electric Railway Museum. Every weekend the old cars, both closed and open, operate over the tracks for visitors.

The Lower Road

But antiquity in architecture is something else, and residents of these old towns along the Connecticut shore of the Lower Road were obviously proud of their surviving relics from past centuries like the Baldwin House (c. 1645) in Branford, the Comfort Starr (c. 1665), and the Whitefield-Chittenden (1639) Houses in Guilford. (Attention Vermont: In the latter was born an ancestor of Thomas C. Chittenden, first governor of the Green Mountain State.) Guilford is said to have preserved what is perhaps the most varied collection of authentic early houses in New England; Branford and Guilford together have warranted a monograph by professional architects dealing with the seventeenth-century houses in each village and on the road between them.

As we started to approach the outer suburbs of New Haven, the red (or brown) mailboxes of the *Register* started to peter out, then disappeared when the city delivery zone was reached. In the country they had been mixed with the bright yellow of the Middletown *Press* and the green of the Hartford *Times*.

At New Haven we arrived at the place where the three Boston Post Roads had converged to form a single route to New York. We were 72.5 miles by railroad from Grand Central Station. In early Post Road days we should have been approximately 87 miles from the Fort which stood at the foot of Broadway, on the site later occupied by the Customs House, opposite the Bowling Green. For many years this was the western terminal of the Old Boston Post Road.

Chapter 23

The Post Road:
New Haven to Greenwich

FROM THE TIME the first horseman rode out of New York with the mail for Boston, New Haven has been a Post Road town. It was the place where he turned north up the Quinnipiac River on the way to Hartford where, according to plan, he "should have a fresh horse constantly lye." In that January of 1673, New Haven was thirty-five years old. For many more years New Haven and Hartford amounted to being Connecticut Colony, and even with statehood, the two towns continued long to share the importance of a joint capital city.

There was a natural, or built-in and jaundiced, rivalry between the two towns. Long before Hartford took to bragging of its insurance industry, or New Haven to point with pride to Yale College, each was looking toward maritime sources to bring it supremacy. Added to its general shipping, New Haven developed an enormous oyster business, and Hartford went to rolling cigars. Neither place was content simply to be on the Post Road.

When the turnpike fad hit Connecticut, first New Haven, then Hartford, started to build pikes to bring country trade into town; and some genius even chartered the Hartford *and* New Haven Turnpike Company. Then, canals seemed for a while to be the sure way to make a city prosperous, and locks were built around the rapids of the Connecticut River at Windsor, causing Hartford to assume that the river would henceforth become the major traffic artery in New England. New Haven decided the time had come to deliver a devastating stroke.

Had not New York's master work, the Erie Canal, already proved what an inland waterway could do for a town? Well, keep your eye on New Haven's Farmington Canal. This was to be that city's truly magnificent attempt to drain off its share of inland commerce. On the Fourth of July, 1825, while massed bands played and cannon belched, the first earth was moved for the great waterway that was —eventually, said New Haven citizens—to connect the St. Lawrence River with Long Island Sound, at New Haven.

The planners had taken care that the Farmington Canal system would give Hartford a wide berth. It was to head north through Hamden, Southington, Plainville, Farmington, Avon, and Granby, then into Massachusetts to Northampton. Almost exactly ten years later, it actually did reach Northampton, and thus the first leg of the miracle canal that was to pile riches on New Haven had been finished.

Another celebration was called for. Citizens lined banks, bridges, and locks to greet the first boats as they passed through on their way south to Long Island Sound *and* New Haven. Buntings fluttered at Farmington, flags were flying at Plainville, Southington, and Cheshire. Half of New Haven waited at Hamden, and bonfires lighted the gaily painted canal boats like the *Wildfire* and *The Rising Sun* all the way to the Long Wharf in New Haven itself.

New Haven to Greenwich

It was a noble effort. It brought some new commerce to New Haven, but not enough and at far too great a cost. Basically the canal was a failure, and though New Haven banks continued to pour money into its operation, the toll charges never amounted to more than a pittance. By 1847, the company was ready to call it a day. Operation was suspended, the canal was abandoned and the right-of-way sold to railroad interests. The experiment had cost more than $1,500,000. Meanwhile, Hartford had boomed into an important fresh-water port, yet things sort of evened up over the years. In 1960 Hartford's population was 162,178; New Haven's was 152,048.

Among the long-established products that have brought both fame and population to these cities are those made in Hartford by the Colt's Patent Fire Arms Manufacturing Company, and in New Haven by the Winchester Repeating Arms Company.

Samuel Colt's contribution, mentioned elsewhere in this book, went into history as The Peacemaker; that of Oliver Fisher Winchester became known as "The Gun That Won the West." It is probable that no other Yankee trademark goods are more widely known than those of Colt and Winchester. The latter weapon is now manufactured by the Olin Mathieson Chemical Corporation which, at 275 Winchester Avenue, New Haven, still maintains the Winchester Gun Museum. This collection totals more than 5,000 items. The museum is at street level. You simply walk in. The curator Mr. Thomas E. Hall, is a man well fit for this superb display of firearms that attracts a steady flow of visitors.

In New Haven there is no need to speak of Yale University. I know of no other "college town" where an educational institution is more integrated with town life than New Haven and Yale. Yet I dislike to leave them without mention of a fictional student of Old Eli named Frank Merriwell who for twenty years was the incomparable hero of *Tip Top Weekly,* a five-cent branch of the dime novel industry. The stories were written by Burt L. Standish, pseudonym of Gilbert Patten, and they ran to a grand total of some 20 million words of pulp-paper biography.

The Post Road

"You are a cheap cad," Frank told the overdressed Harvard bully.

I never got to Yale myself, though my heart was long set on going there, as was the case with many of my generation; and the reason, I fear, was neither William Graham Sumner nor William Lyon Phelps, nor yet Ted Coy. It was because of the peerless Yale athlete —and scholar—Frank Merriwell. You'd think that by now the great university could have given him some sort of a degree, perhaps just an honorary B.S., posthumously, so to speak. But they haven't.

From New Haven to Kingsbridge, New York, as I knew, we must shun the great main turnpike as much as possible if we were to see the towns that were served by the old Boston Post Road. To do so we occasionally had to leave US 1, but not for long; and I shall not confuse myself and the reader by bringing up the matter. For the purpose of this account we remain on the Post Road to New York City.

In Milford we passed a sign indicating we actually were on the Boston Post Road, with not even a passing mention of US 1. On the way into the town we were reminded that Milford had been the center of the shellfish trade for which New Haven was famous. Near the railroad tracks were monstrous heaps of oyster shells—20-odd acres of them, we were told—said to have been made in aboriginal times when Indians came here to feast. About a block off Milford Green was the Eels-Stow House (c. 1689), once the home of Captain Stephen Stow and his wife, Freelove Baldwin Stow. Then we drove to Milford's ancient burying ground, to see one of the most remarkable monuments ever erected in respect to the War of the Revolution. It was in memory of Captain Stow and forty-six American soldiers, and erected "by the joint liberality of the Connecticut General Assembly, the People of Milford and their contributing friends."

Then: "Who shall say that Republics are ungrateful?" asked the marker. The chiseled legend relates how "two hundred American Soldiers in a destitute, sickly and dying condition, were brought from a British Prison Ship . . . and suddenly cast upon our shore, on the first of January, 1777. . . . The Inhabitants of Milford made the most charitable efforts for the relief of these suffering strangers; yet, notwithstanding all their kind administrations, in one month forty-six died, and were buried in one common grave. . . ."

Good Captain Stow was buried with them, for it was he who "took charge of these poor wretches in the Milford Town Hall and nursed them through the smallpox, who cared for and tended them, who heard their last messages and closed their dying eyes, and ended all by giving up his own life that so many of them should live." (The names of the forty-six who died are inscribed on the monument.)

Connecticut and Massachusetts are well furbished with markers and monuments to figures of the Revolution, who for the most part were fighting men, cited for prowess in killing British. Milford's marker to Captain Stow and forty-six more is heart-warming in its compassion.

Stratford is now a residential suburb of Bridgeport, but back in Post Road days it was important as the place where you ferried the wide Housatonic River. The ferry began operating even before the first postrider came through here on his way to Boston. Much later Madame Sarah Knight arrived here, from Boston, riding side-saddle all the way on her justly famous trip to New York, in December 1704, and crossed with the ferryman without incident. On the other side, she and a companion "baited our horses and would have eat a morsel ourselves," but the tavern's "pumpkin and Indian mixed bread had such an aspect, and the barelegged punch so awkward or rather awful a sound" that they left without food or drink, and proceeded to Fairfield. I still have no idea what barelegged punch was.

There is no mention of Bridgeport, or of any other town, in Madame Knight's journal until Fairfield is reached, though in that place they "met with good entertainment, and lodged." Yet because in our time Bridgeport is between Stratford and Fairfield, let's keep it in sequence. At the time of the Revolution it was called Stratfield, and consisted of perhaps a dozen houses. When the first United States Census was taken (1790) the settlement listed 110 citizens. Ten years later, after money was raised by a lottery, and a toll-bridge built across the Pequonnock River, the place was named, with more accuracy than imagination, Bridgeport.

Even before the steamcars came, in 1840, Bridgeport was doing all right. Incorporated in 1836 as a city, the local boosters' club was fairly panting for industries to add to its chief manufacturing plant. This was a salt-works, with its several windmills pumping water from the Sound into the evaporating pans. When the first antecedent of the New Haven Railroad whistled for Bridgeport, the boys were ready. How ready they were for Metropolis can be gauged by the population census; for every decade between 1800 and 1930, the town "showed an increase of 40 per cent." In 1950 it was the third city in Connecticut, with 158,709 boosters present.

In Post Road days, before the railroad, according to historian Stephen Jenkins, the Bridgeport mail arrived by coach between 8 and 10 in the evening, "its arrival being announced by the guard's horn as it entered the village"; there was but "one newspaper subscribed for, the New York *Journal of Commerce,* which was permitted by its owner to be generally read." The railroad soon changed Bridgeport's ways, however; the town not only "took all the papers" but published four of its own, including one named Bridgeport *Advertiser.* By 1848 the city chartered a railroad, the Naugatuck, that *started* from Bridgeport.

Only a little later, an observer marveled at the many things made in Bridgeport. They included "hats, corsets, shirts, firearms, varnishes, metal goods, cartridges, machinery, and "after about 1863, Wheeler and Wilson Sewing Machines." This last was a triumph indeed, if only because the Bridgeport boosters "stole" it from Watertown, Connecticut, where it was first established ten years previously. (One is prepared to believe it was one of Bridgeport's boosters who invented the old gag that laid them in the aisles when worked up by the minstrel shows:)

INTERLOCUTOR: So, Mr. Bones, you did not become a singer, as your mother hoped?

MR. BONES: No, sah. She tried to make a Singer out of me, but I turned into a Wheeler and Wilson.

Other magnificent things happened. One after the other Bridgeport watched as Bridgeport Brass made clocks, then hoopskirts, telephone wire, trolley wire; and mergers produced Union Metallic Cartridge, Parker Guns, and The Remington Arms Companies.

When a youngster, I often accompanied my parents on trips from our home in Vermont to New York City; and of all the places we passed through between New Haven and Grand Central depot, Bridgeport was incomparably the most alluring. That was the winter home of the Barnum and Bailey circus. It was where I became alert, to sit close by the car window. Although I knew Mr. Barnum was dead, and that I no longer could hope to see him plowing a field with an elephant, as he was reputed to have done in former years, I also knew that Barnum and Bailey wintered their menagerie in Bridgeport. I had seen the rows of animal houses near the railroad tracks. It behooved a boy to watch everything as he passed through this magic land. And I did watch, not only then but for many years more. But never once did I catch sight of a circus animal.

Nor did I ever see the man whom the great Mr. Barnum made into a world-renowned figure. This was Charles Sherwood Stratton, who lived in Bridgeport, who became known the world over as General Tom Thumb. It seems that, while staying overnight at a Bridgeport hotel, Barnum saw this midget who stopped growing at six months and remained two feet and one inch tall until well into his teens. The great showman struck a quick bargain with the parents, and took charge of the newly christened Tom Thumb, and started the tour which made Thumb a household word. Barnum later built for himself a fantastically hideous residence he called Iranistan. Yet Bridgeport was lucky even with its fires; Barnum's horror was burned flat in 1857.

How fortunate a place is Bridgeport! Unlike Fairfield, Westport, Southport, Darien, and other towns on the way into New York, it is not obliged to dredge its citizens in order to come up with a "noted author" or a bearded "famous painter," in lieu of *Business Men* who have *done things* . . . Sing Spirella, sing General Electric . . . Praise Bridgeport Brass and Union Metallic . . . Cheer Remington Arms and cheer whatever newer style has overtaken Wheeler and Wilson . . . Hurray for E. I. du Pont de Nemours and Company. . . .

Who wants to know where Ella Wheeler Wilcox lived? Or Wilbur L. Cross? Or, for that matter, Mark Van Doren and Van Wyck Brooks? Or Kay Boyle, Lewis Gannett, Samuel Clemens or even James Thurber?

Rather let us sing, sing, sing of Union Spirella Remington, and Bridgeport. . . .

We had by now passed into Fairfield County, and somewhere along here we had come within what many native Yankees consider the New York orbit, and resent it. But not all of them, as witness Mr. Odell Shepard. This long-time professor at Trinity College, Hartford, welcomed the newcomers in his *Connecticut Past and Present*. Commenting that New York's "Dormitory," as he termed the Connecticut shore west of New Haven, was filling up "with new people who are good for us," he admitted that though the back roads of the region might be somewhat sophisticated, they "will never be either metropolitan nor neglected." He said that the treatment of an old decaying farmhouse by "an intelligent person from the city is indicative of what he and his kind can do for the State as a whole. He puts in new sills, new beams and rafters, new floors. He paints it inside and out. He leaves all that was good in the old structure and gives it a double lease of life." Mr. Shepard did, however, regret the obvious loss of what he delicately called "one of the most interesting phases of Regionalism—the peculiarities of speech." In other words, the so-called Yankee accent was disappearing.

Well, in regard to newcomers, back in the 1830s, when Yankees were leaving *their* native states in great number, many of them to settle on or near the Post Road in New York City, the long settled residents of Manhattan became so alarmed at this invasion of "foreigners" that the New Yorkers sought to get the situation in hand by founding exclusive clubs or societies to keep the newcomers in their place. No less a personage than Washington Irving, a hardshell New Yorker, was the moving spirit of the Saint Nicholas Society of New York, whose avowed purpose was to "combat the social influence of New Englanders" in that city.

An earlier intolerance was that which came to a head right here in Fairfield County; and near the town line of Fairfield-Westport still stands a granite marker to The Great Swamp Fight, in which the white settlers massacred or sold into slavery the remaining members of the Sasqua and the Pequot tribes.

Historians of the Boston Post Road seem agreed that no portion of this highway presented such difficulties as did the terrain along Long Island Sound. If it wasn't boulders and rocks, it was bogs, inlets, or navigable streams. Darien, for instance, was in no hurry for better roads. Everybody there owned a sloop but not a horse and wagon; and thus they fought against building a bridge that would block traffic along its Five Mile River. It was a port of call for some fifty steamboats in the Sound trade, and Darien's commercial center was moved several times in order to intercept this traffic. It was not until the railroad came, in the 1840s, that Darien began to count as much on land transport as on waterways.

The Post Road

The Post Road had been in business more than a century when a French visitor, M. Brissot de Warville, came along here in a carriage, and "at Fairfield finished the agreeable part of our journey. From this town to Rye, 33 miles, we had to struggle against rocks and precipices." He did not know which to admire the more in the driver—his intrepidity or dexterity. "I cannot conceive," he wrote in his journal, "how he avoided twenty times dashing the carriage to pieces and how his horses could restrain themselves in descending the staircases of rocks. One of these is called Horseneck; a chain of rocks so steep that, if a horse should slip, the carriage must be thrown into the valley two or three hundred feet."

In his book on the Boston Post Road, Stephen Jenkins makes a good deal of the Dorothy Quincy-Aaron Burr romance, which took place in Fairfield, where Aaron Burr, Sr., second president of Princeton, was born. When Boston was under siege by the British, in 1775, several members of the Hancock and Quincy families fled down the Post Road, to stay a while with the Burrs. Along came Aaron, Jr., a "fascinating and brilliant young man," says Mr. Jenkins, "whom no woman could resist." One thing led to another, and Miss Quincy, already engaged to John Hancock, head of the Continental Congress, seemed about to forget her promise when Madame Lydia Hancock made it clear, to the fascinator Aaron, that "his room was preferable to his company, and so left the field clear for Hancock."

John Hancock lost no time. He came to Fairfield in August, 1775, and was wed to Dorothy in the Burr House, which for many years was pointed out to tourists as the scene of the marriage, although it was destroyed by fire two years after the wedding when British raided Fairfield and put more than 200 houses to the torch, "leaving no pre-Revolutionary structure in the town," as Mr. Jenkins sadly remarked.

Six miles beyond Fairfield, in Post Road times, was a regular way-stop called Green Farms in old stagecoach schedules. Somebody named Morehouse kept the tavern there. Green Farms is near what became Southport after Fairfield was burned and many of the refugees built their new homes there. Southport was the native home of Joseph Earl Sheffield, who began life as supercargo on a vessel running the British blockade in 1812, made a fortune in the cotton trade, and another building railroads, and gave more than a million dollars to Yale College for what was named, in his honor, Sheffield Scientific School.

One account of Southport says that after Fairfield was destroyed, "most of its *influential* citizens" went there to live, and erected "the many dignified substantial homes bordering its hilly, elm-shaded streets." I did not investigate this matter, but am prepared to believe it from glimpses of what looked like estates.

On the way to Norwalk we passed what Mr. Jenkins called "The Peat Swamp," which, he assured readers, bore an unsavory reputation in Post Road days as the resort of bad characters who would not hesitate, should opportunity offer, to pilfer from or rob the mails and passengers. When Washington came through here on his inaugural tour of New England, he observed that "the Destructive evidences of British cruelty are yet visible both in Norwalk and Fairfield." A few days after the Fairfield attack, the British struck South Norwalk, "and burned property reckoned worth $116,000." Norwalk, like Fairfield and other towns destroyed by British on the Connecticut shore, was later included in the Firelands Grant of the Western Reserve. One of the towns became Norwalk, Ohio.

We were a little surprised that Norwalk, according to a local marker, was where Nathan Hale came when "he started his secret journey into the British lines, by ferrying the Sound to Huntington, Long Island." He was not heard of again until word of his execution as a spy was received. It had seemed to me as if Hale rated markers and memorials in too many towns of southern Connecticut for them all to be authentic. Yet, no man who took on the assignment young Hale accepted, as the sole volunteer, could possibly have too many reminders that he died a patriot when the path of duty turned out also to be the way to glory.

The Post Road

And glory, too, to Norwalk for its fine record of keeping the memorable events of its past where its citizens, as well as strangers, can know what went on here in former times. But I could not blame the town for failing to memorialize what went into history as The Norwalk Horror, although this disaster took a higher toll of lives than could be charged to all the raids made by the British on the town.

One day in 1853, the locomotive engineer of a New Haven passenger train failed to see a low-ball signal set against him at an open drawbridge in Norwalk. Forty were killed and eighty injured, and suits for damages all but wrecked the railroad. But the telling effect of the disaster was that it jolted Connecticut into forming a state railroad commission armed with all the powers of regulation.

The consolidated modern city of Norwalk includes a number of communities. Among them is Silvermine, on Silvermine Creek, which of recent years has become noted as a summer home for painters, vying in this respect with Mystic, Old Lyme, Kent, and a few more places. We did not visit Silvermine. I wanted to see the street where, I'd been told, one James Knapp "produced the first derby hat ever made." I had supposed this hat to have originally been a product of Derby, England, though I recalled, too, that in Canada this type of hard hat was known as a bowler. Forty years ago I arrived in British Columbia, fresh from Boston, wearing what I think was perhaps the only derby hat on the West Coast. I seemed to remember it was a Knox and that the Knox was made in Connecticut, perhaps even in East Norwalk. It was a wonderfully good hat. When, after wearing it every day in the logging woods, I prepared to leave for Oregon, I nailed it fast to a Douglas fir stump. And there, as I later learned, it stayed, resisting the winds, rains, and snows for another twenty years.

Yet, it is futile to look up old sweethearts. In East Norwalk I learned that the Knox derby, made there for half a century, is now a part of the Hat Corporation of America, manufacturers of the

Knox and several other brands. We headed west out of East Norwalk for Stamford.

As long ago as 1830, Stamford was becoming a commuter town. It had some 4,000 inhabitants, the *Advocate* newspaper, and its alert citizens had already learned that the quickest way to New York was to take a stagecoach to the Saw Pits, as Port Chester was called, then board a steamboat to the metropolis.

But late in the fall of 1849, when the railroad came, both the Post Road coaches and the Sound steamers started to feel the new competition. As they did almost everywhere else, the steamcars attracted new industries and also, in the case of Stamford, brought "a continuous influx of New York businessmen who came to make their homes in Stamford."

In Post Road times, the distance from Norwalk to Stamford was generally listed as 10 miles, with one stop between. This was called Middlesex, and is now Darien, named for the Isthmus where, according to Keats, who was a better poet than he was historian, "Stout Cortez," rather than Balboa, stood silent on a peak to get his first view of the Pacific Ocean. To be done with Middlesex-Darien, it was once a parish of Stamford.

There have been some other changes made. The New Haven railroad says the distance from Norwalk to Stamford is 8 miles, and between them are crowded the stations of places named Rowayton, Darien, Noroton Heights, and Glenbrook. It is obvious that those "New York businessmen" who began coming, in the 1840s, to "make their homes in Stamford" were not alone. All the way through this region to the end of Connecticut, at Greenwich, are estates, links, country clubs, yacht clubs; and the long train platforms and the tiny depots are completely characteristic of commuter country.

The commuters *got* their trains too. About all I can remember about the commuter business is that once upon a time, in the early

The Post Road

1920s, the New Haven Railroad operated approximately 150 passenger trains on this division daily. (Its continuous controversy with its patrons is too well known to need comment.)

When historian Jenkins last visited this neighborhood, in about 1910, he paused at Darien, which he had known for many years, to observe that, "except for the thunderous noise of passing trains, the place is as quiet and inactive as in the old coaching days." Born in 1857 at Mount Vernon, New York, Stephen Jenkins knew this western sector of the Post Road like a native. In Noroton he talked with ancients who could remember when that faded village was a bustling place of stores, taverns, post office, and the tide-mill, a time when farmers brought their grain to be ground and their produce for shipment by vessel to New York. "But now (c. 1910) the farms are gentlemen's country estates, and nothing is shipped to New York or anywhere else, and the tide-mill runs no more. . . ."

Of Greenwich, he wrote of the treaty by which, in days before the Post Road, this town became the western boundary of Connecticut; and among its early settlers was John Mead, whose descendants, still living in Greenwich in 1910, Jenkins said were "numbered by legions." Mr. Jenkins was clear eyed in matters of history, and displayed skepticism in regard to the local claim that General Israel Putnam performed here what a Fourth of July orator of imagination called "his leap into fame." This illusion was an event of 1779, when Putnam was here in command of the handful of Continental troops stationed in and near Greenwich. The British attacked in such overwhelming force that Old Put told his few men to disperse while he would ride to Stamford for reinforcements.

Then, near what was the home of a Captain Hobby, Putnam rode down a flight of seventy-four stone steps that led up the face of a steep hill from the Post Road, while his British pursuers, appalled at the rugged descent, paused on the brink to fire several shots at the fleeing enemy.

Well, Jenkins mustered several reasons for his disbelief, doubtless knowing well that the legend would not only persevere, but would grow more wondrous by the year. Which, of course, it did. Old Put just happened to be one of those characters who were born to become legends. And, thus, in good time, what had been simply Captain Hobby's House is now Israel Putnam's Cottage, complete with *bronze tablet,* authenticating the legend.

Today it is difficult if not impossible for a stranger to say where Greenwich leaves off and some other community begins. It is likely that old residents there have a sense of living in a community set apart from greater New York, but I would not know how to go about explaining it. In Revolutionary times, Greenwich, being a border town, where Tories were at least as thick as patriots, became a sort of No Man's Land and the lawless elements, or bushwhackers, became known as "Skinners." The Skinners played no favorites, but moved in where chance offered pillage. Cooper had Skinners active in his popular novel, *The Spy,* which was subtitled, "A Tale of the Neutral Ground." But things quieted down after the war.

What the Neutral Ground's border-type harassments could do to everyday life was seen by the Reverend Timothy Dwight, pastor of the Greenfield Hill Church in Fairfield town, not long before he became president of Yale College. He was writing of the Boston Post Road's extreme western sector and its environs:

Amid all this appearance of desolation, nothing struck my eye more forcibly than the sight of this great road, the passage from New York to Boston. Where I had heretofore seen a continual succession of horses and carriages, and life and bustle lent a sprightliness to all environing objects, not a single, solitary traveller was visible from week to week, or from month to month. . . . The very tracks of the carriages were grown over and obliterated; and where they were discernible, resem-

The Post Road

bled the faint impressions of chariot wheels, said to be left on the pavements of Herculaneum.

For once, at least, the road to Boston had moved a classic eye to comment.

Chapter 24

The Post Road: Rye to Kingsbridge

GREENWICH is the last Connecticut town on the old Boston Post Road. Here a bridge crosses the Byram River and you are in the State of New York and the Town of Rye. In early days travelers from Port Chester took stage either at Rye or Greenwich. The new village was then known as the Saw Pits because of a mill and boat-building shop near the mouth of the river. After about 1739, a ferry started business between what was called Rye Port and Oyster Bay on Long Island.

In early times Rye was shown on the schedules of stage lines to be 32 miles from New York, and with three regular stops—East Chester, West Farms, and Kingsbridge—between Rye and the end of the line.

The Post Road

The end of the line was not an immutable place, yet it varied little until after the railroads came. Call it near the lower end of Broadway, or near the Bowling Green, or perhaps near Federal Hall in Wall Street. Any of these is accurate enough for staging days. The New York terminus of the Boston stages was usually some tavern or other, and for many a year it bore the name of John Fowler.

At the junction of the Post Road and Purchase Street stood an even more famous tavern than Fowler's. This was Haviland's place. George Washington had given it his accolade not once, but twice and, after having passed through many hands, it is now the village hall of the city of Rye.

An account of the origin and progress of what is now Rye, New York, is far too complicated for mention in anything less than a monograph. Let's say only that Rye was once Hastings and was believed by its settlers to be in Connecticut, whose legislature in 1655 declared it to be not one but two villages, Hastings and Rye. Within a decade or so, New York took cognizance of this settlement. It claimed Rye-Hastings for its own, along with another village which its proprietors said was Harrison's Purchase in Connecticut. The squabble continued for many years, or until a King's Order in Council placed Rye-Hastings-Purchase "forever hereafter to be and remain under the government of the Province of New York."

The Post Road through Rye originally followed the ancient Indian trail called the Westchester Path. Little enough was done to improve it until after 1800, when the Westchester Turnpike Company was organized and, encouraged by the first bridge to cross the Harlem River, removed some of the boulders and straightened a bend or two.

But no matter that New York won in the matter of provincehood, Rye and other nearby towns were to suffer the penalties of being border country. During and for long after the Revolution, as was the case with Greenwich, this whole region from, say, Stamford to Pelham was the Neutral Ground, celebrated, as we have said, by James Fenimore Cooper.

Though born in New Jersey, Cooper was reared in Cooperstown, New York, in his father's manoral-type headquarters, and in 1811 married Susan, daughter of John Peter Delancey, in the Delancey home, Mamaroneck, on the Boston Post Road. This was the ancestral home of the Delanceys, called Heathcote Hill. (Later sold, and moved to a spot described as 404 West Post Road, it became a tavern, then a restaurant, and finally the ultimate American institution of strictly modern times, a gasoline station.)

The young Coopers lived three years in the Delancey home. It was probably here that the budding novelist, whose first book was something of a failure, got the suggestion that resulted in his first great success, *The Spy*. It came from the brilliant John Jay, statesman and jurist, the outstanding citizen of Bedford, in Westchester County.

Jay's story concerned a real person, Enoch Crosby, a patriot spy in the Revolution who, posing as a royalist, was bitterly persecuted by supporters of the American cause. Crosby performed heroically against the British who were then in possession of New York. Jay's eloquence about the Westchester spy moved young Cooper to new eloquence of his own. Changing Crosby to "Harvey Birch," Cooper made him cunning, mysterious, dedicated, and driven by patriotism as if by a demon, and, wrote Carl Van Doren, "as lonely as a hero in a Byronic poem." Cooper had "already hit upon the formula of flight and pursuit, and knew how to handle the characteristic suspense of fiction."

The Spy made young Cooper a literary figure of mark. New printings were called for both here and in England. A French translation appeared. Cooper immediately followed with *The Pioneers,* for which he invented Natty Bumppo, a character who comprised not only Daniel Boone, but also the essences of the backwoods frontier as represented over the decades by Ethan Allen, Buffalo Bill, Dick Deadeye, and Kit Carson.

Although *The Spy* was written in Scarsdale, and most of the later Leatherstocking Tales in Cooperstown, Mamaroneck has continued to remind prospective visitors and all tourists that James Fenimore Cooper was formerly a resident at 404 West Post Road. (It's a shameful thing, but Cooper had no use for Yankee heroes. Critic

The Post Road

Van Doren observed that "Cooper cultivated his animosity toward New England, which furnished most of his later villains.")

Somewhere along the Post Road here in Mamaroneck, US Route 1 enters Larchmont. Once called Munro's Neck, this property in 1845 passed into the hands of Edward K. Collins "whose Scotch gardner planted a group of larch trees, specifically to shut off the view from the Post Road." This resulted in Larchmont Manor, "a restricted residential park." I am not sure what the status of present Larchmont is among exurbanites, but it still has a big yacht club and a characteristic suburban railroad station on the New Haven.

The nearby community mentioned briefly as Harrison's Purchase has a New Haven station known merely as Harrison. In Purchase was an estate of a character known (throughout the Far West) as Ben Holladay, the Stagecoach King. Ben was something special in his time. A big, black-bearded and brassy hillbilly dynamo who cornered the Western stage lines, made a whopping big pile, and sold out when he saw the first train heading for the Rockies.

Mrs. Ben Holladay loathed the frontier and all in it and, for the sake of her Ben, fairly crashed into, though never quite entered, "Eastern Society." Here in Purchase, Westchester County, New York, he bought one thousand beautifully wooded acres and in their middle built what a United States senator from Oregon said was "the goddamdest little cottage ever seen outside Newport, Rhode Island." Ben agreed. It was of stone and in it were more than 200 rooms. Ben named it Ophir Place. It "cost seven thousand dollars a month just to run her."

With his stagecoach money, Ben plunged into steamships and railroads, and the Panic of 1873 staggered him. Another three years and his financial power was broken. It was never to be regained. Ophir Place was sold. A year later it came into the hands of Whitelaw Reid, publisher and political leader. While being wired for electricity, the main house caught fire and was destroyed. Holliday's biographer, Ellis Lucia, writes that Ophir was rebuilt by Reid's father-in-law, Darius Ogden Mills, who had made his pile in California banking and Nevada's Comstock Lode.

Today a large part of Ophir's thousand acres is the campus of Manhattanville College of the Sacred Heart. This site is in Harrison's Purchase. In this town, on my visit, there seemed to be still plenty of open spaces, presenting a vista of many large estates, well hedged, the one from the other. Among them, incidentally, is that of Blanche and Alfred Knopf, the publishers, whose unique place is virtually a sort of international forest, with a vast variety of domestic and exotic species, to the delight of silviculturists.

New Rochelle is of course noted as the old Huguenot town. Settled shortly after the Edict of Nantes in 1685, when several hundreds of thousands of French Protestants left their native land, small groups came to America to settle in Massachusetts and New York provinces. Among these were families named Revere and Faneuil. One of the New Rochelle group was Benjamin Faneuil and one of *his* sons, Peter, returned to Boston to become famous as the financial sponsor of that town's Faneuil Hall, later called the Cradle of Liberty. (Paul Revere, son of Paul and Deborah, was The Horseman of the Revolution.)

The first settlers of New Rochelle were scattered along the Boston Post Road on 6,000 acres purchased from John Pell, of Pelham Manor, along with a generous lot granted free by the Pells on which to erect a French church. When Madame Knight came riding along here, in 1704, she found New Rochelle "a very pretty place, well compact, well fenced and cleared all along as we passed." All of which, together with "three fine taverns," would have made her "content to live there."

Not so Timothy Dwight, president of Yale College, whose bilious eye saw "the old French houses, long buildings of stone of one story, with few and small windows, and high steep roofs, as ill-suited to the appearance of this fine ground. . . ." Nor was the church, "built by the same people in the same style," much to look at. But New Rochelle became a township in 1788, an incorporated village in 1858, and in 1899, a city.

By that time, the late Citizen Tom Paine had gradually recovered some of his just fame as the author of *Common Sense, The Rights of Man,* the *Age of Reason,* and *The Crisis* papers. ("These are the times that try men's souls. . . .") Back in 1794, the State of New York had presented Paine with the confiscated estate of a convicted Loyalist. Paine lived on this New Rochelle farm, to die in 1809, in New York City. Because of his notorious agnosticism, no consecrated ground was permitted to receive his body, and he was buried on his own farm. Ten years later his remains were exhumed and taken to England. Where they are now is unknown.

As early as 1839, a few admirers placed a Paine monument on his grave. Later this was moved a few yards, and rededicated in a ceremony that warranted a salute of thirteen guns. And today, (1961) in spite of Theodore Roosevelt's "dirty-little-atheist" remark —today, with a Paine Avenue, a Paine Monument, the Paine Cottage, and the Paine Memorial House, New Rochelle has been described as being pretty much in the Paine business. Yet, among New Rochelle's "tourist attractions" cited in many guidebooks is a statue of an even more controversial character than Paine. This is the monument to Jacob Leisler, erected by the Huguenot Historical Association, in memory of a *de facto* lieutenant governor of New York, charged with high treason and hanged in 1691, though later —and much too late—he was cleared of the charge.

Other listed "Points of Interest" are the College of New Rochelle, opened in 1891 by Ursuline nuns as a boarding school for girls, and in 1904 chartered as a Roman Catholic college for women which, in 1961, had an enrollment of some 900 students.

Pelham is but 2 miles on the Post Road from New Rochelle, and one cannot leave the neighborhood without mention of Thomas

Pell, first lord of Pelham Manor. He came here from Fairfield as a landlooker and trader who could have had few peers in all Connecticut. In 1654 he bought from local Indians a large tract of land which, though claimed by and within the jurisdiction of the Dutch, Pell managed to get "transferred" to New York Colony and its title confirmed by New York courts. There were boundary disputes, too, but Pell held fast; and later, when his nephew John became manor lord, he was happy to sell the 6,000 acres wanted by the Huguenot refugees on which to build New Rochelle.

During the Revolution there was no little fighting in the general neighborhood. This included the battles of White Plains and Pell's Point, a number of hit-and-run raids, and a great deal of looting. As the war gradually faded into the past, its events began to take on the flavor of romance. And when, some half a century ago, it was rumored in New York that the city administration planned to do away with a stretch of the Boston Post Road in the Bronx, a citizen, William O. Giles, whose home happened to be built on the site of old Fort Independence, in the Bronx, appeared to make protest. Presuming on the lack of historical knowledge of the city's rulers, Giles put on a fine show of indignation as he took the floor. "Gentlemen," he declared, "you may destroy many historic landmarks in this city, and nothing will be said. But should you destroy *this* ancient historic road, you may be sure the public shall hear of it. It will not stand for the abolition of this road made famous and sacred by the *ride of Paul Revere!*"

It was magic. Apparently neither the Mayor of New York nor any of his street commissioners knew where Revere *did* ride. But they knew well enough where Mr. Longfellow rode, and the meeting closed with a unanimous vote to leave the Boston Post Road exactly as it then was, circa 1897. Historian Stephen Jenkins observed happily that as a result of Giles's well-timed bluff, this part of the Post Road remained inviolate for many years more.

Sixty-odd years later the streets and highways of Upper Manhattan and the near mainland have undergone such changes that nobody save antiquarians can be certain how and where the first Boston postrider made his way after he had ferried Spuyten Duyvil

The Post Road

Creek at the northern end of Manhattan Island, soon to be known as Kingsbridge. We know only that he moved east to the banks of Westchester Creek and there followed the Indian trail that led him into the Connecticut River Valley.

Yet, both topography and habit combined to keep the Boston Post Road pretty well in line with the original route, and when it became the fashion to number roads and highways, US Route 1 was applied to the former post route from New York to Boston. Even though, as previously pointed out, US 1 was neither the first nor the only post route between the two cities, the figure serves well enough for the Shore Route from Massachusetts Bay to Kingsbridge, New York.

To the intervening generations of dwellers of the Bronx and Westchester County, the Boston Post Road has remained an accepted fact. It was there in the beginning; it was there still 270 years later. Natives and old-timers alike think of it and designate it as the Boston Post Road, or simply as the Boston Road, rather than by its official number.

I used sometimes to wonder if these and other dwellers in present Greater New York have a sense of living in a distinct community, of belonging to an entity like that of a country town or village; or were they content, and even proud to be one of the 8 million or so faceless citizens of America's incomparable metropolis? Although no thought of anything like a "survey" entered the effort, now and then I put some such question to natives, or long-time residents of Manhattan Island and its suburbia and exurbia.

Several replies were vague, but more were positive: yes, this or that resident felt he "belonged" to his community, rather than to New York City. For instance, one of the most articulate was Mrs. John Angell, a native of Pelham. She replied to my query with one of her own.

"Whatever made you think we so-called New Yorkers might not be human beings?" she demanded. *"Of course* we identify ourselves with our community. Not just New York City. When I was growing up in Pelham, I felt just as cozy as any native in a small isolated village." In those days she was Miss Adelaide Townsend. After school at Vassar, she returned to marry a Pelham man, and to start rearing a family.

Years later Mrs. Angell recalled that the Boston Post Road loomed large in her home town. Where it bisected Pelhamdale Avenue, the Boston Road was a good basic point of reference—so many blocks north of, or south of. Growing up in darkest Prohibition, she remembers that the Post Road achieved the reputation of harboring a speakeasy in every block of its damp way through Pelham.

Now and then, on Split Rock Road, which was once the private driveway from the manor house of Thomas Pell to the Boston Post Road, she thrilled to the pageants staged in memory of Anne Hutchinson, the much troubled puritan of Massachusetts Bay, and of Providence Plantations, who at last came to settle here in far-away Pelham, only to die victim of a massacre by savages.

More exciting than pageants, Mrs. Angell recalls, was the truly tremendous occasion when, for a money-raising campaign, she donned a Red Cross uniform and went boldly out on the Post Road, to flag down truck drivers, romantic characters all, for donations. "They were most generous, too," she added. It was also right here on the Post Road where the young woman saw her first long-haul passenger stages, for distant places like Boston and Portland, Maine.

Like any small town, Pelham had its local characters, and notable among them was "The Artichoke King," who was believed to have a tight monopoly of that vegetable beloved of Italians. The "King's" gorgeous home was just off the Post Road, and it was a sort of period elegance in Pelham.

Both Pelham and other nearby communities developed some highly professional Post Road bums—male panhandlers who had their favorite corners or blocks, and youngsters learned that these characters lived "somewhere in New York," owned their own homes, lived well, and had fine automobiles in which they drove to their favored working places before they changed to carefully costumed shabbinesses to make their first pitch for the day.

Then, on Pelhamdale Avenue for many years operated a street

car which, so all Pelhamites devoutly believed, was the original inspiration for the immortal Toonerville Trolley of cartoonist Fontaine Fox. Pelham youngsters were proud of this creation, and happy to share the famous piece of rolling stock with the rest of the United States. . . . Could there, after all, be any doubt that Pelham was not a distinct community?

We left Pelham for Kingsbridge, the last stop on the original Boston Post Road before Manhattan Island, by following signs indicating US 1, with an occasional reference to the Boston Road, to West 228th Street and Broadway, and were met by a friend who gave us needed assurance that we had at last reached Old Kingsbridge.

Chapter 25

Kingsbridge to the End of the Line

WHERE *IS* KINGSBRIDGE, New York? I think we came there by way of Kingsbridge Road to Broadway at West 228th Street. I know there is a Marble Hill station on the New York Central, and another listed as "Sp'n Du'vil," which I had less trouble to translate than to pronounce correctly. Somewhere in the general neighborhood are still other stations labeled Kingsbridge and Spuyten Duyvil.

Marble Hill is the northern tip of Manhattan Island; and around this eminence used to wind the creek called Spuyten Duyvil, which is also the Harlem River. Later, when a ship canal was projected to cut the river through to the Hudson, the Spuyten Duyvil portion was filled in bank to bank. Today, on the ancient creek bed stand,

The Post Road

among other things, the eleven 14-story apartments called Marble Hill Houses.

Nobody could have visited Kingsbridge with a better guide than greeted us on arrival, the Reverend William A. Tieck, president of the Kingsbridge Historical Society, who is also pastor of St. Stephen's Methodist Church, Marble Hill, New York, and the author of a booklet, *God's House and the Old Kingsbridge Road,* which had no little to do with the founding of the local historical society.

Over lunch, Mr. Tieck confessed his "obsession with the fascinating history of the Kingsbridge area." Knowing he was born and reared in Colorado, I wondered what Boston Post Road country could possibly offer against, say, Cripple Creek or Leadville, or Central City, or Denver. He began pitching at once. "I know you plan to trace the Boston Road to the Battery tip of the Island," he said, "yet your story does not really begin or end till you get to Kingsbridge. This was the first land-link between Manhattan and the Mainland." (I turned wary.)

We walked later to present West 231st Street and Broadway, to see the place where the Albany Road and the Boston Road parted. It looked to be against a ridge; and this was confirmed by an old photograph, taken on this spot in 1893. It has all the clarity and detail of a Brady picture. The ridge shows a mansard-roofed mansion, a church, and a long business block, all standing amid profuse conifers and broad-leaf trees.

Across the foreground is Spuyten Duyvil Creek, reflecting images of a hotel and restaurant, of trees, and the bridge itself. On the structure and on street corners are old-fashioned street lamps. The morning light is strong; a horse and buggy at the curb project a black shadow on a store front. Another picture, from a slightly different angle, reveals the tiny island and "Wading Place" which Indians and early settlers used until John Verveelen established a pole-boat "ferry" in 1669. Then, in 1693, twenty years after the Post Road came into being, traffic warranted a bridge not far from the Wading Place. It was built by Colonel Frederick Philipse, a manor lord whose vast acquisitions had been consolidated in the Royal Patent of Philipsburgh. Philipse named it the King's Bridge, honoring William III of England.

Because Colonel Philipse was first of all an excellent business-man, this first bridge over the Harlem River was a toll bridge, and here begins the bitter struggle that enlivened the Marble Hill region a long time. It could well have been called the War of the Bridges. It presented a heroic and determined Good Guy in Benjamin Palmer; and an unrelenting and villainous Bad Guy in Colonel Philipse. The reader should know that this account is partisan history, that the Good Guys *must* win, or there is no story. As such it is a part of the regional wars of the farmer-renters against the manor lords.

The way Kingsbridge historians tell it, Philipse, who not incidentally had been associated in business with Captain Kidd—*the* Captain Kidd—had scarcely started to collect his bridge tolls, when the pioneers around Marble Hill began to show resentment. Most of them did little more than talk mean; but Benjamin Palmer made an effort to build a free bridge across the creek, or river, in the narrow part, a few rods from the toll bridge. He was stopped by some sort of trick court order inspired by Philipse.

Time passed. Palmer continued his agitation, selected another spot on a line with present 225th Street, and prevailed on fellow farmers to help him to lay a free bridge. Actual work began. Philipse was unrelenting. During the so-called French and Indian War period, Palmer was "twice pressed into military service in Canada at the instigation of Philipse" and was obliged to pay soldier-substitutes to take his place. "But," said Palmer, "I continued building the free bridge until finished."

Historian Tieck relates that the new span was dedicated on January 2, 1759, when "a fine fat Ox was roasted on the Green, and thousands from the city and country partook of the Ox, and rejoiced greatly." It was commonly called the Free Bridge, or the Farmers' Bridge, but was also known at various periods as Dyckman's Bridge,

The Post Road

Hadley's Bridge, and Prince of Wales Bridge. The important thing was that the Free Bridge quickly left the toll bridge almost bare of traffic.

Benjamin Palmer, the mover and shaker, seems never to have been given proper credit for his "contribution to the social and political advancement of the commonalty." That is, not until one day in 1959 when, in the auditorium of Public School 122, on West Kingsbridge Road, the Kingsbridge Historical Society dedicated a bronze tablet to mark the site and the significance, as well as the two-hundredth anniversary of the famed old Free Bridge. You may be certain I saw the proud marker while I was in the community.

Both bridges were of great strategic importance during the Revolutionary War. In June, 1776, General Washington, after a personal inspection of colonial defenses in this area, ordered a small, square fort to be built atop Marble Hill. This was to command both the King's and the Farmers' bridges. In late October that year, when Manhattan had become no longer tenable, the fort was abandoned by the Americans, and soon was occupied by the British, who renamed it Fort Prince Charles, for a brother-in-law of King George. The British also had to repair both bridges, which had been dismantled by the retreating patriot forces. Then, in January, 1777, Fort Prince Charles was cannonaded from Spuyten Duyvil Hill, in an engagement that was part of the larger Battle of Kingsbridge. Lest tourists should feel need to know more, Mr. Tieck described the site of this fort as "occupying the high ground in the angle between present Van Corlear Place and 227th Street."

There was still another bridge across the Harlem River to the mainland right after the Revolution. This was near present 130th Street. It shortened the distance on the Boston Post Road between New York and New Rochelle, where the new road joined the old, by more than four miles. Because it had a notable effect on Kingsbridge traffic, this is the place to mention it.

In earlier days people going to New England were more or less

240

satisfied to make the long trip to Kingsbridge in order to pass to the mainland. It is of course possible that the Philipses, who operated the toll bridge at Spuyten Duyvil, were too powerful in affairs of the Province for anybody to propose a short cut. In 1774, however, Lewis Morris, Esquire, of the Manor of Morrisania, and John Sickles of the Township of Harlem, had sufficient influence to induce the Provincial Assembly to empower the petitioners to erect a bridge over Harlem River and that "the said bridge when so built shall be and is hereby declared to be a free and public Highway for the Use Benefit and Behoof of all his Majesty's Subjects whatsoever."

This indicated a free bridge, but nothing came of it just then. Before anything more than preliminary work could be started, the Revolution appeared, full-blown, at Lexington and Concord. It was 1790 before the New York State Legislature granted Lewis Morris a franchise to build his bridge; and he, in turn, transferred the right to John B. Coles, who built the Harlem Bridge and road in 1798. From this time on, traffic to the mainland by Kingsbridge must have taken a decided fall. Four miles saved by travelers to Westchester and points in New England was not to be ignored.

By this time Levi Pease of Boston had got his first United States Mail contract, and extended his stagecoach line through to New York. Pease was doubtless ready to drop Kingsbridge from his stage schedules, save on runs connecting with New Jersey coaches, and to add Harlem Bridge to his regular stops. I do not know if he cut the Boston to New York fare to allow for the lesser mileage.

One thing is certain. Use of the new or Coles bridge over the Harlem must have blighted taverns in the Kingsbridge area; and may have also brightened the business aspects of taverns between Harlem village and New Rochelle. It wasn't long before this route became known as the New Boston Post Road, to distinguish it from the Old Post Road—the Albany Road—on Manhattan Island. The new Boston Road branched from the old at Fifth Avenue and 91st Street and ran northeast for a mile and a half across Benson's Creek and the Harlem farmlands to Cole's new bridge.

This Harlem Bridge cutoff was the first major change in the

The Post Road

Boston Post Road for more than a century. It may not have changed time schedules very much when spread over the whole system of more than two hundred miles; and anyway, by 1798 the running time of the better lines, such as Pease's, was still improving. Yet the new Harlem Bridge route was notice that there was nothing immutable about any "permanent" highway, not even a post road with the added convenience of milestones. Indeed, even milestones themselves were not immutable, and when in 1813 New York City's government was moved from Wall Street north to present City Hall Park, the point of computation of distances moved with it, and the old Fourteenth Milestone was moved across Spuyten Duyvil Creek and set up anew in Westchester County, on the mainland.

Long before the present era of throughways, many of us can recall times and places where a new paved highway almost overnight radically changed the flow of traffic. The old dirt road was left to the surviving horse-and-buggy and farm-wagon trade. The village or small community which did not and perhaps could not shift its business district to meet the new conditions was doomed to senescence. It might come slowly, but come it did. Even a post office could not save it after Rural Free Delivery was introduced. It was too late for a railroad. One general store might survive.

You passed through these communities that had suffered the ultimate rejection, which was a paved road. There was neither balm nor hope left in these Gileads, these Lost Nations, Four Corners, and Bingvilles. They had reached the final insult the United States of the twentieth century could offer—*a dirt road.* And I happen to believe that their few residents are by now not only resigned to their fate, but delighted with their great good fortune.

In regard to the milestones on Manhattan Island, I had the pleasure to meet Richard J. Koke, the outstanding authority on these "silent sentinels of the stagecoach era." He is a member of the Kingsbridge Historical Society, and is also Curator of the Museum of the New York Historical Society. In a monograph on this subject, Mr. Koke observed that the stagecoaches coming down the Post Road from Boston first came within sight of Manhattan Island while descending the slope of Tetard's Hill in Westchester. After crossing Spuyten Duyvil Creek over the King's Bridge, they had hardly rounded Marble Hill when the passengers observed, "on their right, going south, the most northerly of the milestones." This was Number 14.

As the coach lumbered on, at a charge of four pence per mile, New York currency, the little milestones along the west side of the highway "announced each passing mile with regularity and gave the travellers heart that their long jogging journey would soon end." On they went, rolling by taverns and scattered country estates, to pass close to the village of Harlem, then through McGown's Pass, and down the island to glimpse the First Milestone outside the city. (This stood on The Bowery, a little south of Canal Street.) Within another few minutes the stage drew up to the door of John Fowler's Tavern, "near the Collect Pond at the edge of the city." At this period, Fowler's place was a sort of unofficial end of the New York and Boston Post Road. Just beyond Fowler's stood the stone Debtor's Jail, and then Broadway "which continued on south in a straight line to Fort George and The Bowling Green."

Remarking of milestones, Mr. Koke said there had been so much confusion due to a lack of knowledge that "several separate series of stones on different locations were erected at different dates." He believes that the very first stones on Manhattan Island were those placed in 1769 along the west side of the Post Road from the Bowery near Canal Street to the King's Bridge.

Study of old maps and city records indicates that the early post-riders and the first stagecoaches left the city by way of City Hall Park, Park Row, The Bowery, and Fourth Avenue to about Madison Square; then east to Third Avenue, to meander north and west to enter Central Park at 92d Street and, emerging from the Park at 110th Street, continued northward along present St. Nicholas Avenue and Broadway to Kingsbridge.

That even one of these fourteen stones of 1769 should have survived is perhaps remarkable. It had marked the ninth mile when it stood on St. Nicholas Avenue "exactly opposite the north line of West 133d Street." This survivor of one hundred years was, in 1950, when Mr. Koke saw it last, in a private garden at 473 West 152d Street. The legend cut into its face was still legible. It read: "1769 9 mile from N York."

It seems unlikely that the locations of these long-forgotten Post Road milestones will become a matter of argument, even in Third Avenue saloons, a community famous for heated discussions; but Mr. Koke has gone to some care to list them, and so, just in case:

Milestones Erected in 1769
along the Post Road Leading from
New York to Kingsbridge

1st Milestone.   *The Bowery, west side, just south of Canal Street.*

2d Milestone.   *Fourth Avenue, at southwest corner Astor Place.*

3d Milestone.   *Where Madison Avenue and East 26th Street intersect.*

4th Milestone.   *East side Third Avenue, midway between East 45 and East 46th Streets.*

5th Milestone.   *West side Second Avenue at East 62d Street.*

6th Milestone.   *Northwest corner Third Avenue and East 81st Street.*

7th Milestone.   *In Central Park, west of Fifth Avenue between 97th and 98th Streets.*

8th Milestone.   *St. Nicholas Avenue, west side, between West 115th and West 116th Street.*

9th Milestone.   *St. Nicholas Avenue, west side, exactly opposite north line of West 133d Street.*

10th Milestone.   *St. Nicholas Avenue and 153d Street, southwest corner.*

11th Milestone.   *Broadway, west side, near West 170th or West 171st Street.*

Kingsbridge to the End of the Line

12th Milestone.   *Broadway, west side, at or near West 190th Street.*

13th Milestone.   *At a point east of Broadway between Academy and West 204th Streets.*

14th Milestone.   *Broadway, west side, in what is now the Harlem Ship Canal.*

In later years milestones were laid along the New Boston Post Road, as the Harlem Bridge Cutoff came to be known; and others appeared still later in the Borough of the Bronx, in the Boroughs of Brooklyn, and Queens, and at least one stone in Richmond, on the Richmond Turnpike, or Victory Boulevard.

By the time steam railroads were taking over transportation between major towns, New York City was swarming with either horsecars, cablecars, or "the brazen vulgarity of trolleycars," and the milestones of the stagecoach era were falling, one by one, to vandals, street-accidents, and the continuous erosion of time and weather. The Boston Post Road had become an antiquity.

Chapter 26

New York City in Post Road Times, 1789

WHAT WAS NEW YORK CITY LIKE when the Stagecoach Era began on the Old Boston Post Road?

It will be recalled that the first regular mailcoach service between Boston and New York got under way in 1785, when Levi Pease of Boston expanded his Boston–Hartford line to include the fast growing city on Manhattan Island. Although postriders still carried the mails everywhere, Pease within another year won the first contract in the United States to carry mail in his coaches.

Thus encouraged, Pease cut the passenger fare from four pence a mile to three pence; and announced to the public that his mail and passenger coaches would forthwith make the trip from Boston to New York in four days, in summer, and five-and-one-half days in winter.

New York City, 1789

By 1789 Mr. Pease was being referred to in the trade as The Stagecoach King. He had earned it. And now he was equipped and ready for the greatest single transportation emergency in eighteenth-century America.

This was no less than the formal organizing of the United States, the inauguration of its first President, and the meeting of its first Constitutional Congress. All of these mighty events were to take place in the first capital of the new republic, which was New York City, already the capital of New York State.

In this year of 1789 New York City had a population of some 30,000 people. Philadelphia, the recognized metropolis, claimed 40,000; Boston, 16,000. Winning the honor of the seat of government was a handsome prize. Throughout much of the Revolutionary War, New York City had been occupied by the British. It was also widely believed elsewhere to harbor the most notorious crew of Tories in the country.

New York was already cosmopolitan. To begin with there were the old Dutch families, no longer the rulers, but still to be reckoned with. About half of the aldermen elected in 1789 had Dutch names. Jews, English, French (mostly Huguenots), Germans, Scotch, and Irish had moved in. There was a scattering few of Welsh, Poles, Portuguese, and West Indians. And one of every fourteen New Yorkers was a Negro slave. Bond or free, Negroes comprised about one-tenth of the population.

A large majority of the city's population lived south of present Houston Street. The first Post Road milestone outside the city proper stood on Bowery Lane near Canal Street; and the third milestone was way out in the country—or about where East 26th Street now intersects Madison Avenue. Before the year was out, the first Vice-president of the United States was to lease what was considered an "elegant *country* estate" in the Village of Greenwich, at Varick and Charlton Streets.

If you were to name the principal streets of the city in that period, they must have included present Pearl, Broad, Wall, Cortlandt, John, Broadway, and naturally, the Bowling Green and Bowery

Lane. Near the very tip of Manhattan was the uncompleted Fort called the Battery which, in 1789, had begun to disintegrate. Until October 5 of that year, the post office was in the home of Postmaster Bedlow, 8 Wall Street. When it was moved to the home of the new Postmaster, Sebastian Bauman, at Broadway and Crown (Liberty) Street, a protest was raised against its remote location.

But before the year was done, business at the New York Post Office was to undergo so notable a spurt that the newly elected Postmaster General, Samuel Osgood, observed in his report of 1790, that "the franking of letters may have been extended too far." This was one way of indicating that the first session of the First Congress had been a success.

A City Directory of 1789 would have listed 169 taverns and public houses, and doubtless ignored the common run of grogshops, for there were known "to be 333 licensed drinking places in New York," or more than one to every one hundred inhabitants.

Though there is no record that strangers found New York wanting in the number of dispensaries of alcohol, the immense influx of visitors during the inaugural year taxed the capacity of inns and taverns as never before, and also that of the scores of boarding and rooming houses.

Over in Philadelphia, a French innkeeper was advertising that his place was "not like that of an American-run house." He did not put twelve beds in one room. Every lodger had a room to himself. "At my place," he bragged, "you don't have to get out of bed, to go to the window, for Jeanette never forgets the chamber pot." (Were New York chambermaids to be no less diligent?)

It is not to be thought that the up-and-coming people of New York, both state and city, did not appreciate the honors being heaped upon them by the United States. As soon as the Continental Congress selected New York as the temporary capital, the City Corporation engaged Major Pierre Charles L'Enfant, the Paris-born veteran of the American army, to renovate the old City Hall into

New York City, 1789

what was renamed Federal Hall. One imagines the City told the Major to shoot the works. In any event, he did so, to the extent of $65,000. It was a cost, as Architect Fiske Kimball later observed, that "far outran the funds available"; but "the New Yorkers, hoping the handsome building would help them to retain the capital permanently, were reconciled." (It was of course the same expensive Major L'Enfant who surveyed the site and made the plans for the new Federal City on the Potomac.)

Cost what it might, the New Yorkers got their money's worth from the quarters they had provided as a gift to the Federal government. In this refurbished City Hall was to meet the first National Congress. In it the first President was to be inaugurated. Federal Hall was as splendid a gesture as a city could make to a nation. It did nothing to lessen the gift if the State Legislature, to ease the tax load, authorized New York City to stage a series of lotteries.

The Mayor of New York, in 1789, was James Duane, who was succeeded late in the year by Richard Varick. At this period New York's mayor was nominated by the governor, who was then George Clinton, and formally confirmed by the State Council of Appointment. Property qualifications and other restrictions permitted no more than approximately 10 per cent of the adult male population to vote in municipal elections, which tended to make them very dull indeed. Although the Sons of St. Tammany had appeared in several colonies before the Revolution, the society in New York was still little more than a club given to holding an annual picnic at which noble toasts were drunk to proclaim the *Rights of Man,* and a sort of official hymn sung, the closing lines being: "Then pass the bottle with the Sun to Tammany and Washington." One of Tammany's leading members in 1789 was John Pintard, wealthy merchant, and on the roster appeared names already familiar, like Roosevelt and Livingston.

Policing the fast-growing city had become a municipal headache. But the crowds of visitors who came to town for the inauguration may well have been impressed by the variety of officers detailed to preserve law and order. These included a high sheriff and his deputies, a high constable and sixteen elected constables, a chief marshal and his deputies, and the City Watch.

The City Watch was the nearest thing to a conventional police force in the town. Its members carried sticks, wore painted leathern hats, and served under the command of two captains, who reported to the Common Council. Yet it was a *night* watch only, in 1789, and went on duty each evening at seven, starting with a little parade to their posts from the watchhouse near City Hall. Come daylight, these period-cops promptly disappeared, and the town was left to the assorted sheriffs, constables, and marshals.

Now and again the town faced an emergency too great for all of its law-and-order forces combined. Still fresh in mind was the so-called "Doctors' Riots" during April 1788, when Governor Clinton called out the Militia to handle the mobs of more than 2,000 who were searching the houses of doctors suspected of robbing graves.

During the inaugural year, however, there seem to have been no such major incidents. Indeed, the night watch met the emergency due to the veritable hordes of strangers with no more than the average number of incivilities which were at one time believed to have greeted outlanders in later years by New York policemen.

Doubtless the watchmen tired of directing vast numbers of country bumpkins to Federal Hall, and the Executive Mansion, or to the City Tavern, or the John Street Theater, and even to the unsavory neighborhood just east of Chatham Square. Yet, meanwhile, the Common Council had reason to commend officially three brave watchmen named "Culbertson, Schofield, and Gobel" who were also given awards of cash for "having seized dangerous robbers in the night."

There was no element of contention or surprise in the election of George Washington as President. Even before the Constitution was adopted, public opinion had fixed on him. On April 6, 1789, the

New York City, 1789

Continental Congress formally proclaimed his election, and sent a messenger to Mount Vernon with the formal notification. By the sixteenth, the President-elect was on his way north to the seat of government. After parades, salutes, and other festivities all the way from Alexandria, Virginia, to Elizabeth Town, New Jersey, he was met by the Committee of Congress, and escorted to New York by water. The party came ashore near the foot of Wall Street.

"And there," so wrote Elias Boudinot, New Jersey statesman, to his wife, "we saw many thousands of the citizens waiting with all the eagerness of expectation to welcome our excellent patriot to that shore, which he had regained from a powerful enemy by his valor and good conduct. . . . Here he was met on the wharf by many of his old and faithful officers and fellow patriots who had borne the heat and burden of the day with him . . . and who now joined the universal chorus of welcoming their great deliverer (under Providence) from their fears. . . . It was with difficulty a passage could be made by the troops through the pressing crowds."

Never before had New York or any other American city seen a gathering of such magnitude. Taverns, private houses, mansions, all had been overflowing for days. Make-shift tents were being set up in open lots even as the President landed. One may judge from old letters, diaries, and newspapers that the one man they had come to see did not disappoint them. In the midst of the brilliant array of uniforms, moving slowly between banks of cheering men, women, and children, the somber figure of Washington, in plain blue coat, buff waistcoat and breeches, seemed to stand apart, and a little remote, from all else. Here was the national hero, and he looked, as thousands tried to say, then or later, the way an American hero should look.

For another seventy years and more, the bards, the sweet singers, and the poets who saw him plain in New York, on this day of days, tried to immortalize George Washington in some happy arrangement of words, in some deathless phrase that would ring down the centuries. I wonder if any of them did better than these commonplace eye-witnesses who told one another that Washington even *looked* the way he should. And that was enough, for these, his countrymen, had looked into their own hearts and told what they saw there. . . .

The procession paused at No. 3 Cherry Street, which had been prepared for General Washington's official residence; and from there he was conducted to the house of Governor George Clinton. That night the city was "brilliantly illuminated," and the ale houses and tavern taprooms had a night to remember. And so, one may presume, did the night watch.

Yet, the climax was yet to come. A week still intervened before the inauguration, set for Thursday, April 30. Hundreds more visitors were coming into town every day. Where they were to lodge was a question. But entertainment was no problem. To a large majority of the visitors, who had never been there, New York City itself was already something to see. If Philadelphians could be condescending in the matter of population, let them, but Boston, with only half as many people as New York, could not.

In their entertaining study of New York as it was at this period, Frank Monaghan and Marvin Lowenthal remarked that even in that ancient time the city was a "paradise for shoppers." In the shops were a glittering array "of things that had never been seen in the best establishments of Hartford or Albany or Trenton." Here were tailors and stylists who knew the latest thing in Paris and London. Here were dealers in fine wines and fine tobacco, including cigars from Havana, snuff from Scotland. There were several booksellers, many dealers in wallpapers. In Maiden Lane was William Griggs, whose advertisement in the *Daily Gazette* said he was proud of his "Plate and Plated Ware." At 81 Queen Street was John Jacob Astor, ready to sell "Piano Fortes," and anxious also to "Pay Cash for all Kinds of Furs." At 22 Wall Street was Hugh Smith, who would exchange some of his linens just imported from London for "Potashes."

There were as yet no department stores, but at 79 William Street was the emporium of John Turner, who advertised all manner of "imported Mullins, Mullinets, Irish Linens, Indian dimities, Fustians, Sattins, Persians, Brocades, Genoa Velvets, Bombazeens, Shaloons, Nankeens; Chip and Leghorn Hats; Lute Strings; Figured Oil Cloths; Black and White Beaver Hats; & c & c" for a full column of solid type, in the *Gazette*. John Shephard, 23 Hanover Square, tailor to ladies and gentlemen, was offering cloths for men's formal attire in colorings showing the possibilities of the early Federal period. These shades included Bottle Green, Ravens Gray, London Smoke, Queens Drab, Scarlet, Garnet, Mouse's Ear, Parsons Gray, and Mulberry.

In comparison to New York's superb shops, the city's theater fare seems meager. What was not called "the Theater District" was confined to the north side of John Street between Broadway and Nassau. It was a large wooden building painted red and in it was appearing "The Old American Company," the star of which was Mr. John Henry. Mrs. Henry was the leading lady.

The "season" of 1789 ran from April 14 to December 15, but the house was dark during August. There was no stove in the theater. The many big candles may not have been blinding, but they were known to drip wax steadily upon the audience. The President, the Vice President John Adams, and Governor George Clinton attended at least one performance of Sheridan's *School For Scandal*, which was given eight nights. Shakespeare held the boards at other times, with *The Merry Wives of Windsor, The Tempest,* and *Richard III.* And it was here in the John Street house where a comedy, *The Contrast,* by Royall Tyler, was first produced. Tyler is known as the first American playwright.

During 1789, the Henrys occasionally filled in with a pantomime, *Robinson Crusoe,* and something called *The Shipwreck.*

Other attractions during the inaugural year were a zoo of wild animals exhibited at 28 Wall Street; a wax works show at 14 William Street; and Bowen's Wax Works on Water Street. Bowen was an up-and-coming showman. *His* wax dummies "moved their heads, winked, and performed other feats." Bowen also had an effigy of "The President of the United States sitting under a canopy in military dress." Among the admiring spectators one afternoon were

"The President and his Lady and family and several other persons of distinction."

Then, there were the so-called public auctions, the "Vendues." Announced almost continuously in the *Daily Advertiser,* and conducted by professionals, these affairs were something of an entertainment, though the more sophisticated considered them the noisy efforts of wholesale merchants to rid themselves of merchandise of all sorts that had failed to find favor with retail storekeepers. The lively, witty auctioneers put on a good show to excite their audiences; and at proper intervals their confederates in the crowd started flurries of bidding to pressure the gulls to action. It is possible that the "surplus army-goods" business originated in these auction rooms, as witness the offering of "42½ dozen ramrods" to the highest bidder.

And at last came the day, April 30, which broke clear on Manhattan Island, and began with a cannon salute from the Battery near the Bowling Green. New York City was already astir. By ten o'clock the members of Congress and other eminent persons were assembling at Federal Hall in Wall Street, and were discussing a matter of some importance: Should the head of the state be addressed as His Highness, His Excellency, or how? It was agreed he should be simply Mr. President.

A little after noon, troops were at their stations, carriages were in line, and the Senate Committee arrived at 3 Cherry Street to inform George Washington that the Congress of the United States awaited his arrival. Mr. Washington was ready: "He bows deferentially to the committee, and Colonel Morgan Lewis rides to the head of the column, and the inaugural procession is under way."

Dragoons, artillery, grenadiers, as brilliant in new dress uniforms as they had been colorless and often shabby in their fighting clothes: then Highlanders in bright tartans and kilts; and then the troops of the line, less ornamental, but smart enough; and finally the coach of state, bearing the President. It was a magnificent job with decorated panels, and borders of flowers and cupids supporting festoons.

The route from the Executive Mansion to Federal Hall was a good half mile. Within the latter the members of Congress had been sitting impatiently for an hour and ten minutes before the sergeant-at-arms announced arrival of the President. The members came to their feet as Senator Ralph Izard, South Carolina, conducted Mr. Washington to the seat under its crimson canopy and presented him formally to Mr. Adams, the President of the Senate.

Things now began to move with dispatch. Mr. Adams informed Mr. Washington that Congress was ready to witness his oath of fealty to the Constitution. The President-elect replied that he was ready to take that oath, and with Mr. Otis, clerk of the Senate, leading the way, he proceeded to the balcony opening out of the chamber, being followed by Mr. Adams, Chancellor of New York Livingston, Governor Clinton, Roger Williams, Richard Henry Lee, and Generals Knox and St. Clair and Baron von Steuben.

Somebody pointed out that a Bible had been forgotten. One was hastily brought, and placed on a crimson cushion held by Clerk Otis. With its pages open to a chapter of *Genesis,* the first President laid his right hand on the book and repeated, after Mr. Livingston, the oath. Then: *"So help me, God!"*

Chancellor Livingston turned to the vast crowds in the streets, windows, and tops of houses. "Long live George Washington, President of the United States!" he cried. The flag of the new republic was raised over Federal Hall. Cannon at the Battery let go. The Spanish man-of-war in the harbor fired fifteen guns. Bells pealed. President Washington bowed to thronged Wall and Broad streets, then was escorted inside to the Senate chamber, where he read his brief inaugural speech.

The President was obviously nervous, his hand shaking. It was a disappointing address to some in the chamber, including Senator William Maclay, of Pennsylvania, who confessed to his diary that he was hurt because Washington was "not first in everything."

Maclay had "wished all set ceremony in the hands of the dancing-masters and that this first of men had read his address in the plainest manner, without ever taking his eyes from the paper." It pained the Senator that "this great man was agitated and embarrassed more than ever he was by the levelled cannon or pointed musket. He trembled, and several times could scarce make out to read, though it must be supposed he had often read it before."

Senator Maclay was known to suffer terribly from rheumatism, and the very next day, when Congress got down to work, he objected to and corrected alleged blunders made by Secretary Otis, and wrote, privately, of "the vacant, silly laugh of the Vice-President." It seems probable that his remarks on Washington and Adams were in part due to unusually severe pains in the joints.

The city of New York, capital of the United States, gradually returned to its normal life, proud among the nations of the world, with its new status as the seat of government of glorious America. Yet, all was not quite settled. An almost incredible indignity was in store. At the second session of the first Congress, held in the same Federal Hall which New York had presented as a gift to the United States, Congress, on June 28, 1790, and by a majority of one, voted to move the capital to Philadelphia, for a period of ten years, then on to the banks of the Potomac River in a region to be called the District of Columbia. . . .

Was ever the gift of a generous people so ill repaid? Note, too, that this repudiation of New York was carried by a majority of one. I choose to think that although the hellish arthritic pains of Senator William Maclay of Pennsylvania may in no manner have ceased between the first and the second session of the first United States Congress, he was doubtless as usual in his seat on that tragic day in June 1790, when gloom settled over Manhattan, and the boys in Federal Hall started to pack their carpet bags for Philadelphia, the new seat of government of the United States.

The New Yorkers were shocked to their roots. One of them wrote

that "our city will be deserted and become a wilderness again, peo-
pled only with wolves, its olden inhabitants." But he recovered soon
and remarked that "I see no reason why we should be in such a fever
about Congress moving away, so long as the old Hudson continues
to roll to the sea."

He was right. It was already too late for New York City to be
affected much or long by the loss of Congress. The Erie Canal alone
was to be worth more commercially to New York City than a
permanent Congress. By 1830 at latest, New York had passed Philadelphia in population. A decade later there was obviously no longer
any contest.

By then it was also obvious that New York was the kind of town
that Got the Railroad as soon or before anybody else did. Before
railroads were even thought of, New York was the kind of town that
got the first post road in North America.

A single reference will indicate the great influence the United
States Post Office had on transportation. In 1824 Levi Pease, the
Stagecoach King of New England and New York, died, aged eighty-
four. Since the time of his first through mail coach to New York, the
time of carrying the New York and Boston mails had dropped from
six nights and six days to a matter of thirty-six hours. One may still
believe it is not too late to hope for a fine mural in each of the
terminal cities, showing mail coaches of Levi Pease's New York and
Boston Line.

Acknowledgments

My *interest* *in* *the* *subject* of this book is
of long standing. It was present when I first began
working on what much later was published as *The
Story of American Railroads,* which contained accounts of several old lines that served New York
and New England; and it continued when I went on
to consider the endless migrations from that part of
country, the result of which was *The Yankee Exodus.*

Early and late, both Yankees and Yorkers used
the Old Post Road, the first highway so designated
in North America. Most of the institutions in which
are preserved the facts and legends and myths of
the Post Road are near or on the Road itself. Among
them are several of the greatest collections in the
United States, or elsewhere. I am especially indebted
to the American Antiquarian Society, of Worcester,
Clifford K. Shipton, Director, and to its staff, including Miss Mary Brown; the Boston Public Library, Clifford Lord, Director, and its staff, including
Mrs. Elizabeth Wright; the Public Library of the
Town of Wethersfield, Connecticut, and Mrs. Lor-
raine Backman, Reference Librarian; the Kingsbridge (N.Y.) Historical Society, and the Reverend
William A. Tieck; the New-York Historical Society,
and Richard Koke and Sylvester Vigilante; the New
York Public Library, and Mrs. Shirley L. Spranger,
of the American History Room. I must also mention

the Public Library Association of Portland, Oregon, William Wood, Chief Librarian, and staff members Miss Elizabeth Johnson and Miss Louise Prichard.

Then, there is the New England Council, Boston, with Director Gardner Caverly and staff, especially Charles Grinnell and Robert Hassett, all of whom made suggestions and offered help of the most valuable sort. At the Boston office of the American Automobile Association was Mrs. Jean O. Erickson, who cheerfully computed the mileage of various sections of the Old Post Road between Boston and New York.

In both New England and New York, and elsewhere, were many individuals with some special knowledge, and a great deal of good will, to whom I tender thanks for help given. Among these friendly collaborators are:

Frank H. Buxton, Norman Dodge, Howard Cady, Mrs. Thomas H. Carroll, John N. Makris, Frank O. Spinney, Catherine Fennelly, David McCord, Oliver Jensen, Thomas E. Hall, Mr. and Mrs. Ralph Briggs, R. E. Brummer, Ed Brummer, Mr. and Mrs. Karl D. Edwards, Holman A. Holbrook, Mr. Ernest Dana, Blanche Smith, Wayne Smith, Mr. and Mrs. Lewis Gannett, H. L. Sullivan, and Dr. Kenneth Williams.

Miss Esther Watson prepared the manuscript for the printer. My daughters, the Misses Sibyl Morningstar and Bonnie Stewart Holbrook, helped to prepare the index.

Stewart H. Holbrook

Bibliography

Abbott, Katherine M., *Old Paths and Legends of New England*, New York, 1909.

Allen, Gardner, *A Naval History of the American Revolution*, Boston, 1913.

American Guide Series, Connecticut, Massachusetts, New York, Rhode Island, 1937, 1938, 1940.

Amory, Cleveland, *The Last Resorts*, New York, 1952.

Andrews, Edward Deming, *The People Called Shakers*, New York, 1953.

Arthurs, Stanley M., "The Old Boston Post Road," in *Scribner's Magazine*, Vol. 44, November, 1908.

Bacon, Edwin M., *King's Dictionary of Boston*, Boston, 1883.

———, *A Guide Book*, Boston, 1903.

Benét, Stephen Vincent, *John Brown's Body*, New York, 1928.

Berger, Max, *The British Traveller in America*, New York, 1943.

Brown, Henry Collins, *The Story of Old New York*, New York, 1934.

Cadman, Paul F., and Allan Forbes, *Boston and Some Noted Emigrés*, Boston, 1938.

Canby, Henry Seidel, *Thoreau*, Boston, 1939.

Chase, J. E., "Old Coaching Days," in *The Nation*, Vol. 99, December 3, 1914.

Connecticut Tercentenary, "A Brief Account of the Collins Company, Collinsville, Connecticut, 1935."

Crawford, Mary Caroline, *Little Pilgrimages among Old New England Inns*, Boston, 1907.

De la Torre, Lillian, *Elizabeth Is Missing*, New York, 1945.

Earle, Alice Morse, *Stage Coach and Tavern Days*, New York, 1900.

Farnsworth, Albert, "Shays' Rebellion," in *Massachusetts Law Quarterly*, Vol. XII, No. 5, February, 1927.

Fitzpatrick, John C., *The Diaries of George Washington*, 4 vols., Boston, 1925.

Forbes, Allan, and Paul F. Cadman, *Boston and Some Noted Emigrés*, Boston, 1938.

Forbes, Esther, *Paul Revere and the World He Lived In,* Boston, 1942.

Garlick, Harriet T., "Tales of Ye Olde King's Highway," in *Daughters of the American Revolution Magazine,* Vol. 50, June, 1917.

Gough, John B., *Autobiography,* Springfield, Massachusetts, 1870.

Hale, Edward Everett, *A New England Boyhood,* Boston, 1927.

Heimann, Robert K., *Tobacco & Americans,* New York, 1960.

Hill, F. T., *The Story of a Street,* New York, 1908.

Holbrook, Stewart H., *Lost Men of American History,* New York, 1946.

————, *The Age of the Moguls,* New York, 1953.

Holmes, Oliver W., "The Father of New England Stage-Coaching," in *Journal of Economic and Business History,* Vol. 3, Feb., 1931.

Howe, George, *Mount Hope: A New England Chronicle,* New York, 1959.

Howe, M. A. DeWolfe, *Boston Landmarks,* New York, 1946.

Huntoon, Daniel T. V., *History of the Town of Canton, Norfolk County, Massachusetts,* Cambridge, 1893.

Jenkins, Stephen, *The Old Boston Post Road,* New York, 1913.

Kirkland, Edward Chase, *Men, Cities and Transportation: A Study in New England History, 1820–1900,* Cambridge, 1948.

Knight, Sarah Kemble, *The Private Journal of a Journey from Boston to New York, in the Year 1704,* Boston, 1920 (and other editions: New York, 1825; Albany, 1865; Norwich, 1901).

Koke, Richard J., "Milestones Along the Old Highways of New York City," in *The New-York Historical Society Quarterly,* July, 1950.

Kouwenhoven, John A., *The Columbia Historical Portrait of New York,* New York, 1953.

Longfellow, Henry W., *Tales of a Wayside Inn,* Boston, 1915.

Lowenthal, Marvin, and Frank Monaghan, *This Was New York,* New York, 1943.

Lee, W. Storrs, *The Yankees of Connecticut,* New York, 1957.

Lucia, Ellis, *The Saga of Ben Holladay,* New York, 1959.

Monaghan, Frank, and Marvin Lowenthal, *This Was New York,* New York, 1943.

Morse, Sidney E., *Morse's School Geography,* New York, 1840.

Moore, Mabel Roberts, *Hitchcock Chairs,* New Haven, 1933.

Powell, Lyman, *Historic Towns of New England,* New York, 1902.

Rawlins (John E.) Post, Grand Army of the Republic, Marlboro, Massachusetts, *The Story of the John Brown Bell,* 1910.

Roberts, George S., *Historic Towns of Connecticut River Valley,* 1906.

Shepard, Odell, *Connecticut Past and Present,* New York, 1939.

Stiles, Henry R., *History of Ancient Wethersfield, Connecticut,* c. 1904.

Bibliography

Summerfield, Arthur E., *U.S. Mail: The Story of the United States Postal Service,* New York, 1960.

Thomas, Robert B., *The Farmer's Almanac,* various years.

Tieck, William A., *God's House and the Old Kingsbridge Road,* Kingsbridge, New York, 1948.

Trumbull, Benjamin, *A Complete History of Connecticut,* 2 vols., New Haven, 1818.

Twichell, Ginery, *A Sketch of the Life of . . . , In Early Life a Stage Driver, etc., etc.,* Boston, 1883.

Twichell, Ginery, Obituary of, *Worcester Daily Spy,* July 24, 1883.

Webb, Walter Prescott, *The Great Plains,* Boston, 1931.

Whitehead, Russell F., *An Architectural Monograph on the Boston Post Road,* in "Whitepine Series," Vol. 6, No. 1, February 1920, Saint Paul, Minnesota, 1921.

Wilson, Rufus R., *New York in Literature,* Elmira, New York, 1947.

Winsor, Justin, Memorial History of Boston, 4 vols., Boston, 1881.

Index

Index

Index

269

Index

Index

About the Author

Stewart Holbrook is one of the distinguished writers on the American scene. Descended from a long line of New Englanders, he is uniquely suited to his subject, the Old Post Road. He was born in Vermont, went to school in New Hampshire, and the town of Holbrook, Massachusetts, was named for one of his family.

Mr. Holbrook has been a newspaperman, a semi-pro ballplayer and, before serving in France with the American field artillery, was an actor in a repertory company which, he says, was possibly the worst ever to tour the Canadian provinces.

After the war, he bought in Boston an elegant derby hat and a round-trip ticket to Vancouver, British Columbia. Three years later, he nailed the bowler to a Douglas fir stump in the timber and took off for Portland, Oregon, where he edited the *Lumber News,* and began writing for a living. He now makes his home in Portland with his wife, Sibyl, and two daughters. His hobby is painting pictures in a style peculiarly all his own.

Mr. Holbrook is the author of a number of books, among them *Holy Old Mackinaw, Ethan Allen, Lost Men of American History, The Yankee Exodus, The Age of the Moguls, The Columbia River, Dreamers of the American Dream,* and *The Golden Age of Quackery.*